Intimate Economies of Development

Aspirations, desires, opportunism and exploitation are seldom considered as fundamental elements of donor-driven development as it impacts on the lives of people in poor countries. Yet, alongside structural interventions, emotional or affective engagements are central to processes of social change and the making of selves for those caught up in development's slipstream.

Intimate Economies of Development: Mobility, sexuality and health in Asia lays bare the ways that culture, sexuality and health are inevitably and inseparably linked to material economies within trajectories of modernization in the Greater Mekong Sub-region. As migration expands and opportunities proliferate throughout Asia, different cultural groups increasingly interact as a result of targeted interventions and globalizing economic formations; but they do so with different capabilities and expectations. This book uniquely grounds its arguments in interlocking details of people's everyday lives and aspirations in developing Asia, while also engaging with changing social values and moral frameworks. Part and parcel of a widening landscape of mobility and contingent intimacy are the ever-present threats of infectious disease, most prominently HIV/AIDS, and human trafficking. Thus, impact assessment and targeted interventions aim to address negative consequences that frequently accompany infrastructure development and market expansion. This path-breaking book, drawing on more than 20 years of ethnographic research in the Mekong region, shows how current models of mitigation cannot adequately cope with health risks generated by wide-ranging entrepreneurialism and enduring structural violence as dreams of 'the good life' are relentlessly enmeshed in strategies of livelihood improvement.

Chris Lyttleton is Associate Professor of Anthropology at Macquarie University, Australia.

T0347930

Routledge Studies in Development, Mobilities and Migration

This series is dedicated to the growing and important area of mobilities and migration within Development Studies. It promotes innovative and inter-disciplinary research targeted at a global readership.

The series welcomes submissions from established and junior authors on cutting-edge and high-level research on key topics that feature in global news and public debate.

These include the Arab Spring; famine in the Horn of Africa; riots; environmental migration; development-induced displacement and resettlement; livelihood transformations; people-trafficking; health and infectious diseases; employment; South-South migration; population growth; children's wellbeing; marriage and family; food security; the global financial crisis; drugs wars; and other contemporary crisis.

Gender, Mobilities and Livelihood Transformations
Comparing indigenous people in China, India and Laos
Edited by Ragnhild Lund, Kyoko Kusakabe, Smita Mishra Panda and Yunxian Wang

Intimate Economies of Development
Mobility, sexuality and health in Asia
Chris Lyttleton

Crisis and Migration
Critical perspectives
Edited by Anna Lindley

Intimate Economies of Development

Mobility, sexuality and health in Asia

Chris Lyttleton

Routledge
Taylor & Francis Group

LONDON AND NEW YORK

First published 2014
by Routledge
2 Park Square, Milton Park, Abingdon, Oxfordshire OX14 4RN

and by Routledge
711 Third Avenue, New York, NY 10017

First issued in paperback 2016

Routledge is an imprint of the Taylor & Francis Group, an informa business

British Library Cataloguing in Publication Data
A catalogue record for this book is available from the British Library

Library of Congress Cataloguing in Publication data
Lyttleton, Chris.
  Intimate economies of development : mobility, sexuality and health in Asia / Chris Lyttleton.
    pages   cm. – (Routledge studies in development, mobilities and migration ; 2)
  Includes bibliographical references and index.
  1. Mekong River Region – Social conditions.   2. Mekong River Region – Economic conditions.   3. Sex – Mekong River Region.   4. Public health – Mekong River Region.
  5. Economic development – Social aspects – Mekong River Region.   6. Mekong River Region – Emigration and immigration – Social aspects.   I. Title.
  HN690.8.A8L98   2014
  306.309597'8–dc23
  2013039318

ISBN 13: 978-0-415-78727-7 (pbk)
ISBN 13: 978-0-415-81773-8 (hbk)

Typeset in Times
by Out of House Publishing

This book is dedicated to Nook and Sudjai

Contents

Figures and tables

Figures

Tables

Acknowledgements

I owe massive thanks to numerous people in different locales, communities and government sectors all over the region: they are far too many to name but this in no way reduces my profound sense of gratitude. I hope the following chapters make it very clear the depth of my debt to so many people for sharing their time, their feelings and thoughts, not to mention everyday practicalities of sharing food, drink and the chance to talk about life. I am glad to be able to re-voice my thank-you's here to each and every one. I also want to thank the folk accompanying me and helping me gather details, narratives and shared experiences in wide-ranging lifeways across the region over many years including A-Pu, Pouyer, Tadum Sayarath, Santiphap Luangbouheuang, Chittaphone Santavasy, Manichan Keoviriyavong, Sisouvanh Vorabouth, Mukdawan Sakboon, Soontree Reuanmoon, Paul Cohen, Patchareepan Ravangban, Li Yunxia, Deng Rei and Zhang Nan, to name just a few. They have to a person been wonderful. Advice and encouragement as I put the text together has come from many sources, let me simply single out Allan Beesey, Lisa Wynn, Paul Cohen and James Loneragan. Collegial support has been an absolute godsend from my colleagues in the Anthropology Department at Macquarie University in allowing me the time and back-up to do the legwork leading to this book, with a special note of gratitude to Payel Ray who has been a constant source of assistance. Institutional support in many places has also been vital. I wish to express deep-felt gratitude to friends and colleagues at UNESCO, Chiang Mai University, Norwegian Church Aid, Yunnan Health and Development Research Association, GTZ, Mae Tao Clinic and the Asian Development Bank, in particular Thapin Phatcharanuruk, Zhang Kaining, Margrethe Volden, Minavanh Pholsena, David Feingold, Heather Peters, Elizabeth Vochten, Terrence Smith, Soe Than Lwyin, Emi Masaki and Randy Dacanay, as well as the numerous government officers who provided help and guidance along the way. At different stages, funding for research has come from AusAID, ADB, UNESCO, Norwegian Church Aid and Macquarie University.

Chapters 2 and 5 contain excerpts of material I have previously published in *The Australian Journal of Anthropology* 2011, 22 (3); *Asian Studies Review* 2011, 35 (2); *Culture, Health and Sexuality* 2011, 13 (suppl.2); and a monograph published in 2008 by UNESCO titled *Mekong Erotics: Men Loving/Pleasuring/Using Men in Lao PDR.*

Abbreviations

AAC	Asian AIDS Committee
ACMECS	Ayeyawaddy-Chao Phraya-Mekong Economic Cooperation Strategy
ADB	Asian Development Bank
ASEAN	Association of Southeast Asian Nations
B	Thai Baht
BEZs	Border economic zones
CDC	Centers for Disease Control
CPPCR	Committee for Protection and Promotion of Child Rights (Burma)
EIA	Environmental impact assessment
FAO	Food and Agriculture Organization of the United Nations
FSW	Female sex worker
GBC	Golden Boten City
GFE	The girlfriend experience
GMS	The Greater Mekong Sub-region
GTZ	German Society for Technical Cooperation
HIV	Human Immune Deficiency Virus
ID card	Identity document card
IDU	Injection drug user
IOM	International Organization of Migration
KAPs	Key affected populations
MAP	Migrant Action Program
MARPs	Most-at-risk populations
MMN	Mekong Migration Network
MSM	Men who have sex with men
NAch	Need for achievement
NCA	Norwegian Church Aid
NGOs	Non-governmental organizations
OECD	Organisation for Economic Co-operation and Development
PWID	People who inject drugs
RETA	Regional Technical Assistance Project
SARS	Severe Acute Respiratory Syndrome

SEZs	Special economic zones
STIs	Sexually transmitted infections
TBBC	Thailand Burma Border Consortium
UK	United Kingdom
UNAIDS	Joint United Nations Programme on HIV/AIDS
UNDP	United Nations Development Programme
UNESCO	United Nations Educational, Scientific and Cultural Organization
UNFPA	United Nations Population Fund
VCCT	Voluntary confidential counselling and testing
WHO	World Health Organization

Introduction

I come to desire the pleasure of desire itself. In fact it could not be otherwise. If desire were satiated, if it were not deflected onto a demand for commodities, the fashionable replacement of which knows no limits, then not only would the growth of wealth come to a halt, but the whole social nexus of civilization would fall apart.

(Adam Smith in Buck-Morss, 1995: 452)

This book is about desires and development. Not desires *for* development in the sense of a 'road to the modern', but desires as fundamental components of social change. At face value, wishful dreams and development programmes might seem awkward bedfellows in a world where subjective wellbeing is considered the stuff of existential grappling and development is more concerned with bricks and mortar of social and economic engineering. But, as Stiglitz (2011) wryly reminds us, "trickle-down economics may be a chimera, but trickle-down behaviorism is very real". Stiglitz is right: desires for a better life filter far and wide as people seek to emulate a preferred lifestyle, nowhere more so than in areas where development actively introduces broader opportunities. In fact, mimicry has a long history if, for example, we think back to an earlier era when the foibles of colonists were resolutely copied in imperial capitals dotting the globe. But these days longings for 'what the other has' perhaps reach further than before as neoliberal expansion is generally credited with loosening more traditional constraints and fostering myriad forms of entrepreneurship. Indeed, highly contagious aspirations have become part of daily life in even the most remote parts of the world as infrastructure development, migration and diverse forms of media stimulate perceptions of what is possible and what is needed and how best to achieve both. The production of desire, restlessly internalized in the notion that we can and should live the 'good life' – and moreover, that the responsibility to achieve this lies with us as individuals – has become a normative aspect of life almost everywhere. Reality is, of course, not so forthcoming.

As such, while often unspoken and certainly unmeasured, fostering desires is a crucial substrate of programmed interventions aimed at improving everyday life in developing countries. Of course, socio-political and economic contexts vary depending on which developing country and which particular group one is considering. So too, the specific nature of longings and aspirations is never homogenous no matter how much trickle-down might have taken place. Nevertheless, there is common ground in the process by which people's lives are fashioned by global forces that transform not only worldviews and everyday material conditions but simultaneously "our most intimate inner processes: emotion, cognitive style, memory, our deepest sense of self" (Kleinman and Fitz-Henry, 2007: 55). One reason that these global figurations intrude so deeply into who we are is due to a simple but often overlooked fact. Capitalism is, first and foremost, a form of social interaction that tailors how people think and feel. "Capital, of course," as Hardt and Negri (2009: ix) explain, "is not a pure form of command but a social relation, and it depends for its survival and development on productive subjectivities that are internal but antagonistic to it." As capitalism(s) spreads via this painstaking colonization, so too, it inspires previously unentertained and ineffable hopes, nowhere more so than in areas undergoing targeted development.

Numerous philosophers, such as Adam Smith (quoted above) or Marx, have stressed that capitalizing on desires is central to the ways in which people angle for, and exploit, advantage within changing economic orders. So too, affect more generally is regarded as central to contemporary globalization wherein "the formation of our tastes, and thus of our desires and satisfactions, is necessarily bound up with the proliferating differences of capitalism and their seductions" (Moore, 2011: 24). From this vantage point, aspirations cease to be idiosyncratic emotions that emanate from the individual psyche but are part of much larger cultural systems of shared meaning, including wants and needs. To this end, among his vast abstractions, Deleuze offers one crystalline point: "It is not that 'I' have desires; it is from desire that an 'I' or subject is effected" (Colebrook, 2002: 116). Furthermore, as he and Guattari argue, intensification of desire as it flows (unevenly) within different social formations is a primary producer of human sociality. Put more simply, being subjectively shaped by wants and needs is one of the most fundamental elements of our existence as social beings. In what follows, my intention is to detail how modernization generates particular currents of sentiment and styles of self-making as it offers new options, creates new connections and leverages new lifestyles throughout much of the world.

Even beginning with the relatively banal suggestion that desire is what forms and connects us as human subjects, observations linking aspirations and global circuits of value find little currency among development planners. As they too grapple with how to improve the common lot of their would-be beneficiaries, development agents tend to think of connections as being built in more conventional ways – through markets and trade and roads that will deliver a steady movement from A to B. But, even if seldom within the orbit of development planning, how desires circulate is central to visions of modernization. In a world where millions seek to find their feet amid changing economic structures and heightened mobility, Appadurai reminds us of one persistent fact: social life unfailingly unfolds through "practices of intimacy" which, as he explains, embrace "the work of sexuality and reproduction, the webs of nurture and of friendship, the heat of anger and violence, the nuance of gesture and tone" (1997: 116). These everyday moments of interpersonal connection largely go unnoticed precisely because of intimacy's very mundaneness. This does not make them unimportant: quite the contrary. It is often the smallest of human gestures, the most personal moments of human interaction – the affectionate glance, the swallowed grimace, the automatic clap on the shoulder – that form the fabric of social life and the grounding of human existence. We can put it another way, material economies are never separate from intimate economies in the ways people experience their lives, nor should they be disconnected in our analyses. How we envisage and understand the interface of these nuanced and sometimes contradictory dimensions for those under the sway of development assistance and economic transformation is the aim of this book.

Self-making in the Mekong

Regardless of whether we think of them in material form or more abstract yearnings, regardless of whether we detect them as prompted or prevented from becoming part of embodied hopes and dreams, how aspirations inform or stimulate what we do remains integral to the politics of everyday life. But while desires can, of course, range all across the emotional scale from relatively superficial whims to profound longings, there are also important ways in which they are framed and structured as part of development processes. The politicized role played by affect (a term taken to mean, in sum, the cultural and contingent nature of emotions) is arousing increasing interest within social formations in Asia where, for example, Rofel (2007: 3) tells us that the spread of infectious yearnings and passions creates "a desiring subject" pivotal to the transformation of post-socialist China. Given their centrality in "new forms of emotional labour and to responses to the precariousness of neoliberal workplaces" (Wetherell, 2012: 10) in China or anywhere else, Wetherell suggests the pressing question then becomes whether, in fact, affective practices can be "exchanged for other kinds of capital such as material wealth?" (ibid: 112). In what follows I will demonstrate how intimate relations do indeed become valorized, albeit in unpredictable ways, through both speculative and sometimes dehumanizing processes of self-making prompted by development trajectories.

What follows is not a political economy of development that scrutinizes allocations of material and financial resources. There are many other existing analyses of this sort (see, for example, Santasombat (2008), Ganjanapan (2000) and Glassman (2010), to mention only three). Here, we take a different tack. This book is about affective economies and delivers quite different insights. For typically, rather than seeing them as central to processes of accumulation and exchange, we are far more likely to take for granted that emotions are infectious as we effortlessly share in, or have trouble avoiding, prevailing sentiments emanating from those around us. The fact that we often do not register this transaction is part and parcel of intimacy's seemingly private functioning. Taking stock of how development evokes and transforms the immeasurable, intangible and sometimes invaluable emotional substrates to everyday lives, and how this profoundly mediates development's practice and impact, relies on deeper examination. This, in turn, places firmly centre-stage another taken-for-granted assumption, in this case, that contemporary free-market structures are not only more efficient but that they actually generate shared wants and needs. In this light, to speak of different economies – financial, political, symbolic, intimate and so forth – we imagine orchestrated systems geared to managing flows in circumstances of sometimes scarce or limited availability. How this happens is entirely dependent on social context. "It should be obvious," Dumont suggests, "that there is nothing like an economy out there, unless and until men construct such a thing" (quoted in Buck-Morss, 1995: 439). It is in this sense that I approach affective economies as processes that manage emotions, which is to say, determine how they are mobilized, channelled, negotiated and exchanged, and, in the course of which, take on value. We can thus follow Ahmed who suggests that "emotions work as a form of capital; affect does not reside positively in the sign or commodity, but is produced only as an effect of its circulation" (2004: 120). Put another way, how people feel as they grapple with orchestrated change is not restricted to individual psychology. The social character of modernization's affects – excitement or sadness at leaving for the big city, dismay at egregious working conditions, elation at first-time mobile phone ownership, hostility over land encroachment, or any other of the sentiments underpinning social change – circulate in complex ways. As such, an evolving emotional circuitry constitutes social groups through its movement, as it both informs and responds to development's insistent interventions. In short, the myriad and ambivalent ways people engage with capitalism's proffered dreams is fundamental to how market expansion is organized, encouraged and, in turn, experienced.

In parts of Southeast Asia, perhaps even more so than in other parts of the developing world, a prominent dimension that girds contagious visions of modernization are widely promoted notions of 'Community, Competition and Connectedness'. Repeating these three Big-Cs as a campaign chorus, regional policies champion a new architecture of rapid economic integration within the Greater Mekong Sub-region (GMS), a core body recently constituted within Asia. Governments and aid agencies energetically conjure visions of diverse modes of supply chain production woven together by new corridors of trade and labour migration. A number of concrete initiatives, backed by billions of donor dollars, have already established its skeletal framing. Numerous hardware and policy developments are now stitching together a new skin for this geo-body ranging from tariff streamlining through to expedited customs and immigration through to concrete thoroughfares being carved through feebly resistant mountains. Subsistence, cash-crop production, industry and services intermingle as infrastructure, commodity flows and supply chains channel a more 'modern' consumer consciousness throughout the region. "New forms of knowledge create new forms of sociality which have the potential to create new ways of seeing, doing, feeling and being" (Moore, 2011: 22). Nowhere is this truer than in the now pulsating connection of hinterland and urbanized areas of the Mekong countries where previously hostile polities are now traversed by far-reaching labour networks, circular mobility and accessible technology that bring into close contact strongly contrasting ideas and mores of modernity.

In aiming to clarify the nexus of material and intimate economies, we must first be clear that this is not the sacrosanct realm of the private, as much as we are led to believe it is. Intimate relations are a formative part of our everyday lives: they are born of affect, central to a sense of self and the unavoidable means by which we connect to others. As such, they also share a wide gamut of emotional dimensions from nurturing, affection and desire through to struggles over social and economic power. Intimacy is certainly inner-directed, defined by dictionaries as "pertaining to…one's deepest nature", "private and personal action", "close personal relationship", "sexual"; but intimacy is never simply a private concern as it is also controlled, manipulated and/or embellished by outside interests (Boym, 1998: 500). And, we might add, structured by the ways capital is exchanged and accumulated. For beyond its private markings, intimacy is at heart an aspiration for something shared; a narrative, Berlant tells us, "set within zones of familiarity and comfort: friendship, the couple, and the family form, animated by expressive and emancipating kinds of love" (1998: 281). The rub is, of course, that the public institutions of intimacy – the family, trusting camaraderie of the close and the dear, and so forth – seldom endure as stable forms when "romance and friendship inevitably meet the instabilities of sexuality, money, expectation and exhaustion" (ibid). Intimate relations are thus also the sites of contestations over power and identity. It is precisely this insistent instability that prompts intimacy's creative range of expression, none more so than in the equally volatile way that social relations are transformed by targeted interventions. Taken together, and this is the key point, contemporary neoliberal entrepreneurialism, and development initiatives that assist its expansion, can and do implicate aspirations and intimacy in both normative and exceptional ways. And, as I will reveal, it is the implicit vulnerability within intimate relations emerging as an integral part of changing material economies that should be a concern to well-meaning attempts to mitigate risk and unwanted consequences of structured interventions.

Bringing our focus to the unpredictable and unstable role of intimacy within development trajectories is important in that it allows us to demonstrate how changing economic structures impact on an individual's subjective sense of self, every bit as much as the more quantifiable dynamics of agricultural change, transformed labour markets or spreading consumerism. To do so, I will take a number of different examples from parts of Southeast Asia, in particular the borderlands where multiple Mekong countries adjoin. The ways different people and groups in these areas manage their lives, as much of the world around them is refigured, brings to mind what is so often forgotten within development blueprints – that capitalism is at heart a historical formation informed by both material and immaterial dimensions of social interaction. Some take an almost religious position on this process: "Humanity and its soul are produced in the very processes of economic production" (Hardt, 1999: 91). There is no doubt the very scale of global capitalism lends itself to such images of all-consuming influence. But even when choosing a more modest stance on how economic structures impact on the sense of self, one must stay conscious of the fact that specifics always vary. Diversity remains one of capitalism's irreducible elements despite the limited vocabulary used to address its "styles and subjectivities" (Tsing, 2009: 150) and it is precisely its productive instabilities that consistently engender new affective practices which form the focus of this book.

Variability in capitalist structures is often attributed to the temporal and evolutionary framework underlying the rise of modernity and its subsequent stages (Jameson, 2002). In this perspective, modernization, as a strategy to turn premodern into modern via core structural changes, ushered a generalized transition from agriculture to industry. Subsequently, in much of the industrialized world, the dominant engine of capital growth moved from industry to services and information. A corollary movement takes place away from manual labour and into the domain of affective labour through practices that produce immaterial goods – knowledge, information and so forth. Thus, affective labour gains increasing prominence within, for example, service industries in the sense "that its products are intangible: a feeling of ease, well-being, satisfaction, excitement, passion – even a sense of connectedness or community … What affective labour produces are social networks, forms of community, biopower" (Hardt, 1999: 96). Some place this step-like evolution as fundamental to the growth of global consumerism. Indeed, analyses of diversifying networks of supply and demand often show how central affective labour has become to the latter-day spread of capitalism and its reliance on services, outsourcing and casualization. Others remain more sanguine about transition being either sequential or equivalent to a global sea-change and caution against forgetting numerous circumstances of gut-wrenching labour found all over the world, regardless of the shift to service and information economies (Tsing, 2009). This is certainly true in the examples to be used throughout this book where entrepreneurship and exploitation frequently co-exist as tandem aspects of social change, and where gruelling exertion and punishing surveillance are common even as people seek consumerist pleasures found glimmering in emergent economic opportunities.

In what follows, we will traverse the Greater Mekong Sub-region (Myanmar, Thailand, Cambodia, Vietnam, Laos and part of China) to uncover precisely how affective dimensions of human life – in this case, the dynamic, creative and sometimes oppressive practices of intimacy – inevitably and inseparably dovetail with more concrete life changes brought about by economic and infrastructure development. While the specifics differ, we can detect similar processes of self-making taking place through affective practices throughout the Mekong region: as much in the rubber fields of North Laos as in the garment factories at the Thai/Myanmar border, as much in 'gay' encounters in downtown Vientiane as the massage shops in Southern Thailand, as much in opulent casinos in special economic zones near the China border as in ramshackle beer-bars along new roads crisscrossing the region. In the process we will approach development, migration, sexuality and health as four interrelated phenomena. To do so, I aim to address particular shortcomings in current thematic approaches.

1. *Migration and social fields*

Glick Schiller has alerted us that analyses of migration and mobility seldom manage to consider

> daily social activities that unite migrants and natives within workplaces, neighbourhoods and leisure activities. They also disregard the forces that construct differences, such as the intersections of the global political economy and local forms of differentiating power, including those that racialise, feminise, and subordinate regions, populations and locations.
>
> (Glick Schiller, 2009: 26)

I intend to consider both. In a region characterized by multiple forms of movement and multiple modes of regulation, global capitalism insistently makes hopes and dreams central to its expansion in ways that require ongoing and often embodied negotiation. As specific behaviours do indeed 'trickle-down', it is clear this process doesn't occur unassisted: fantasy needs an object, emulation needs a subject and the capacity to aspire needs a roadmap. This combination takes shape in the unremarkable and unreported ways that populations and individuals find themselves prompted to move in search of something better. But while mobility might provide an opportunity to embrace new ways of being in the world, this does not guarantee escape from forces that disempower as much if not more than they empower. One way or another, as roads and policies bring an ever more diverse range of peoples together under the guise of opportunity, interactions between itinerant and non-itinerant peoples are an important staging ground for new forms of social and economic relations. We will see that under the frameworks of donor and state development programmes, the capacity to aspire and the intimate practices this promotes have taken on a wider set of possibilities and permutations than ever before as local awareness of strategic choices is broadened through vibrant circuits of media, meanings, bodies and practices. The self-making processes that take place as part of an expanding frontier are refracted through rubrics of power that determine how one is either assimilated into, or marginalized by, new hierarchies of value and human capital. Cultural, social and economic difference is often at the heart of these circulations determining the extent to which one feels one belongs, or what one has to do to belong. At the same time, various forms of state and regional surveillance seek to set effective monitoring and policing mechanisms that guarantee a migrant's 'sense of self' conform to social and political norms and ensure where necessary that enduring hierarchies are, in fact, maintained.

2. *Managing intimacy*

A central premise of this book is that discussions of international development seldom explore the extent to which the specific nature and dynamics of people's interpersonal interactions, both within and beyond local communities, determine the contours of social and economic change. Intimate relations are a case in point. I refer to these as relations that are physically and emotionally close (or at least appear to be) and take shape in a shifting landscape, where, as one example, reproductive labour is drawn into transnational flows of bodies and capital (Constable, 2009: 50). Thinking specifically of sexual connections, Hubbard (2011) has pointed out that, short of a focus on sex trafficking, international political economy seldom considers sex as central to contemporary globalization. He insists that this occlusion prevents us from seeing "the importance of sexuality both in decisions to migrate and in migrant lifestyles within world cities" (ibid: 3). Hubbard's interest is on how 'landscapes of desire' animate urban environs. But migration and intimacy are not simply formative elements of self-making in cities. Moore (2011: 96) agrees that we need to grasp the fact that "modernisation and nation-building depend on the proper management of intimate relations", but adds that, in this context, international development remains an arena where "modern understandings of sexuality have been extensively deployed, but in ways which frequently escape critical attention". Closer scrutiny does indeed show that social spaces transformed by development programmes, whether in cities or not, are inevitably a product of the relationships constituted within these spaces, and furthermore that evolving market-based connections emerging as part of development's promise frequently have intimate and sexual underpinnings. People and institutions embrace and exploit this in different ways as affective practices become entrepreneurial choices. In so doing, geography, sexuality and development become closely linked.

3.   *Development and disease*

Part and parcel of the widening landscape of intimacy accompanying mobility is the ever-present threat of infectious disease. One might categorize vulnerability to HIV or other infectious diseases facing mobile populations in specific ways:

> in absolute terms (people are unprotected), in relative terms (exposure to higher than average risks), epidemiologically (exposure to higher risks of infection), medically (inability to get optimal quality and level of care), with respect to human rights (exposure to discrimination), socially (deprived of some or all social rights and services), economically (inability to offset risk of infection or access to care) and politically (inability to get full representation or lacking political power).
>
> (Wolffers et al, 2002: 459)

Apart from the commonplace notion that development status and HIV spread are interrelated, detailed consideration of how development initiatives transform aspirational strategies that, in turn, feed into any or all of the above risks, is missing. For example, growing human rights discourses are bringing attention to the diversity of sexual cultures, but these understandings still fit awkwardly within targeted health programmes. Quite simply, this is because desires – in particular overlapping the domain of sexuality – and their place in growing consumer consciousness are such subjective aspects of being. When sexuality is discussed in development programming, often as part of the Millennium Development Goals' focus on HIV and maternal health, it is typically addressed within static gender frameworks, attempts to place non-normative sexualities into catch-all categories or generic notions of health-based negative externalities. In most cases, sexuality is side-lined as unpredictable and immeasurable. But does this make the place of desires as a fundamental part of growing consumer capitalism any less important to development programmes' outcomes and concepts of mitigation? Rather than seeing sexuality as something in need of correction or regulation (usually via negative sanctions), examining how intimate relations and human capital become deployed as an integral part of people's strategies to engage in new market opportunities is crucial if we are to understand the complexities of development's impacts on physical and mental wellbeing and how to better address potential and/ or real health dilemmas that emerge.

4. *Mitigation*

Finally, in order to address unwanted consequences, the concept of mitigation has become a core but contentious element of contemporary development practice. After 60 years of reflection on how foreign aid affects people in both empowering and debilitating ways, the concept of minimizing 'collateral' damage has become a central operating principle in much OECD development planning. Impact assessments are mandated in order to ameliorate outcomes. But has there been adequate attention to the limits of this thinking? In following chapters it will become clear that when we consider development's intrusion into how people actually think and feel we see that mitigation is currently a clumsy tool, and not yet equal to the complex dynamics of social and interpersonal relationships that are at the heart and soul of development's impact. Bruno Latour (2008) describes the double-bind facing social change makers in his aptly-titled essay, "It's Development, Stupid! Or How to Modernize Modernization?". Modernization, he writes, is, in essence, a "continuous movement toward a greater and greater level of attachments of things and people at an ever-expanding scale and at an ever-increasing degree of intimacy" that, in a complex set of nested outcomes, requires "the normal duty of continuing to take care for the unwanted consequences all the way, even if this means going ever further and further down into the imbroglios". Given the proliferating range of interventions as donors seek to improve the lot of the less fortunate, precisely how to mitigate unintended consequences that emerge from intimate attachments becomes a central, albeit unrecognized, problem for development planners. This is particularly relevant in areas such as the GMS with its high ethnic diversity and intensely orchestrated intersections of vastly discordant levels of human, social and financial capital.

The practice of contemporary impact assessment in the GMS raises a further and very glaring contradiction. The ethos of entrepreneurialism relies on people taking a chance, on people taking risks. This premise is fundamental to the sensibilities sweeping through the region. Yet at the same time, millions of development dollars go into supposedly mitigating unwanted consequences, based on a pre-emptive logic of 'measure, avoid and/or compensate'. There is a very basic tension here. On the one hand, people are encouraged to try their hand in market engagement in freeform ways one cannot anticipate and, on the other hand, we work with a logic that suggests we can anticipate and take care of undesired consequences before they happen despite the fact that aspirational endeavours are premised on their unpredictability. The impossibility of any resolution seems lost on programmers and policymakers who champion the alchemical magic of the market at the same time as programmatically asserting the ironclad assurance of impact assessments and viability of mitigation. It is not only planners who maintain a schizophrenic approach to the ability to contain risk. The many migrant, mobile and/or marginal individuals called upon to be foot soldiers in expanding economies of the region are buffeted mercilessly by the viscerally incompatible combinations of intoxicating aspiration and (self-) imposed subordination to the point that grasping and avoiding risk becomes an ever-more alien expectation. As Latour (2008) notes, mitigation aims to plumb the depths of a combination of greater intimacy and surrounding imbroglios in its attempts to take care of the downsides of social change, even as this implies it must remain perpetually at odds with its mission.

First steps: locating connectivity

In order to shed light on the many paradoxes and incongruities that emerge in the project of structurally and discursively engineering modernization's trajectories, we turn attention to development and its affective economies in the Greater Mekong Sub-region (GMS), which sits between Northeast and South Asia forming a strategic crossroads for trade and communication. It is, according to its chief financial backer the Asian Development Bank (ADB), "a natural economic area" that can be best advanced through what it terms "the corridor-development approach" (ADB, 2012: 4) via which expanding capital markets are the key driver of regional growth. As such, it is a region fired by dreams of cooperative development that will jump-start economic growth and livelihood improvement for the millions of poor people residing in the adjoining nation-states. It has become the terrain of an ambitious infrastructure programme that aims, with large amounts of money, to insert the skeletal structure that might support these goals. While concerted market penetration is decades old in many parts of the GMS, and disenfranchisement associated with ethnicity and migration is a commonplace occurrence in the region, I wish to demonstrate a more nuanced engagement. Under the enthusiasms of spreading neoliberal sensibilities and integrated regional development the colliding trajectories of aspirations, intimacy, mobility and health have become ever more apparent.

I draw examples from different parts of this region: from the previously poppy-covered fields of North Laos to the downtown beats of rapidly modernizing Vientiane, from proliferating 'pit-stops' and ethnic ghettoes along new economic corridors through to 'special' enclaves dotting the borders that, in one zone might be sweatshop production sites, in another might be pleasure palaces catering to mobile gamblers or, in a third case, drug-riddled red-light zones created for cross-border dalliances. It has been popular to think of situations such as these as zones of exception, as unique spaces operating with a different set of rules and expectations. This might have some basis in fact, but I will aim to show more. For it is the common links that overarching GMS visions seek to cement that, in fact, make these non-exceptional spaces even as they market their 'specialness'. Indeed, both within and beyond these special zones, locals and non-locals are seemingly enthused by the entrancing qualities of the GMS vision, endowing the region with exemplary and progressive characteristics full of opportunities for its residents and lessons for analysts. "The GMS is also worth understanding for those of us living outside of it because it is an integral part of the broader world in which processes of 'globalization' and 'regionalization' are occurring ... Like other world regions, the GMS is being conceptually produced with boundaries marking it as a distinct place of development", the unveiling of which Glassman imagines will offer "a true metaphor for the world in which we all live" (2010: 2).

Visions of the importance of the GMS such as these radiate in many directions – unsurprising given the massive amount of money spent in stitching together the architecture of this dream. How dreams become activated and experienced is a far more tenuous project to uncover. Central to our concerns are the ways interpersonal connections become the substrate of precarious subjectivities as inspired aspirations find an uneasy fit with the ambiguous reality of development's deliverables. Foucault offers us his version of the contemporary connectivity and community being championed by development agents in the GMS:

> We are in the epoch of simultaneity: we are in the epoch of juxtaposition, the epoch of the near and far, of the side-by-side, of the dispersed. We are at a moment, I believe, when our experience of the world is less that of a long life developing through time than that of a network that connects points and intersects with its own skein.
>
> (Foucault, 1986: 22)

It is the pulsing points on the various GMS skeins that we now turn to.

Chapter summary

The following chapters build on fieldwork carried out by myself, either alone or with research colleagues, in GMS countries over the past 20 years. Chapter 1 introduces the conceptual and geographic terrain where lives are transformed by intersections of the material and the intimate. Chapter 2 is about the exploration and exploitation that take place in frontier zones as ethnic women's sexuality becomes a formative element of market expansion. I focus on how aspirations and structural violence typify development's intrusions into settings where rubber plantations blanket remote hills and forested domains are cut open by

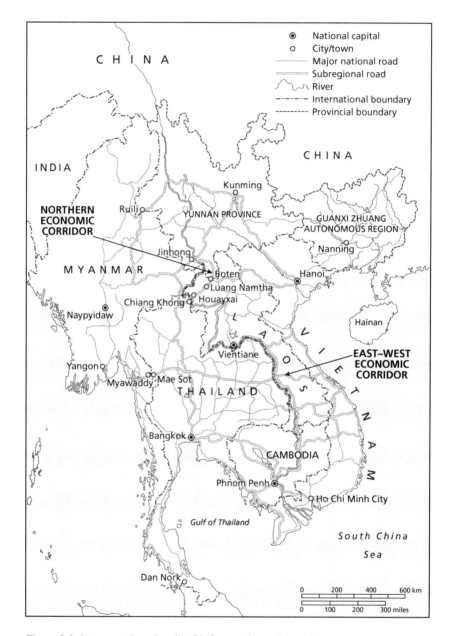

Figure 0.1 A new patchwork quilt: GMS countries and corridors

new highways. Chapter 3 moves us from blacktops to blackjack and takes us deeper into 'special' border locales where, in the interests of establishing market value, red-light trade towns and over-the-top casinos manufacture enticements premised on sensual and sexual excess. Chapter 4 describes the underbelly politics of the growing precariat in the GMS and the profound affective responses that emerge. We canvas how a global marketplace rationalizes labour regimes that debase migrant workers and in so doing promote volatile relations predicated on emotional and physical security. Chapter 5 then shows us how aspirations remain resilient and creatively linked to the speculative project of attaching value to human capital in embodied and intimate ways. Chapter 6 is about aiming to address health dimensions emerging from the valorized intimacies described in each of the preceding chapters through rubrics of predicting and pre-empting damage. Pseudonyms have been used throughout.

1 Ethnicity, capital and the architecture of mobile hopes and dreams

> *To the degree that identity has come to rest, at once, on ascription and choice, conviction and ambiguity, ineffability and self-management, it has embedded itself in a human subject increasingly seen, and experienced from within, as entrepreneurial. Not least in enacting her or his otherness.*
>
> (Comaroff and Comaroff, 2009: 50)

In the late 1600s, Dutch philosopher Baruch Spinoza argued that we should recognize that affect is crucial to our capacity to act. For him, a central dimension of humanness is the importance that the 'capacity to be affected' has for our ability to act meaningfully in this world. One of Spinoza's concerns was to uncover the work that fear and joy do in mobilizing political subjectivities, a focus that makes his work timely and evergreen. For our purposes, he evokes a fundamental premise – affect is a constitutive rather than a derivative quality in political practice, that is to say, the ways people actually feel is indispensable in the (re)constitution of the social body (Ruddick, 2010: 24). Applied to our interest in populations in the GMS, this means that the potential to improve one's life (the object of so much development machinery) cannot and should not be separated from an emotional engagement in the process. The capacity to aspire to, or desire for, something better is central to making appropriate and/or opportunistic choices that change one's life. Or, in the terms I am using to frame this perspective, to understand development and its contingent impacts, material and intimate economies should be conceived as indivisible.

Spinoza distinguishes *potentia* – an innate capacity to act – from *potestas*, a top-down control of knowledge that dominates and alienates its audience. *Potentia* or empowerment is achieved through the social nature of becoming active, where emotions are understood and inform communal action rather than the prescriptive frameworks (*potesta*) that encourage passive observance of the rules (ibid: 26). Three hundred years later this is eerily familiar to key tenets derived from recent decades of development programmes – participation of local communities is essential, top-down delivery is anathema to sustainable outcomes. But there is more to this picture. According to Spinoza, in order to mobilize *potentia*, the capacity to act must emerge from a complex interplay of affect and reason which,

Figure 1.1 Akha woman musing at a monthly market

in turn, entails collaboration with others. "These collaborations," Ruddick summarizes, "stem from our desire to reproduce 'joyful' encounters and avoid painful or discomforting ones" (ibid). Passive engagement of the emotions causes 'inadequate ideas' and thereby limits the capacity to act. On the other hand, active engagement creates a sense of accomplishment (joy) through positive collaborations and achievements. This brings us back to the crucial point that Spinoza recognized so many years ago – affective practices are central to the unfolding of modernization and social mobilization processes. Or in the catchphrase of legions of neo-Spinozists: 'You can't have effect without affect.' In this chapter we move beyond a narrow focus on joyous engagement to lay the geographic and conceptual groundwork necessary to profile the ways that aspirations and other sentiments, such as fear and envy, longings and satisfactions, are part of shared affective economies circulating throughout the GMS (and beyond).

The geographic field of our enquiry into these economies was given official definition in 1992, when six Asian countries entered into a (literally) groundbreaking programme of cooperation and development. The agreements created a new entity, the Greater Mekong Sub-region (GMS), transposed over prior cartography in order to highlight its geopolitical importance. Its strategic goal is to revitalize Asian regionalism. Its collective target is more than 300 million people living in countries linked by the Mekong River: Cambodia, Lao People's Democratic Republic (forthwith Laos), Myanmar, Thailand, Vietnam as well as Yunnan Province and Guangxi Zhuang Autonomous Region of the People's Republic of China. Based around billions of dollars invested in infrastructure, growth policies plan to use abundant natural wealth – timber, minerals, coal and petroleum, hydropower – to boost local economies. They also intend to embed more open, market-based systems to create a competitive bloc in an area more recently familiar with war, strife and political conflict. The transition from widespread subsistence farming to diversified supply chain production is regarded as crucial for reducing economic disparities and developing the region's human capital, even as its actual implementation is far from straightforward.

Market penetration is not new, but it has been given huge impetus under the GMS framework. Given the scale of interventions across this terrain, in particular in the agriculture sector (where resettlement, cash-cropping and contract farming have been furiously leveraged), the first two decades of GMS programming have delivered profound impacts on everyday life. Some people have benefitted as economies have indeed grown noticeably across the region. So too, there are many who might not consider their lives improved as "'pre-capitalist' agricultural workers are not only dispossessed and transformed into wage workers, but most often pushed into motion spatially. These displaced workers have commonly migrated across regional divides to relatively urban centres in Thailand and Vietnam, swelling the ranks of the informal and precarious labour markets" (MMN, 2013: 167). For others, perhaps even the majority, sorting out a livelihood remains a fraught mix of imposed interests intermeshed with insistent aspirations. Everyday lives are simultaneously supported and/or shoehorned by policy directives and infrastructure roll-outs in often incongruous ways, in the course of which hopes and dreams end up deployed in a vast range of directions. This is the nature of development's pointillist canvas– die-hard optimism sitting awkwardly next to life-sapping exploitation – details obscured if we rely only on soft-focus. Closer scrutiny shows that, one way or another, development programmes and policy mandates continue to transform lifestyles and landscapes in the GMS in often contradictory ways, as mobility becomes routine and new states of being take centre-stage.

Fields of dreams

Creating economic corridors was earmarked as 'the first strategic thrust' of the GMS programme that, substantially supported by the Asian Development Bank (ADB), began in earnest in the early 2000s. Indeed, newly upgraded highways and feeder roads have greatly improved 'physical connectivity' and facilitated cross-border trade, investment and labour migration. In so doing, national polities are physically stitched together with a new architecture that continues to transform local livelihoods and diverse aspects of everyday life. In terms of regional planning, priority has been given to 'clearing the way' through concrete infrastructure. The 'software' aspects of development, that is, how people will actually use the roads, comes in their wake (ADB, 2007: vii). The ADB's emphasis on first laying roads might well remind one of a phrase from a movie. It's about a vision; one might say a vision for development through concrete transformation. In the Hollywood version, Kevin Costner has a revelation – a baseball field will bring life back to his rural community. "If you build it, he will come" he hears in a dream. Shoeless Jackson, that is. He does come, back from the past to create a new future and so too do people – in the final shot we see an endless stream of cars snaking down the highway through the evening dusk on their way to the field. Brought together by the building of this diamond, turning what was cornfields into an icon of American culture. They came to watch the baseball just as they came to watch the movie. *Field of Dreams* was a big-time commercial hit.

Cut back to the GMS where big-time dreams are also common currency. A glossy brochure released in 2004 touted the wonders of Golden Boten City to be carved out of remote forest flanking the Northern Economic Corridor just inside the Lao border with China. The Chinese/English text trades in the language of fantasy as heavily as any Hollywood scriptwriter. After listing the preferential state policies it enjoys to promote import, export and opulent entertainment, this free-trade zone is wishfully described as: "The promised land for freedom and development, wide-world for adventure and fortune. A place where: elite and wisdom [sic], luxury and desire, legend and dream, mystery and fact, all go beyond your imagination." In fact, the investors were seriously hoping the business men and women they attract could very concretely imagine the benefits as they spend 48 pages in this brochure telling of wonderments to be established in Golden Boten City. It, too, might have been subtitled "Field of Dreams" (although, as we will see, happy endings are not guaranteed).

The Upper Mekong is a previously remote area that has often been the subject of ambitious, albeit unrealized, dreams of regional integration. Take, for example, the nineteenth-century British and French missions in search of land-based trade routes to link mainland Southeast Asia with China. So too, cross-border links have at times been etched by spiritual rather than economic mapping. Cohen (1999) describes transnational Buddhist revivalist yearnings inspired by the charismatic and peripatetic monk Khruba Bunchum, who in the 1990s carved a sacred cartography through reliquary-building tours along routes that are remarkably homologous with roads subsequently constructed by the GMS programme. By the early twenty-first century, concrete freeways have become the more prominent symbol of utopian visions as the GMS programme has built corridors for traders, truckers and tourists to move rapidly through previously remote and hinterland areas of neighbouring states (see Figure 0.1 on page 12). Connecting highways and ring-roads linking the six GMS countries are core elements of visions of regional economic cooperation. Border points have been upgraded, customs protocols streamlined and border towns are booming. Bridges have been built, airports with international runways established and troublesome rapids in the Mekong exploded so large cargo boats from China can run unimpeded. Same premise as the movie – in this case plural: "If you build it, they will come." Provide thoroughfares and people will come together to experiment with, or exploit, newfound opportunities. Of course, roads and infrastructure development are about more than just people movement. They also envisage other types of mobility: goods and ideas, trade and commerce. But the notion of integration via these corridors relies most fundamentally on people interacting with people. Roads are magnets as well as thoroughfares. Despite being about movement they are also about openings, about connections, about opportunities, about new forms of economic and social engagement. For thousands – perhaps millions – they represent new choices due to the passage they provide. People come to roads as much as they move along them. And people connect in any number of social and commerce-related interactions, from the clinical handshake over a cultivation contract through to a sexually intimate sojourn with a village woman all in the name of economic integration. Invited, not in this instance by a Hollywood icon, but instead an equally global symbol of modernization – a gleaming blacktop, a new asphalt artery called in tabloid fashion a 'new economic corridor' – that is, in similar fashion, transforming lives.

Befitting this vision, it is not just investment brochures that trade in optimistic rhetoric. The ADB GMS website intones "The rich human and natural resource endowments of the Mekong region have made it a new frontier of Asian economic growth. Indeed, the Mekong region has the potential to be one of the world's fastest growing areas."[1] Bringing such projections into a practical scale of management, the GMS has become a high profile development zone fuelled by donors busily advocating the requisite buzzwords: connectedness, competitiveness and community. Hopes that these manoeuvres will be synonymous with rapid livelihood improvement take root at all levels: from the high-story policy think-tanks prophesying competitive advantage through to hand-in-the-dirt subsistence farmers wondering precisely what they might compete with as market economies become the chief mainstay of everyday social relations. What is far less clear is what it means for the many millions of poor people to become 'connected' in a subjective sense within this contrasting political, economic, cultural and geographic terrain. As mentioned, the scale of impetus to change people's lives in this region is huge, stemming from massive funds soaked into numerous hardware

Figure 1.2 Local labour on the Northern Economic Corridor

schemes geared to assisting in market diversity. But while 'community' is seen as a logical alliance based on cultural proximity and shared programme goals, a closer look at the region shows a more complex reality. At one level, the spread of market capitalism has been pronounced and profound in its reach into even the most remote parts of the GMS where technology as the conduit of commodity desire and wage labour as the conduit of capital have become part of daily life in ways unimaginable a decade or two ago. At another level, the region is fraught with ambiguities inherent in the shift to new economic sensibilities. Jean and John Comaroff, so precise at pointing out paradoxes within global workings, write that neoliberalism:

> appears both to include and to marginalize in unanticipated ways; to produce desire and expectation on a global scale, yet to decrease the certainty of work or the security of persons; ... above all, to offer up vast, almost instantaneous riches to those who master its spectral technologies – and, simultaneously, to threaten the very existence of those who don't.
>
> (Comaroff and Comaroff, 2001: 8)

It is exactly this ambivalent mosaic of everyday life that the roads cutting through the mountains or crossing borders at new checkpoints complicate in both material and immaterial ways. Even as they streamline the physical topography and bisect national cartography, they introduce peaks, troughs and crossings of an altered social landscape: new opportunities, new pitfalls, new projects of self-making, new threats to wellbeing.

Ethnic intersections: time-worn and heartfelt

Although the GMS countries, except the two Chinese provinces, belong to the Association of Southeast Asian Nations (ASEAN) and share in the goal of collectively orchestrated policies, there is little in the way of recent history that guarantees any sense of cultural or political uniformity for regional plans. The slogans promoting community and connectivity paint over a vast canvas of economic and cultural variation. The GMS encompasses the financial powerhouses of Yunnan and Thailand, the rapidly growing economy of Vietnam alongside the improving but less stellar performers of Laos and Cambodia and the recently unshackled resource-rich but opportunity-starved Myanmar. It is politically diverse: the past 50 years have seen bloody confrontations and sometimes horrifically damaging attempts at different modes of governance from uneven command economies, isolationist autarky, dictatorship and haphazard democracy.

Nowadays, liberalized trade policies have earmarked a newfound commitment to minimally fettered market relations even as the wide variability in human, social and environmental resources means this integration will play itself out in uneven ways for years to come. Future uncertainties notwithstanding, this book is not about the bumpy trajectory facing regional economic growth per se. Rather it is about how the attempts to build both physical and symbolic roadmaps may well deliver economic corridors, but that these concrete tarmacs are emblematic of a far more profound set of changes. That is to say, how people use opportunities in ways that both embrace and exploit the increased range of social interactions available to them is uncharted and unpredictable. And yet, how sentiments implicit in capitalist social formations – the heady aspirations and the dehumanizing realities – are, in fact, given substance within and beyond ethnic bounds is central to the way change is unfurling in the GMS.

One fact is obvious: both the concrete roads and ephemeral visions of progress in the GMS embrace a vast mixture of peoples and cultures that defies ready assimilation into neat blueprints. The region is populated by ethnic groups with different ways of being and thinking that prompt complex and sometimes ambiguous relations between politicized bodies at the macro level and contradictory and sometimes ambivalent interpersonal relations at the micro level. In the past, divergent aspirations have led to some groups seeking active distance from state-led modes of governance and socio-economic integration. Hence James Scott's (2009) assertion that millions, who historically lived in stateless societies in Zomia (a putative region covering mainland Southeast Asia), managed to avoid assimilation into larger lowland polities by strategic withdrawal and geographic dispersal into the mountains. Core residences of Zomia's disparate 'state-avoiding' populations were the cool hills that flank the adjoining border areas of Lao PDR, Thailand, Southern China, Myanmar and Vietnam – also called the Southeast Asian Massif. These days the GMS (adding Guangxi to the mix) is home to roughly 65 million people from ethnic minority groups. But, as Table 1.1 makes abundantly clear, even today physical dispersal and social distance mean accurate headcounts are hard to come by.

What is more clear-cut is that a large percent of the lowland rice-growing peoples in the GMS belong to the Tai-language group born of a thousand-year diaspora heading south from China and forming a cultural area "comparable in some respects to say that of the romance languages in Europe" (Turton, 2000: 3). This cultural collectivity is easier to count as it comprises majority national populations (ethnic Thai in Thailand, Lao in Laos), regionally dominant populations within national boundaries (Shan or Tai-Yai in Myanmar) and considerable sub-populations (Dai in China and Tai in Vietnam). For many centuries, Tai populations have distinguished themselves by etching idioms of backwardness, primitiveness and ethnic inferiority to distinguish non-Tai groups. The extent to which Scott's survival strategy treatise characterizes the historical cut and thrust of state/non-state relations is still debated. What is less contentious is that a longstanding dichotomy in Southeast Asia – minority/majority, lowland/highland, people that belong/people that don't – has endured as a structuring device governing social, economic and political relations between different ethnic groups. "Since time immemorial," as Formoso (2010: 320) puts it, "lowland rice growing peasants have despised 'tribesmen' living in nearby hills. But at the same time as they negated their cultural existence, while their rulers attempted to assimilate these backward peoples, they were pragmatic enough to take advantage of their economic resources and of their situation as 'bordermen'." Still today, prejudices underpin political and social domination of minority groups throughout the region.

Ongoing discord between central and peripheral populations centres heavily on political security, land use and access to resources. Some years ago it was estimated that between 30 million and 80 million people depend on shifting cultivation in

Table 1.1 Ethnic groups in the GMS

Major ethnic groupings in the GMS

Major groups	Cambodia	Yunnan (PRC)	Laos	Burma	Thailand	Vietnam
National majority peoples						
Khmer	6,467,000					
Han		24,692,000				
Lao			3,000,000			
Burman				21,533,000		
Thai					59,000,000	
Kinh						65,051,000
Highland peoples						
Tibeto-Burman		7,468,884	159,500	9,692,008	620,800	32,432
Sino Thai		2,059,800	674,085	3,362,400	758,000	5,099,997
Hmong-Mien		1,233,100	260,000	10,000	155,000	1,079,700
Mon-Khmer	115,961	1,280,700	854,449	2,380,100	1,577,857	2,880,395
Austronesian	255,000			7,000	3,115,500	590,000
Subtotal	370,961	12,042,484	1,948,014	15,451,508	6,227,157	9,682,524
Other		542,100			1,423,000	
Ethnic population estimate	6,873,961	37,213,584	4,948,014	36,948,014	66,650,157	74,733,524

Note: the enumeration of population by major ethnic groups is not accurate or up-to-date. As a result, in all countries except Thailand, the ethnic population estimate is less than the estimate for total population. In Thailand, the ethnic population estimate seems to indicate that some people have been counted as both an ethnic minority and Thai.

Source: Asian Development Bank quoting Grimes (2003); (cited in NGO-Forum, nd)

the Asia-Pacific region, most frequently ethnic minority groups (FAO, 1993: 12). While resettlement and modernization have dramatically reduced the ability to perform swidden, processes of assimilation and state attempts to control subsistence patterns and other aspects of minority life consistently introduce social conflict and tension across ethnic lines (Gillogly, 2004). A common characteristic of minority or indigenous peoples is thus marginalization that in the past may have led to conflict and/or flight but nowadays leads to orchestrated resettlement and migration as well as more generally poorer health, lower educational opportunities and a more insecure livelihood. Hierarchies, based on social and cultural capital (or lack of), continue to structure ethnic relations, but prior distinctions are giving way to new avenues of social discrimination. No longer can stereotypes based on economic production (swidden), on topography (highland dwellers) and on geography (border areas) be blanketly applied. Peripheral zones are no longer outside the circuits of economic growth (if they ever were). Rather, minority identities have become front and central due to insistent migration that fosters circuits of national and transnational exchanges and development programmes that, for their part, bring modernization directly to the doorstep of the previously excluded.

Throughout Asia, diverse development programmes aim at 'civilizing' minorities through social engineering projects geared to nationalist conformity, such as fluency in the national language, conversion to a recognized religion and entrance into the world economy. The GMS programme might inadvertently assist with the first two, but it is unabashedly, at the behest of its member governments, leveraging the third of these elements through opportunities for economic diversity. Conventional modernization approaches, cash-crop production, expansion of education promoting lowland values and, most potently, consumer consciousness and wage labour consolidate the move to conformity. But pressure to assimilation also creates profound ambiguities as it both beckons and preserves distances. Difference doesn't disappear as long as maintaining boundaries and hierarchies of 'otherness' remains a core element of the ways a nation produces its citizen body through defining who belongs and how. On the one hand, rapid social change, ushered by new roads and land-use policies, is profoundly disjunctive for minority groups as the "absorption of alien power is accomplished through the dissolution of normal boundaries of the self and cultural identity: identity is submerged in a chaos of differences" (Tapp, 2010: 97). On the other hand, cultural groups recognize that identities can and do change as they find innovative ways of contesting and re-establishing the very tenets of cultural survival and, at times, a willingness to endure imposed social change (Duncan, 2004: 6).

One way or another, the juxtaposition of cultural systems plays out in competition for social and material resources fostering new forms of subjective experience. This process is anything but predictable in its outcomes: "the consequence of this intensification and diversification of exchanges with an enlarged outside world is that the highlander's self-perception is more ambiguous and blurred than before" (Formoso, 2010: 330). The idea of a transformed world with new parameters and knowledge systems is central to the visions of development in the region. What is missing is details clarifying the (blurred) social and affective experiences brought about by opportunities and altered lifestyles throughout the region. As we will see, new roads, factory enclaves, expanding commercial agriculture, casinos and other service industries in frontier towns collectively create intense cultural crucibles that, due to their reliance on itinerant labour, in turn foster hostile affective economies of prejudice and fear in face of migrant inflows even as they feed on the spread of consumer desire central to much mobility in the first place.

"Borders," as Donnan and Wilson (1999: 64) neatly summarize, "are zones of cultural production, spaces of meaning-making and meaning-breaking." The conjunctions and fractures taking place all over the GMS, as people connect and disconnect in the name of economic diversification, mean that frontier zones are fundamentally heterotopic in the sense that they are discordant spaces marked by internal heterogeneity (Saldanha, 2008: 2083). Heterogeneity is prompted not just by movement of people. It is also generated by market forces that increase the mobility of capital, sites of production and of flexible labour with the combined effect of being able "*both* to breach and buttress sovereign borders, *both* to extend and to constrain the regulatory ambit of states, *both* to valorise the local and cast it into force fields well beyond itself" (Comaroff and Comaroff, 2009: 47, emphasis in original). Despite these profoundly equivocal forces and the powerful economy of alterity that makes 'otherness' such a potent mode of productive distinction (and, as pointed out by the Comaroffs at the start of the chapter, one that is ever-more embedded in entrepreneurial sensibilities), we need to remain conscious of the growing silhouette of 'community' also being espoused by donors as people throughout the region are increasingly brought together within an infectious consumer consciousness that expands a 'neoliberal subjectivity' beyond cultural and national bounds. Boundaries might separate adjoining political and geographic entities but they also attract people and institutions with an interest in pursuing interactions across these borders. In so doing, frontier and/or special zones inspire insistent jockeying for advantage as difference and prejudice sit alongside a shared desire for livelihood improvement and the fruits of development.

Remapping social spaces

In much of the GMS, national borders have divided ethnic populations that had previously shared common territory and social structures. At other times, they create new cross-border communities premised on trade and social exchange. From any point of view, frontiers and borders are special zones. They provide diverse opportunities for economic and social relations as they promote entrepreneurial and exploratory forays into neighbouring territory. Borders are also the sites of intense regulation to ensure ventures and relationships supposedly stay within the best interests of the neighbouring nation-states and more concretely those of the communities flanking each other. It is here that policies encouraging economic expansion and those seeking to assimilate 'unruly' populations overlap. The intersection of self-making, desires and development doesn't just take place at national borders. Frontier zones are central to this picture in that they are constantly subject to shifting geographical and temporal scales (Hirsch, 2009).

Figure 1.3 New roads open forests to new vistas and cross-border engagements

Depending what frame of reference one chooses, frontiers in the GMS depict border zone, and sometimes peri-urban, enclaves (throughout the GMS) through to sub-national regions (within unevenly developing nation-states) through to nation-states depicted as regional frontiers (Laos, for example) through to the whole GMS (as ADB has characterized it). Invigorating this evolving boundary-scale is incessant movement that underpins frontier capitalism as a preferred mode of economic expansion. Mobility is precisely what the new economic corridors are premised on – movement within and between countries. Not only is internal migration significant – out of the hills, out of the villages – so too cross-border movement is huge throughout the GMS.

Mobility has historically been encouraged by availability of land in frontier areas as lowland farmers encroach into the periphery and make contact with other cultural groups. At the same time, minority groups have been involved in wide-spread trade relations in parts of Central and South Asia as well as within Southeast Asia for thousands of years. While mobility and migrant labour is nothing new, it is being given a major shift in scale and complexity as regional cooperation gathers steam. In the process, frontier zones and most specifically national borders have been the focus of intense development targeting. In the late 1980s, then Thai Prime Minister Chatichai Choonhavan is famous for prioritizing market relations within ASEAN through his injunction to "turn battlefields into market places". Thailand's economy boomed in the latter decades of the twentieth century and regional and economic integration became a logical way to ensure expansion of this growth. In the early 2000s, alongside assistance from the ADB, border economic zones (BEZs) – often referred to as special economic zones (SEZs) – were established throughout the GMS as cornerstones to furthering regional integration.

Of course, other objectives underlying attention to borders are also relevant, such as formalizing trade in areas historically hard to regulate and controlling labour migration flows by containing them in border areas. In the early 2000s, four sister-city collaborations were established between border towns in Thailand and their neighbours that coincided neatly with the ADB's economic corridors stitching the region together. Since then SEZs have proliferated in other GMS countries and many of them adopt dubious claims to development of local populations through investment in casinos and other high-cash turnover enterprises. Some suggest that, supported by public and private sectors throughout the GMS, neoliberal expansion has set in train a flexibilization of labour resulting in "downward pressure on labour rights and labour standards" and making exploitation central to regional development (MMN, 2013: 173). While this equation sums up pervasive dimensions of a regional political economy, one cannot cast frontier capitalism as purely oppressive or extractive. There is no doubt the newly labelled precariat suffers multiple indignities. At the same time, optimisms and sometimes improved options are also fuelled in these zones. Marginalization is real and insidious, but development processes are seldom black and white. These zones being connected by multiple development thrusts can also be thought of as social spaces that constitute hugely varied forms of interaction and dynamics between mobile and non-mobile populations.

Despite ambiguities in border life, what is abundantly obvious is that, facilitated by economic corridors and new infrastructure, mobility within the six GMS countries has trended steeply upwards between areas of disparate economic status. In part this is due to previously closed economies opening themselves to regional trade and labour movement. Reports have estimated that the overall number of migrants in the GMS is close to 4 million with 2.55 million of these in Thailand (Lewis et al, 2010), although others suggest the number in Thailand is perhaps much higher (Huguet et al, 2012). Complicating accurate headcounts are the numerous forms of movement throughout the GMS. As agricultural transformations, urbanization and industrialization forge ahead, internal movement into urban and peri-urban areas in Laos, Vietnam and Cambodia is also significant but largely uncounted. Thailand, as a core economic hub for the GMS, remains a preferred destination for largely unskilled workers from neighbouring countries seeking higher incomes. It is expected that GMS migrants will increase to nearly 4.5 million persons by 2015 of which roughly 3 million will move to Thailand (Lewis et al, 2010: 18). Economic disparities provide the obvious impetus behind this movement. According to the World Bank in 2011, Thailand's average per capita income was US$5,281, compared to $804 for Myanmar, $912 for Cambodia, and $1,204 for Lao PDR (AEC, 2013). Poorer countries, however, are not just sending countries; they too receive considerable numbers of in-migrants and other itinerant travellers. Specific investment and construction zones – industries, dams and highways, agricultural areas devoted to rubber and other cash crops – bring large numbers of migrant labour from China and Vietnam into Cambodia, Laos and Myanmar. Moreover, a huge but largely uncounted number move back and forth across borders throughout the GMS in itinerant, short-term fashion, often following seasonal agricultural cycles.

In short, mobility in the region is commonplace and substantial and there is massive variation in styles and duration of movement. Its impact is interwoven across social, political and economic dimensions. While some areas undoubtedly benefit materially from large numbers of migrant residents, shifts occur across other domains as the young and able-bodied leave communities and families are fractured for long periods of time. Inevitably forms of social and cultural reproduction are radically reconfigured in the sending communities just as everyday life is transformed for the many that move. A positive view of this movement summarized in *The Economist* (19 November 2011) sees diasporas as most effective in proximate areas when the interpersonal links are mobilized through: cultural links (family, community, ethnic group) that speed the flow of information across borders; networks of trust, as people are much more likely to believe and follow the advice of someone that seems familiar to them; and finally, most important, connections that help people with good ideas collaborate with each other, both within and across ethnicities. This type of thinking informs much of the rationale for increased linkages promoted by community and connectivity. However, it doesn't occur without anxious oversight. Increased border and migrant surveillance is a product of perceptions that increased flows are also a threat to regimes of order and structures of governance. Meanwhile, the experiences of the migrants themselves are often difficult, dangerous and, at times, bordering on inhumane.

There are further explanations for increased migration in the region, including better access to information and efficient transportation, greater communication capacities due to new technologies and ongoing displacement arising from governance problems. Each of these has its roots in orthodox development analyses where debates continue as to how best conceptualize the interface of development and migration. Rather than seeing migration as a development failure (shouldn't development stop people having to leave?) there are many who cite it as a panacea via the economic and human capital that is returned home. Having said this, the assumption that remittances are in fact a reliable tool of development processes is under constant revision. Some think it helps, perhaps following John Galbraith who famously noted "migration is the oldest action against poverty" (1979: 7) – hence migrant diasporas are considered neo-development agents through money sent home. And then there are those that think it doesn't – migrants, they say, far and away benefit the receiving country. More recently, the notion of 'social remittances' has gained currency as returning migrants bearing 'Western' values are seen as natural and valued brokers of social change (Glick Schiller and Faist, 2009: 13). In fact, this model is not so different from previously imagined mechanisms of modernization. For example, in the 1960s, following prominent theories of the time, it was argued that there is a personality attribute crucial to entrepreneurial motivation – the 'need for achievement' (N-Ach), a contagious value that could be made to spread, virus-like, through even the most recalcitrant of traditional societies. Evolutionary notions of development and their remnants of cultural engineering are seldom repeated publicly these days, but their premises have hardly disappeared. Even accepting that mobile bearers of Western values and the transfer of human capital might, although this is highly debatable, constitute a beneficial element of circular migration for home communities, there remains much in this picture that is not well understood. What is an objective measure of social value? There is no doubt that one way or another, at a global level, hundreds of millions of migrants leave their homes in the quest for livelihood improvement and return as 'bearers of values'. Precisely what values they might garner, and how and where they accumulate, is another cornerstone of our enquiry.

Mobility, health and wellbeing

Regional integration endeavours, land-use controls, shifts in production and workforce, desires to accumulate material and symbolic value (and experience the city lights) taken together profoundly destabilize a sense of permanent place for millions in the GMS. Cultural intersections and collisions are therefore inevitable as new thoroughfares allow increased movement to take place within and between areas of ethnic diversity. At times, these interactions merge seamlessly as part of myriad increasing flows. At other times, frictions and fissures emerge as social and cultural accommodation requires compromise and sacrifice. Very often, in particular for migrants with little social or economic capital and little in the way of marketable skills, this involves accepting work and living conditions that pose threats to physical and mental wellbeing. WHO summarizes succinctly the health dilemmas facing a world with more than 200 million international migrants and more than 700 million national migrants:

approaches to manage the health consequences of migration have not kept pace with growing challenges associated with the volume, speed, diversity and disparity of modern migration patterns, and do not sufficiently address the existing health inequities, nor determining factors of migrant health, including barriers to access health services.

(WHO, 2010: 3)

Tellingly, overall, more than a billion poor people worldwide, including migrants, still lack access to essential medicines.

Within the range of health threats to migrants, new infectious diseases pose increasingly difficult problems for international surveillance, treatment and control. Just as the notion of the border is, throughout the world, under intense scrutiny for its ability (or lack of) to regulate mobile bodies, this is an era of epidemic and borderless contagion of a viral form. Internationally, a resurgent rubric of tropical public health focusing on identification and containment is gaining prominence. In the new millennium, where one is from, one's background, one's movement and even one's gender are central to heightened regimes of control. Border-crossers are monitored and registered for the potential they have to be carriers of infectious pathogens (most recently, SARS, bird flu and swine flu) whose emergence, since the early days of Ebola panic, seems to be accelerating and whose control is increasingly globally coordinated. Since 2005, revised global health regulations have expanded the range of reportable diseases, provided criteria for identifying new epidemic events and specified conditions that mandate the involvement of the international community in outbreak responses (Rodier et al, 2007). Given its global severity, the spread of HIV is one prominent example that has focused our attention on 'hotspots' and attendant risks faced by migrants locked into social and economic relations over which they do not always have adequate control. My concerns in this book are not with epidemiological hotspots per se. Rather, I wish to bring attention to a broader array of connections between mobile and non-mobile groups that create opportunities for transmission of illness and disease. The starting point has to be that often relatively mundane behaviours are the bedrock of social interactions within a changing economic landscape. As such, in what follows I use HIV as an example rather than the sole focus of attention in order to explain how implicit vulnerability and instability within forms of intimacy implicate ensuing threats to health and wellbeing.

Disentangling the logics of social action, I will show how intimacy and emotional connections become significant means by which people seek to gain access to new economic opportunities and/or create buffers against uncertain exigencies of life. Throughout the GMS we can pinpoint health threats based on expanding social networks, and attempts to control these, as people use their bodies and intimate relations as a selective means to gain social leverage. At heart is a prominent equation that exacerbates vulnerability to illness and broader forms of social suffering. Economic expansion increases opportunities for profit-seeking – this is the underlying logic of market growth. But we can state this in another way – economic growth increases the opportunities for exploitation. It leads to a second simple correlation. Exploitation can lead to health threats and the spread of disease, at times through sexual relations. This occurs when economic competition involves social subordination that, when gender and ethnicity are implicated, oftentimes also means sexual exploitation. Mobility is central to these formulations. So too is the manner in which neoliberalism reconstitutes a sense of self.

Neoliberalism and intimate reproduction

Framing mobility and the styles of intimate relations within a political economy of globalization highlights inequalities behind people flows. It makes transparent the fact that transnational migration ratchets up the impact of neoliberal policies in developing countries. Agency, and the complicated ways in which mobility and migration reposition individuals and their intimate connections within chains of supply and demand, is central in this mapping. As neoliberal policies have become consolidated throughout the world, so too they introduce an ever tighter alignment with 'enterprise' as the key social value based on market competition and self-interest. Thus, among the broad ethnic diversity I described earlier, we can also highlight the spread of 'enterprise society' through its most obvious manifestations – the patchwork quilt of economic zones and corridors that foster the proliferation of small-scale ventures both in production and service industries. But it is not enough to scrutinize material evidence of market expansion and diversity of economic ventures, as important as these undoubtedly are. Special zones of various shapes and forms dot the borders. They and the roads that link them are drawcards as well as conduits. Despite being about concrete advancements, infrastructure development is also about openings, about connections, about opportunities, about new forms of economic and social engagement, new forms of pleasure.

   As mentioned, economic arrangements are social relations that foster specific forms of self-making or subjective formations. In addition to people and goods, regional development programmes also envisage other types of mobility – the movement of ideas, changing lifestyles and, above all, infectious entrepreneurialism as the cornerstone of an expanding free market. The dynamics of this entrepreneurialism must be adequately grasped if we are to appreciate the interplay of intimate and material economies and the ways new social relations generate profound effects for a sense of self. This evolving self-making occurs in identifiable, if not always transparent, ways married to contemporary development machinery that aims to improve everyday livelihoods. In this context, neoliberalism acts as a primary catalyst for local change in its role, to borrow Harvey's summary, as "a theory of political economic practices that proposes that human well-being can best be advanced by liberating individual entrepreneurial freedoms and skills within an institutional framework characterized by strong property rights, free markets and free trade" (2005: 2). Or as Rofel (2007: 16) suggests, neoliberalism places "greater emphasis on the idea that individuals need more freedom for self-actualization", thereby informing forms of governance that re-construe "individual citizens as subjects of entrepreneurial choices". Similarly, Ong (2007: 6) centres

Figure 1.4 Cross-border controls at the China–Lao frontier

her influential analyses of Asian subjectivities on the assertion that neoliberalism encourages "experimentations with freedoms" as "promiscuous entanglements of global and local logics crystallize different conditions of possibility". But precisely how this chorus of freedoms and possibilities are imagined and experienced, and the extent to which 'freedom' is an apt term for any of the life changes in the GMS, is in need of further examination.

The search for something better takes people on many different types of journeys. Some become endeavours etched by relentless yearning spread over many years. Others respond to a very specific version of 'freedoms' packaged for immediate consumption. One development site I visited at the Lao/Myanmar/Thai border offers an example of the latter. Dok Ngiew Kham, a sister venture to Golden Boten City, is wishfully and brashly labelled a special economic zone. If one believes its press it has been purposively introduced to help the local economy and its residents. Its mega-casino complex offers a bizarre combination of opulent gambling halls, richly red traditional Chinese arcades, fancy and tawdry hotels, gaudy entertainment plazas and karaoke bars, ramshackle rental units made from prefabricated containers, weird Mongolian yurts on the riverside and a small desultory zoo. The 10,000 hectares of rural land surrounding the casino have been leased from the Lao government for up to 99 years by a well (self-) publicised Chinese entrepreneur, Zhao Wei. They reach down to the heavy Mekong river smack in the middle of the Golden Triangle, long famous as the source of other addictions since the Indochina war. On this particular day – during *Songkran*, a water festival of renewal that marks the Buddhist New Year in many parts of the GMS – several tables inside the casino are swamped with Lao visitors including kids and hunched grandmothers all angling to make a buck (baht) as a nod to the annual festivities. Rather than the more affluent Chinese patrons sitting mute as they intently calculate the odds, the Lao mass around tables urging each other on and cheering when luck turns their way. At the Lao tables, they play a simple two-card game. Nothing as complicated as multiple hands and options, it is a wager, with a low minimum (100 baht, US$3.11), based on whether the dealer will turn over a card higher or lower than its predecessor.

The predominance of Lao patrons is unusual; on any other day the bulk of the clientele in the casino are men who make the trip to this mecca from across China by boat, road and plane. Four Chinese men sit with us during a break from the baccarat. They don't have to travel so far as they are working on a six-month contract in a nearby banana plantation. They come regularly to the casino to try their hand; they also come to find a partner for other forms of relaxation. Here, they tell us, sex, drugs and gambling are a normal expectation, part of a composite package. The freedom Dok Ngiew Kham represents when compared to homeland China is visceral and intoxicating. This is precisely the atmosphere that the millions of investment dollars are seeking to cultivate and capitalize on (and use to ostensibly extend benefits into disadvantaged local communities ringing the complex). Back home, according to these banana-packers, one cannot gamble except secretly; one cannot readily seek outside sexual relations as prostitution is illegal and one's wife is nearby; drugs are severely controlled at risk of serious repercussions. But at the casino all is reversed: "Here," they glowingly describe its siren call, "nothing is illegal. Drugs are everywhere, in your hotel room the police never bother you; so too girls are everywhere – Thai, Chinese, Lao and Burmese, take your pick; and gambling – not only is it legal, it is, of course, why you come here."

These men are revelling in an environment that is perhaps not normally associated with neoliberal prescriptions; but its ethos is hardly exceptional. It requires special zones and accommodating policies; a customized space that is, in turn, utterly dependent on the impressionable bodies, labour and sentiment of many locals and itinerant workers who have quite different experiences with loosening constraints. Entrepreneurial 'freedoms' (or lack of), what they constitute and how they are provided vary dramatically in different parts of the region. Even so, they share one basic premise: individual endeavour and pressure to 'self-actualize' is a central component, conscious or otherwise, of a ruthless pursuit of the 'good life'. Casinos are just one example where people take a chance with what they can muster. As described in a later chapter, here gamblers wager their holdings in the hope of more while local and itinerant women (and men) who 'take care' of them carry their own (mismatched) hopes as they also seek to gain from the (human) capital they place on the table. At its most basic, it is a pattern repeated across the region.

Foucault, in *The Birth of Biopolitics*, famously pointed us to the neoliberal creation of an "enterprising subject" that maximizes his or her own "human capital"

(Foucault, 2008). In development circles, human capital gained credence as a prosaic tool within education programmes, but this thinking now seems somewhat quaint. More recently, it has been charged with supreme importance as a pliable element of human subjectivity fostered by free market sensibilities. For, as Lazzarato summarizes:

> Neoliberal government intervenes in the domain of the social by converting the latter into a function of enterprise. It intervenes to promote multiplicity, differentiation and competition of enterprises and to incite and constrain each individual to become an entrepreneur of himself/herself, to become 'human capital'.
>
> (Lazzarato, 2009: 120)

To determine what constitutes an 'enterprising subject' in the development zones in the GMS necessarily takes us into the logic of competition as the organizing principle of an expanding market. While the 'otherness' of ethnic difference might always remain important as an element of social and human capital (the economy of alterity), it is a more generic reliance on social inequalities that characterizes the spread of neoliberalism throughout the region. Underlying this ethos lies a very basic premise. For competition to function it is the "freedom of the enterprise and the entrepreneur that needs to be produced and organised" (ibid). Thus, the donors who backstop the GMS programme and its emphasis on connection, competition and community as cornerstones of regional development are in fact echoing the clarion call for opening up spaces of enterprise. Connection is, as I mentioned, the hardware of roads and special zones. Community, in this sense, relies on notions of cross-border ethnicity and culture as the meeting place and mode of commodification that can advance an entrepreneurial self. Competition creates the ground rules for how this can be deployed within social and economic hierarchies. It requires constant stimulation, an uneven playing field and the preservation of difference, in other words, the exact social topography of the GMS.

> For neoliberalism, competition like the market is not the result of the 'natural play' of appetites, instincts or behaviours. It is rather a 'formal play' of inequalities that must be instituted and constantly nourished and maintained. Thus appetites and instincts are not given: only inequality has the capacity to sharpen appetites, instincts and minds, driving individuals to rivalries.
>
> (ibid: 117)

Feher adds importantly to our understanding of how this neoliberal ethos sharpens competition by suggesting that a fundamental characteristic of the ability to optimize one's 'capital' is the merging of the productive and reproductive within rubrics of self-entrepreneurship. In earlier Marxist renderings we as sovereign subjects were perceived to have certain inalienable rights – most prominently the right not be taken as a commodity – leaving certain aspects of the human condition, including needs and aspirations (love, religion, culture), to supposedly remain in an existential realm that cannot or should not be subject to market exchanges (Feher, 2009: 23). Such demarcation was seen as crucial to human functioning

> for it is only when the demarcation between the negotiating subject and nego-tiated commodity is clearly established and enforced that the free labourer can safely submit to the laws of the market without losing his or her sense of (moral) dignity and (political) sovereignty.
>
> (ibid: 24)

While human capital was previously framed as the basis for education or vocational skills improvement, it has evolved significantly since then, in both a programmatic and conceptual sense, to encompass virtually all aspects of human life. Its amorphous potential is now taken to subsume even innate qualities, such as genetic traits, and situational aspects, for example the social milieu, including specific relations such as styles of parenting through to what one does with one's body in terms of diet, sex life and exercise, etc. (ibid: 26). In other words, as I noted before, the very stuff that makes up the affective and intimate practices through which everyday life unfurls. In the course of this shift in understanding and experiencing one's human capital, an important divide has been dismantled – arenas that were previously considered inalienable, the social, cultural and moral aspects of society, are in effect reconstituted. Under neoliberalism, any separation between the spheres of production and reproduction is eroded so there is no existential domain, no aspect of our lives including the intimate that lies outside that which can be maximized as human capital. This is not the same as saying anything and everything can be commodified and subjects reduced to passive consumers in a world of diminishing humanity where all is for sale. Rather, it turns individual subjects into active "producers, as entrepreneurs of themselves or more precisely, as investors in themselves" (ibid: 30). Hence, intimate and reproductive labour – care-givers, surrogates, nannies, etc. – has become a global growth industry. At a further extreme, as in the global trade in body organs, or the blood/HIV scandal in Henan, China, one's very life becomes marketable capital (Shao, 2006), and "as strategies of capital accumulation seek to find a new frontier, the generative capacity of life itself becomes financialised in the context of uneven development" (Anagnost, 2011: 214). This spreading frontier finds subjects everywhere and where dignity lies in this new terrain is an open question.

Let me use another illustration. In a small village on the edge of the Northern Economic Corridor we met Orn, a defiantly enterprising 23-year-old Khmu woman raised in a remote part of Laos. As I have described elsewhere, hers is a portentous narrative of change in the region (Lyttleton, 2013). The story she told us when we met in 2009, just as the new road had been completed, isn't about new jobs or skills that infrastructure development has brought her. But it is about how the capacity to act finds its own navigational points, in particular in the intimate relations it fosters.

At the age of 16, barely educated, Orn decided to chance her hand at finding work in Thailand. She crossed the river to a border town in North Thailand, where she lived for some months with a Japanese man working for a local NGO whom she met in a bar. She came back to Laos with money from him to put a corrugated iron roof on her parent's house. She returned to Thailand and followed her boyfriend to Bangkok but they soon split up. She began working in a restaurant and became close friends with other Lao women working in bars. She married a Thai man and bore his child (three years old at the time we met her). After a year, she came back to her home village to organize a local marriage for herself and her partner, and to let her parents, who had no contact with her, know what had happened to her. At this point, the village headman under pressure to detain anyone working illegally in Thailand reported her to the district authorities. She was fined $90, which she raised by selling her necklace and bracelets, and was prohibited from returning to Thailand. Accepting she could not return, within a year she married again – this time a local man, an ex-teacher, from a village near the lignite mine on Route 3 (the Lao section of the Northern Economic Corridor). She now has a second child who was one year old when we met. When we talked with her, she had opened a small shop in her house as a means to make a modest income. She had recently persuaded her two nieces aged 13 and 14 to join her from their more remote village. Her rationale is that on most evenings, truck-drivers from the nearby lignite mine wander in to the village looking for somewhere to pass a few hours. She figures the men will be far more likely to hang out at her house drinking if she can provide them with company. The two young nieces had only been there for one week when we met Orn. They work in the fields during the day but in the evening, they provide the draw-card for customers. But Orn said she was annoyed that these girls have not yet fully understood the logic of her enterprise. They are frightened when the men sit too close and they run away when the men try to hug them. She tells them the men mean no harm. She might well be imagining further relation-ships will take place when the girls get more comfortable. She is hoping to be able to start a small food shop/restaurant if she can save enough money, so men will stay for longer and spend more money. She says she will be able to do this if the girls stay. This she feels will cement her place in the village as the one most actively finding a niche to make money from proximity to the mine. "I can make money here but it all depends if the girls get comfortable with the men."

Whatever moral adjudications her choices provoke, Orn feels she is doing exactly what is being expected of her in the context of new roads, new opportunities and the 'freedom' to use what resources she has at her disposal, in other words be an entrepreneur of herself and her kin. She is, in many respects, the perfect subject of livelihood transitions anticipated by the GMS rhetoric – poor, rural, mobile, female. Her village was, accordingly, subject to various outreach mitigation interventions during road construction to make locals aware of how the world can be turned to their advantage, or at least how to avoid typecast dilemmas of disease and mercenary subjugation. But she, like so many others in the Mekong, responded to a more insistent rhythm of fantasy, in this instance, beckoning her to extend service economies she was familiar with from Thailand and offer the appeal of her young relatives as a means to do so. The finer details of her commercial endeavours hardly fit with normative prescriptions for occupational diversity in the region, but her capacity to aspire and to act is nonetheless transparent in its response to enticements of the moment. We will return to consider Orn's enterprise further, but the point can be made now that she is hardly unique in the ways she internalized contagious aspirations of this brave new world, and devised a plan to make the most of her options. Corner the market and sell beer and proximity to young women to coal-bound truckers. What precisely these raw forays into market relations deliver her, or her nieces, and where safety lies as she submits is another matter.

Human capital and the value of immaterial labour

This merging of the productive and reproductive is important because, when we look at the choices people such as Orn make in the different locales across the GMS, we see that human capital frequently merges intimate sectors of people's lives with more orthodox economic strategies they may employ as the separation between "intimate man and the entrepreneur is no longer tenable" (Feher, 2009: 33). If we were to stop here, it would perhaps be useful enough to see that this framing of human capital has become the bedrock of proliferating notions of entrepreneurship and complicit intimacy in the GMS. But Feher takes another important step. Given that neoliberalism, like any form of capitalism, is a form of social relations there are further implications as we consider the role of human capital in processes of self-making. A major zeitgeist in the midst of globalized and hyper-stimulated markets is the sensibility that it is better to 'grow' capital rather than earn it per se. This is one of the key drivers in the immaterial economies of the world. Hence, the trope of 'appreciate' in the sense of 'make bigger' transfers to the sensibilities we internalize concerning our place in the world and how best to advance our wellbeing. "Insofar as our condition is that of human capital in a neoliberal environment, our main purpose is not so much to profit from our accumulated potential as to constantly value or appreciate ourselves – or at least prevent our own depreciation" (ibid: 27). While this line of thought rests solidly on economic frameworks of growth and maximization, the point should not be lost that any discussion of self-appreciation also implies a sense of emotional engagement in how personal value is understood and optimized as a tool of exchange. And it is no coincidence that the process by which emotions fall within the broad embrace of human capital, in turn, informs the vitality and relevance of affective economies and their role in 'appreciating' one's self-worth. This then becomes the nexus where affective practices are exchanged for material value as individuals actively speculate with multiple and/or different forms of intimate connection. Moreover, individuals become mobile bearers of accumulating values as they move within the region and it is the irrepressible contagiousness of these new sensibilities that fuels development's impact.

The following chapters use many examples to portray the warp and weave of affect blanketing the GMS. The intent is not to generalize the impact of neoliberalism or global circuits of value as either generic across Asia or uniquely dominant in the structuring of the subjectivities of the hundreds of millions who live in the GMS. Rofel (2007: 14) has cautioned us that even though a sexual politics of privatized desires is central to neoliberal mechanisms transforming China, this process is deeply embedded in social, cultural and historical specifics. Indeed, the expansion of affective fields has arguably not automatically entailed a parallel demise in state power that maintains its control over new forms of subjectivity in China (Yan, 2010) and to varying degrees in other parts of the GMS. From a regional vantage point, neoliberalism is taken up selectively with differing outcomes as "the strategy of governing and self-governing is not uniformly applied to all groups and domains within a nation" (Ong, 2007: 4). This is not to say one cannot identify important shifts towards 'human capital' as a key means of self-making and its 'appreciation' throughout the region. But how it is experienced and understood should not be read in any universal sense. So too, it is incorrect to think of shifts in self-making as unambiguously emancipatory. The difficulty is, of course, that one entrepreneur's freedom can readily entail another's entrapment in an economic (and social) sense, or another's sense of transgression in a political sense.

The elevation of supposed 'freedoms' that might inspire the entrepreneurial spirit is usually associated with advanced Western economies where, inspired by Milton Friedman's *Capitalism and Freedom*, the metaphor of liberation underpinning neoliberal spread took hold. Meantime, a more prominent overtone in the developing world has been uneven, and sometimes quite damaging, outcomes associated with structural adjustment. It is nothing new to suggest that the spread of economic structures, especially those based on logics of extraction, have had imperialist overtones for centuries. A rich body of anthropological material evokes the complex, destructive or, at times, enormously creative ways that imposed social change and resettlement is dealt with by locals attempting to ameliorate or avoid its impact. Studies show how individual and social bodies cope or don't cope with cultural confrontation under projects of colonialism and/ or development by emphasizing political dominance. Others highlight the discursive power of economic, social and cultural orders as one worldview displaces or minoritizes another within an economy of symbolic violence. Taken together, inequitable forms of governance alongside politics of ethnic difference promote insidious forms of material and social suffering through structural violence which is "exerted systematically – that is, indirectly – by everyone who belongs to a certain social order … In short, the concept of structural violence is intended to inform the study of the social machinery of oppression. Oppression is a result of many conditions, not the least of which reside in consciousness" (Farmer, 2004: 307).

Hence, alongside the rhetoric of 'freedoms', we can also point to the complex ways oppressive conditions are internalized by neoliberal practices. This is important, because if we elevate entrepreneurialism and ignore structural inequalities then human capital becomes a discursive device to legitimate new forms of control that does more than "reproduce existing regulatory mechanisms and forms of exploitation; it provides enhanced techniques of control through freedom itself" (Comaroff and Comaroff, (2009: 52). It is not simply surveillance that is reconfigured through rubrics of self-control. New economic structures aggravate disadvantage precisely because non-economic or 'cultural' factors – gender, race, ethnicity, religion, age, sexuality, citizen status and so forth – are used by workers to maximize their value through performative self-exploitation, where, for example, as Tsing (2009: 159) summarizes most simply, "a day labourer must perform brawn and availability; a prostitute must perform sexual charm". Furthermore, just as productive and reproductive aspects of self become inseparable, so too opportunity and exploitation, and the diverse dimensions of desire and prejudice that underpin these, become hard to separate. "On the one hand," Lazzarato (2009: 126), also following Deleuze and Guattari, reminds us,

> 'human capital' takes individualisation to its highest degree, since the subject implicates in all its activities 'immaterial resources of the self' that are affective and cognitive. On the other hand, the techniques of 'human capital' lead to the identification of individualisation with exploitation, since the 'entrepreneur of oneself' is both manager and slave of him/herself, capitalist and proletarian.

Or, as Orn's case shows, one's own kin can be drawn into this equation as well.

Not all responses to economic integration and expanding markets are perilous or demeaning, but they are always nuanced. Damaging exploitation of people's desire to be part of a consumer economy can be found within numerous development scenarios throughout the GMS. But, at the same time, acknowledging the infectious appeal of markets, networks and opportunities is also necessary if we are to appreciate the often contradictory ways self-making plays itself out through the mobility and aspirational endeavours people engage in. The potency of modernization's emotional investments is strongly demonstrated in the desires and needs that regional development has seeded. Shared sentiments circulate a sense of the collective envisioned by GMS rhetoric –that this brave new world embraces everyone, the dream of newfound rewards is available to all – even as there is nothing equal or smooth about the frame this vision is hoist upon. For the landscape of affect is a convoluted surface, disjunctive and disjointed. Neoliberal formations create wildly disparate emotional states that characterize social relations: fear, prejudice, intolerance, loss, pain, hunger, hopes, desires, needs, pleasures, satisfactions. It is precisely the ragged movement of these kaleidoscopic signs of affect, rather than their residence within individual psyches, that forms the social body and that etches volatile and intimate social spaces of inclusion and exclusion. This brings us back to the point made earlier that affective economies fashion new forms of subjectivity as individuals align themselves with capitalist desires/structures and that "the subject is simply one modal point in the economy, rather than its origin and destination" (Ahmed, 2004: 121). Desires, alongside other sentiments, circulate and in so doing create a sense of belonging and of marginalization. This then is one essential measure of the impact of development in the GMS that we need to attend to – the ability to generate flows of affect that shape social spaces and thereby individual experiences. Development programmes, and modernization more generally, are heavily invested in the programme of 'trading in signs of affect' and that, as people move between different spaces within the GMS, this process carries a diverse set of outcomes, some of which have specific implications for health.

Capitalist modernity is often depicted as a gradual but unavoidable disengagement from prior 'traditional' and communitarian modes of thinking and feeling. This is a trend discernible throughout the GMS. In turn, this dislodging leads to a form of compulsiveness wherein the 'capitalist' is "primed to repetition without – once the traditional religious ethic had been discarded – having much sense of why he, or others, had to run this endless treadmill" (Giddens, 1994: 70). In sync with this habituated compulsion, capitalism works because commodity desire is intensified by the impossibility of its satisfaction, by its constant mobility from object to object. The escalating uptake of consumer consciousness within less-modernized populations allows an economy of affect to do its work and turns wants into needs, and for many immaterial labour and intimate relations become the catalyst to material value. The GMS is becoming a more integrated marketplace as both donor funding and ASEAN policies formalize and standardize economic systems and mobility of goods and people within the region. But so too eddies and whirlpools of exclusion and disadvantage grow. This is because, at heart, any form of capitalism relies on stratified enclosures as the defining logic of accumulation, and despite disavowal, in turn establishing those who are within and those without as it relies on a disenfranchised and precariat labour force.

> The discourse of enclosures, in other words, must present itself not as a negative force, one that separates, brutalises, and disempowers; but, on the contrary, it also has to wear the mantle of rationality, and project a vision of the future that makes sense to a multiplicity of concrete subjects.
>
> (De Angelis, 2004: 82)

Economic change in the region is about advertised enclosing and embracing as much as it operates through rubrics of difference and otherness. Hence, we get the broad-scale advocacy of benefits to project glowing visions of the future, to expand the enclosures. But it is wrong to see these as 'bad faith' or some sort of deliberate attempt to misinform; rather such manoeuvres should be understood as a profoundly effective discursive means to generate shared responses through the affective economies that gird development processes. Thus the very sense of a multiplicity (GMS residents) implies a degree of uniformity that would never have been previously employed to describe this part of Asia.

Another more instrumental means to bring our focus firmly onto the ways emotions can be a vehicle of change has been formulated by Appadurai (with an echo of Spinoza) in his use of the 'capacity to aspire' as a core aspect of human struggle to overcome adversity. Just like the circulating desires and contingent values we have been discussing, aspirations are cultural in the sense they derive from structures of shared understanding, which is to say we might all want a better life but we don't all imagine exactly the same better life. Importantly, capacities to aspire are a variable skill set that can be broadened or constrained.

> The capacity to aspire is thus a navigational capacity. The more privileged in any society simply have used the map of its norms to explore the future more frequently and more realistically and to share this knowledge with one another more routinely … The poorer members, precisely because of their lack of opportunities to practice the use of this navigational capacity … have a more brittle horizon of aspirations.
>
> (Appadurai, 2004: 69)

This operational potential, thus, becomes a target in a wide range of interventions aiming to reduce poverty's constraints – oddly named 'pro-poor approaches' within donor circles. Appadurai makes the connection to development agents specific as he describes hopes amongst the poor in developing countries nurtured by 'ritualized' practices of NGOs and activists "through which social effects are produced and new states of feeling and connection are created" (ibid: 81). But one might enlarge this orbit and suggest that it is not just NGO interventions that embellish new feelings and connections. In addition to state-driven forces of market liberalization that have transformed earlier socialist modes of economic distribution, development programmes throughout the GMS offer a package of values extolling economic growth as they fertilize the capacity to dream or, I might add, the capacity to exploit. The more interesting question then becomes, when does rhetoric become genuinely linked to forms of empowerment or improvement in capabilities or, put another way, when does the capacity to aspire realistically become the capacity to act, and under what terms does trickle-down behaviourism become an everyday and sustainable reality? Or, in more simple terms, will the choices Orn has made deliver any sort of improvement to her, or her nieces', wellbeing that can be equated in terms of human dignity?

Aspiration and risk

> *There is only desire and the social, and nothing else.*
>
> (Deleuze and Guattari, 1983: 20)

I noted at the start of this chapter that we should see the capacity for aspirations and actions as inseparable, with collective affect being essential to jump-start an engaged politics of social mobilization. However, I have also indicated that the capacity to act does not automatically imply a straightforward trajectory of improved wellbeing as much as we are led to believe and hope that it will.

Figure 1.5 Laos-Vegas on the Mekong: Dok Ngiew Kham special economic zone

What the following chapters will show is that the capacity to act is stimulated at numerous fronts as contagious entrepreneurialism, as well as orchestrated community initiatives, are part of social change happening throughout the GMS. Many of these newfound lifestyle changes are built on a very particular set of affective practices linked to particular spaces and sensibilities. This is not an autonomous landscape. Affect is cultural and contingent, and as such, the ways in which it is part and parcel of new livelihoods can be as negative as they are positive. People are sometimes pressured into positions both uncomfortable and dangerous. At other times, they avidly grab for opportunities fired by the dreams they have been convinced are accessible. Exploitation, as much as enticement, shades the emotional landscape of those embracing new lifestyles as they traverse the Mekong. Hence, as we consider in more detail the combination of intimacy and material change the ultimate goal is to be in a better position to adjudicate how mitigation and preventing damage might be best employed.

For underlying this proliferation of affective practices lies one ever-present reality. Alongside economic expansion, regional integration and the various lifestyle changes this implies, so too the contexts where people take risks proliferate. Many argue, like Latour, that this is part and parcel of contemporary modernity which encourages a form of reflexive and speculative consciousness that emerges from having to deal with ever increasing problems it creates (Beck, 1992: 21). This is not to say people anywhere, anytime have not faced physical and emotional risks throughout their lives. But there is a shift in the register of both practices and perceptions. Under forms of modernity, speculation about potential outcomes undergoes a gradual move away from a focus on visible reality towards a longer time horizon of more amorphous threats, towards what we cannot see and cannot perceive, towards asking in ever more clinical detail for experts to tell us how real the unforeseen dangers are (ibid: 73). Likewise, in developing countries decisions and constraints multiply across diverse fields of action as modernization proceeds. At the same time, forms of bodily and psychological risk radiate as lifestyle and workplace conditions are altered.

I can be more concrete about one specific fact of life. At heart, to be an entrepreneur is to take risks. This is the point of the so-called 'experimentations with freedoms' being encouraged throughout the region with the unstated but ever-present admonition to 'take a chance'. Hence, accompanying the spread of neo-liberalism, fields of risk multiply both in a subjective and material sense as people manufacture, or are made available for, new opportunities. As part of development planning ushering these changes, how people imagine and confront threats to themselves, their families and their communities in the embrace of broadened lifestyles becomes the subject of risk-planning, impact assessments and mitigation programmes. The question to be taken very seriously is whether in fact this downstream planning is able to conceptually or practically deal with the growing array of risks raised by the exploration and exploitation of new opportunities being created by regional development. And is there even a concept of how to safely submit to market rules?

Conclusion

Structural violence perpetuates social inequities and introduces enduring forms of emotional and social suffering as social hierarchies exacerbate poverty and marginalization leads to health vulnerabilities. Just as fear and its more amorphous cousin, anxiety, move between subjects creating fluid collectives of those that share these feelings: so too aspirations feed the longings of numerous people in the GMS who are led to imagine that development will carry them to the 'good life' (that has not yet trickled-down). The dream of something better is shared by millions. As such, desires are omnipresent – not just unquenchable but actively nurtured and shared through affective economies promoted by development programmes speaking of regional connectivity and growth. So when the ADB exclaims "the GMS Program has indeed accelerated; delivering concrete results and contributing to the shared vision of a *prosperous, integrated, and harmonious* Mekong subregion", these are not idle advertising slogans (ADB, 2007: iv, emphasis added). These are signs that circulate within the language of dreams that are packaged by the hundreds if not thousands of development workers and government officials charged with the day-to-day discharging of the 'shared vision'. And yet, their relentless pursuit has an inevitable downside as people place their own bodies or those dear to them directly in line for subjective and physical damage.

In the following chapters, I focus on one aspect of this complex of entrepreneurial forays and newfound threats to environmental, social and/or individual wellbeing. I examine how changing material conditions generate an increasing breadth of intimate relations, some as a means to gain market advantage, others as a form of existential safeguarding amid the destabilizing and often precarious flows that characterize economic expansion. In both instances, intimate relations are born of affective economies wherein dreams and wishes flourish alongside prejudice and oppression in landscapes charged by economic opportunity. At the same time, one can also detect the role of creativity as integral to the 'appreciation' of the self, as human capital is deployed in ever more diverse fashions in both urban and rural sectors throughout the GMS. Although my attention is primarily on border and/or frontier zones, the processes I describe are not unique to these spaces. Certainly, in border areas tropes of exploration, excitement, marginalization and oppression offer a stark profile to the intersection of intimacy and material relations and their place in the circulation of value. But self-making processes are stimulated by flows of affect at multiple registers all over the region as free market ideology entrenches mobility, technology and commodity culture. Migrant and mobile bodies face the same or similar patterns of self-endeavour in urban and peri-urban zones. Similarly, health dilemmas as well as more amorphous concepts of risk spread within diverse populations and within institutional bodies charged with controlling emergent threats at a national and regional level.

Thus, by the end of the book I will consider the arena of individualized and institutional risk assessment within development programming. The ability to forecast and thereby pre-empt is a major challenge as choices are made in environments that simultaneously encourage entrepreneurialism and commodification of human capital. People are asked to 'to take a chance' with faith that the 'magic of the markets' will do the rest. But, within this landscape of unforeseen potential, it is also expected that individuals will understand the risks inherent in changing lifestyle choices so they self-regulate and conform to the demands on appropriate citizenry. To help them with this, we have impact assessment mitigation programmes that aim to shore up any shortcomings. The fundamental tension here mirrors that of development more generally; how to facilitate trickle-down behaviourism (the spread of neoliberalism) in a way that doesn't simply magnify risk and sites of damage. The following chapters reveal the creative and nuanced ways people deal with these contradictory aspects of development throughout the GMS.

Note

1 www.adb.org/countries/gms/overview (accessed 24 May 2013).

2   Frontiers and embodied ambitions

A frontier is a space of desire: it calls; it appears to create its own demands; once glimpsed, one cannot but explore and exploit it.

(Tsing, 2005: 32)

I began by describing how transnational road linkages, together with market diversification and surging consumer desires, hasten social and economic change among widely diverse groups throughout the GMS. Many of these dynamics constellate in border regions where historical opportunism and loosening political

Figure 2.1 The highland frontier in northwest Laos

strictures foster market opportunities and expanding entrepreneurialism. This is precisely what development programmes in the region aim to achieve. But there are also dimensions of change that do not fit within the normative 'technical assistance' blueprint. In settings undergoing rapid change, regional policies readily become personalized and the interpersonal readily becomes intimate for men and women carried forward helter-skelter in the slipstream of rapid modernization.

Not so long ago, I was at a meeting of a United Nations task force on AIDS where some wag quipped that interventions addressing mobility and sexually transmitted disease should be themed "when the rubber hits the road". Here, I follow this direction and examine connections between intimacy, rubber and roads, albeit in a quite different sense than condom promotion. Recent rubber tree cultivation in the hills of northern Laos has been spurred by cross-border connections that, in turn, frequently piggyback on the sexual in these frontier zones. Burgeoning relations between Chinese men and young ethnic women across the border are part and parcel of complex resource negotiations fuelled by contagious dreams of rubber riches. Meanwhile, highways cutting through hills and nearby valleys trigger the growth of supply chain networks that extend well away from the tarmac into hinterland villages. In this instance, young ethnic women, caught up in the back-swell of economic diversification and tightened access to land, become a resource diverted to the new economic corridors.

That roads and other structural interventions should bring different peoples into contact is hardly a novel proposition in development circles. That we should see ethnic relations as almost invariably sexualized in these interactions is a less common conclusion. However, it is a phenomenon that has a long history in both colonial times and more recent waves of nationalist assimilation and global tourism. It occurs in large part because of the way difference creates desire. In simple terms, boundaries demarcate material and symbolic difference. Sexuality permeates geographic and ethnic divides precisely because a sense of difference can be so readily eroticized. In this sense, boundaries become power-ridden sites of enticement, transgression and control. For example, as Shrage (1994: 142) has noted: "More generally when we look at sex commerce cross-culturally and historically, one thing that stands out, but stands unexplained, is that a large percentage of sex customers seek sex workers whose racial, ethnic, national, or class identities are different from their own." In fact, this desire for sexual exploration of 'the other' can be explained easily. Boundaries or borders don't just separate – they create, based on the very differences they signal as defining what belongs and what doesn't. Mandating divides fashions any number of meanings including the desire to possess what one is separated from, to lay claim to what one does not have. In a psychoanalytic sense the equation is simple: borders create difference, difference generates desire. Indeed, imperial histories and travellers' tales offer a rich and often bizarre testament to the time-worn ways in which ethnicity is exoticized and then sexualized by power differentials that infuse frontier locales. Such ready modes of eroticization still proliferate in contemporary times, leading Nagel to emphatically conclude:

Ethnicity and sexuality are strained, but not strange, bedfellows. Ethnic boundaries are also sexual boundaries – erotic intersections where people make intimate connection across ethnic, racial, or national borders. The borderlands that lie at the intersections of ethnic boundaries are 'ethnosexual frontiers' that are surveilled and supervised, patrolled and policed, regulated and restricted, but that are constantly penetrated by individuals forging sexual links with ethnic 'others'.

(Nagel, 2000: 113)

Frontiers have become a popular means of conceptualizing the penetration of difference, as these spaces tend to be less fixed and legibly mapped than geopolitical boundaries. They are volatile and shifting zones where, as Tsing flags above, difference and desire conjoin, where locals are portrayed as unmodernized and local resources as ripe for exploitation. This combination requires particular exploratory mechanisms for those entering these spaces. When borders and frontiers coincide in space and time the impact on ethnicity and sexuality is particularly resonant. Affective networks carved by desire and opportunism that emerge within new lifestyles in these zones are the subject of this chapter. I wish to establish one central point: it is not simply that ethnicity and sexuality are commonplace bedfellows, but more significantly, social change and broadened sexual networks are interrelated outcomes of development processes.

Tsing portrays frontiers as sites where relations are both unpredictable and heavily gendered:

Confusions between legal and illegal, public and private, disciplined and wild are productive in sponsoring the emergence of men driven to profit, that is, entrepreneurs as well as natural objects conjured in their resourceful drives. These men and objects are contagious, recharging the landscape with wildness and virility.

(Tsing, 2005: 41)

Intrusive frontier masculinity may be well-rewarded in the cut and thrust of aggressive land grabs and resource extraction. But on a more subtle level, women's engagements, both willing and coerced, in the social relations and entrepreneurship in these zones should not be discounted or simply subsumed under the spectacle of male aggrandisement. In fact, ethnic women, marginalized as they may be, also actively partake in self-making processes as neoliberal expansion fuels frontier attitudes in the border areas of the GMS. These women, and the men they interact with, together seek new and profitable engagements amid a social landscape that fires aspirations at the same time as it incites exploitation.

There are two prominent mechanisms of ambitious accumulation in frontier zones that I wish to discuss. First, betting on rubber futures has become a burgeoning mode of entrepreneurialism for both investors and small-holders in the borders of Laos and China (and elsewhere in the GMS). Previously disadvantaged ethnic minorities – primarily the Akha in the area that I consider – now grasp rubber as the primary means to achieve newfound aspirations and thereby economic and social elevation. Second, slightly further inland where new roads carve open the landscape, entrepreneurialism operates at a different and more directly embodied level. Here, it is not the flowing latex that conjures heady dreams as much as the labour of young Khmu women who are drawn from all over northern Laos to the monetary seam of expanding drink-shops and their implicit economies of service and sex. It is this movement from rural village to commercial opportunities provided by infrastructure development that shoulders the aspirations of their families, their agents and perhaps most profoundly the dreams of thousands of young women themselves as they seek to become active players in an increasingly in-your-face material culture spreading throughout Laos. Amid the flurry of material bargaining that characterizes the rubber plantations and beer-shop recruitments, we should not lose sight of one important fact: even in its most generic sense, entrepreneurship is predicated on the ability to negotiate risks. The volatile characteristics of capital spread in these zones demonstrate with dramatic clarity that risks radiate in multiple directions. As I will describe, the ability of Akha and Khmu women and men to successfully negotiate this difficult landscape is a work in progress: a process of sexualized self-making that once uncovered can be recognized as all too present in development trajectories and as such often carries specific health dilemmas.

In a recent book Hall, Hirsch and Li examine agrarian transformations in Southeast Asia, in the course of which they bring to our attention how social intimates jockey among themselves for control of land resources. There are ample examples in farming communities in the GMS of interpersonal relations that become fractured as market-based forces insinuate themselves within community structures. These modes of 'intimate exclusion' play themselves out within a complex calculus of economic and emotional vectors as market-inspired claims to resources seek to prevail over social bonds of kinship, friendship and community engagement: "The tension produced by exclusion's double edge," the authors suggest, "is intense at an intimate scale as each villager's assertion of a right to exclude runs up against another villager's claim for access" (Hall et al, 2011: 146). Such processes are well under way in the hills of northwest Laos as villagers angle for a leg-up in the dizzying maelstrom of governance constraints, market freedoms and cross-border movements that nowadays characterize everyday life. But we can also detect nascent and often haphazard dynamics of a reverse process – intimate inclusion. Shadowing the ways frontiers foster new relations based on difference, sexuality itself becomes part of the strategies of capital accumulation in ways that are seldom publicized but often present.

Opium haze to rubber futures

Since the turn of the twenty-first century, rubber plantations have spread rapidly and in seemingly unstoppable fashion throughout much of the long borderlands adjoining Laos, Myanmar and southwest China. This surge in plantation agriculture has swamped previously subsistent hinterland areas populated by minority groups. It has been spurred by the voracious requirements for rubber in China due to the rapid rise of the middle class and the need to furnish both industry and the uptake of automobile consumption. Prompted by entry into the WTO in 2001 and strategically packaged as donor aid, Chinese authorities devised forms of tax relief and subsidies for rubber companies to push across its southern borders. This scheme, trumpeted from large billboards seen throughout northern Laos (and Myanmar), was called the 'poppy substitution project'. Meanwhile, the privatization of rubber cultivation in China since 2003 encouraged many small-holders in the China/Lao borderlands to expand their interests across the border. Once opium cultivation became actively suppressed in Laos and Myanmar, it allowed huge tracts of land in the regions bordering China to be turned into plantations sprouting carefully staggered seedlings.

One case in point is Luang Namtha Province in Northwest Laos. The popula-tion is roughly 90 per cent from ethnic minority groups (Lao population overall includes almost 50 per cent from minority groups). Here, amid helter-skelter land-grabs, numerous villagers converted whatever land they could lay their hands on into contract-farming enterprises for either corporate or kin-based investors from nearby China. This has taken place in particular in the border district of Muang Sing. Here, and in the adjoining Muang Long district, 30,000 Akha form the majority population. The Akha ethnic group are generally held to have moved south from China over the past 100 or so years and in the past typically lived in the mountainous slopes surrounding the Tai Lue who have dwelled in the lowland valleys for much longer (Muang Sing was a small Lue principality dating back to 1792). In recent years, many Akha villages have relocated to the increasingly crowded lowland valleys. Since the Lao and Chinese governments became more accommodating of free-market policies, numerous small informal arrangements between Akha kin from both sides of the border as well as numerous larger corpo-rate planning agreements have turned Lao hillsides in these districts into a wildly proliferating rubber nursery covering tens of thousands of hectares. And with the rubber comes the associated presence of people, as Chinese guest houses, restau-rants and small-scale industry start-ups now dot the valleys. And with the pres-ence of more people, a complex set of nested relations emerge.

As mentioned, land-use changes are recent. Prior to 2004 there was virtually no rubber in Muang Sing. Three years later, figures from the Provincial Agriculture Office showed that by 2007 nearly 10,000 hectares were under plantation in the small hilly district. Before its arrival, the local trade economy in this part of Laos revolved around rice grown by the lowland Tai peoples augmented by a smat-tering of contract crops such as sugar, watermelons, cassava and capsicums and ad hoc arrangements with highland Akha providing forest plants for a Chinese market requiring fresh produce and naturopathic medicine. In the hills, a differ-ent cash crop had a longer history. Until the late 1990s, when opium production was forcibly prohibited, the hills were dotted with a vibrant mosaic of fields of purple, red and blue poppies. For a brief period, this small promontory of Muang Sing and Muang Long was celebrated as tourists flooded the area, in part for its exotic diversity as Akha and other groups would co-mingle in the early morning fog-shrouded markets, and, in larger part, for the appeal of the poppy. Muang Sing was touted by travel books as the opium capital of the Golden Triangle and tourists would wander into Akha villages requesting a sample. Ecotourism posters soon followed, warning of the cultural violations this entailed. Not sufficiently, however, as a number of Western tourists died from overindulging, and I remember on one visit seeing a sad, desultory pile of wet sawdust under an umbrella in the yard of the refrigerator-less (no electricity) hospital doing its best to cool the coffin of an overseas overdose as authorities awaited consular officials from the distant capital of Vientiane.

These districts were also momentarily famous in earlier epochs for other reasons. This was the border zone where the colonial powers inked treaty arrangements over what was to be British and what was to be French during the late nineteenth and early twentieth centuries. Now the colonial remnants – a military barracks and an old market – are rotting as the region entered a development stasis almost as soon as the treaties were signed. The brief period of Soviet assistance did little to change a history of benign neglect. More recently, tourism has also waned significantly alongside the removal of opium. But in place of colonial, socialist or fledgling ecotourist influence, the valleys and hills are heavily infiltrated by Chinese as their material footprint becomes more pronounced by the day. Akha also live on the Chinese side of the border where they are demonstrably wealthier than the Lao Akha, largely because of decades of rubber cultivation. This clear-cut disparity in overt modernity marked by the China/Lao border, only a few kilometres from Muang Sing town, has very rapidly and very effectively engineered an almost unanimous shift in attention. Now that rubber is officially invited into Lao, it has eclipsed all other crops in terms of levels of interest. Endeavours to gain entry into this market have brought about a rabid gold rush of local forest and rice land conversion alongside more calculated and cynical land-grabs by outsiders. Consequently, all eyes now focus on the China border and what cross-border liaisons can bring to bear.

In the midst of this economic and agricultural transformation, Chinese Han and Chinese Akha come and go into Laos in large numbers. For their part, Akha from Lao cross regularly into China for market access, health services and an array of social pursuits with newly acquainted friends and kin. Dreams of wealth resonate everywhere. As I write, rubber is only just beginning to be tapped (young trees take close to eight years before the sap runs) so these yearnings for prosperity have had a lengthy period of gestation and so far little concrete substance on the Lao side. Meanwhile there are a growing number of marriages as the obvious rubber wealth across the border beckons many young Akha women to follow the siren call of a better life with a Chinese husband. So too increasing incidences of coerced sales of young Lao Akha women as wives inside China is an insidious underbelly of the increased cross-border movement. This is a growing trend found along the Myanmar and Vietnam borders as well. Despite the notoriety of the Thai brothels as repositories of Myanmar women, Feingold (2013: 212) notes that (as far as an official reported caseload is an accurate indication) a majority of cross-border trafficking cases from Myanmar are women taken to forced marriages in

China. Back in Muang Sing, the process is gathering steam. Given the desire to experience a modern lifestyle, young women are often invited across the border, either by Chinese men they have met or by local Akha men or women. They then disappear. Informants in a Chinese village we visited reported a typical price of 5,000 RMB for a young Akha woman to be corralled and sold as far afield as Shanghai and Guangdong. Meanwhile, health authorities worry that less visible disease spread is also on the up as cross-border movement brings with it increased sexual networking (Slesak et al, 2012).

Prior to Laos opening its borders and economies in the 1990s, cross-border traffic was most commonly itinerant Yunnanese traders coming in search of fragrant sandalwood, medicinal vines, native sesame seed, pungent bamboo roots and even human hair, sold by the yard-arm, for markets back home. Such petty trade notwithstanding, market expansion and modernist values are very new to these hills, the changes they render are raw and often visceral. It is a brave new world constituted by what Tsing has described as the contagious spread of frontier sensibilities and inventively destructive machinations.

> Frontier culture is a conjuring act because it creates the wild and spreading regionality of its imagination. It conjures self-conscious trans-localism committed to the obliteration of local places ... a distinctive feature of this frontier regionality is its magical vision; it asks participants to see a landscape that doesn't exist, at least not yet. It must continually erase old residents' rights to create its wild and empty spaces, where discovering resources, not stealing them, is possible. To do so it must cover up the conditions of its own production.
>
> (Tsing, 2005: 68)

This origin story of frontier accumulation typifies parts of Laos where rubber investment piggybacks on murky and inequitable contracts leveraged by more savvy Chinese – kinfolk or otherwise – on non-literate villagers where profits over the next 30 years or so are to be split 70/30 or 60/40 in favour of the cross-border investors bringing their market expertise. Lack of clear land ownership titles raises the spectre of further opportunism. It need not simply be in the form of lopsided contractual agreements. A 2007 Study of Communal Land Registration cites rubber in North Laos as one of the key pressures on village unity as communal land is turned into private holdings by unscrupulous villagers or by overbearing government staff, resulting in communal forest land managed by outsiders in contractual agreement with Chinese companies (Seidel et al, 2007: 21). While processes of frontier accumulation might indeed be shrouded in confusion and the eradication of prior communal frameworks, there are identifiable stages in these trajectories. They lead us to one firm conclusion. The inroads of cash crop plantations does not take place simply as a product of the magic of the markets, be they frontier-based conjuring acts, intimate exclusions or otherwise. Rather, intrusions of capital rely very directly both on a number of concrete events and, even more importantly, the integration of new economic engagements within the

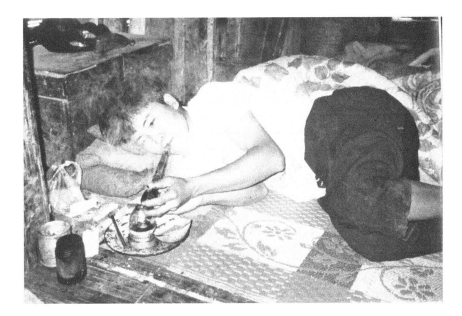

Figure 2.2 Pre-modern dreams

particular way social relations – and the subjectivities these entail – are able to embrace and capitalize on new openings. The manner in which intimate economies are central to economic growth in general, or in this case the spread of rubber, is occasionally mentioned as an aside, as an epiphenomenon of material expansion, but as we will see, they are in fact central to the uptake of entrepreneurial opportunities.

When the socialist mode of economic management became moribund in the late 1980s, Western agencies became the primary conduit of modernization for thousands of rural villages throughout Laos. For example, German (GTZ) and Norwegian (NCA) aid agencies established long-term food security programmes in a majority of the Akha villages in the Sing and Long districts. Project activities targeted clean water, crop diversification, education assistance and primary health care. At the time, the Lao government resources were scarce and most assistance in these villages came from foreign aid. Roads into the mountains were non-existent: access was by harrowing foot trails for the Akha or traversed by the large off-road motorcycles used by the NGOs. No electricity, inclement weather, and unforgiving topography meant opium served as a superb buffer in insecure times. In these districts, Akha were primary producers. Not sold as part of insidious international drug rings as much of the international discourse in the evils of illicit drugs would have us think (Cohen, 2013), but locally bartered as a means to rice, as a means to salt and other basic commodities, as a means to pain relief, as a means to survival. Also, unfortunately, as a means to fuelling the all-too-common human frailty – addiction.

The Western agencies, seeing the primacy of opium in Akha livelihoods, introduced the idea of development-based drug rehabilitation. That is to say, detox leveraged on the promise of a better future through the fruits that they as outside donors could offer. Over a number of years starting in late 1990s, agencies in Sing and Long entreated, cajoled and berated, in moral and almost Calvinistic rhetoric, opium users to give up in the name of modernization, to save their communities from a drug-burdened future and to embrace a 'non-degenerate' life wrapped in the promises of outside assistance. But manoeuvres – well-meaning as they might have been – to rid opium from the area hardly minimized habitual consumption. Without doubt they changed the rules, as well as the commodities at stake. One elderly Akha man I met ruefully talked about a life long-gone: "In the mountains life was better, we had more money [from opium] but nothing to spend it on; here by the road we have less money, but more [desire for] things to buy" (Lyttleton, 2005: 58). Attempts to remove opium gathered steam and ultimately would open the future to the Akha in ways that were both precipitous and, in many respects, savage. Rubber has flowed into the ruptured local economy. At face value, this may well bring about economic security of a sort, and certainly has much more market credibility than opium. But, as described earlier, transformations also occur at a subjective and interpersonal level, themselves terrain ripe for exploration. It is precisely the inevitable exploitation that insinuates in subtle ways between the men and women parlaying their future that concerns me here. The second stage of this trajectory – resettlement into the lowlands and into the world of wage labour – makes this more apparent.

In 2003, opium was officially banned and enforced through strong-arm intervention in Muang Sing and Muang Long (and elsewhere). Akha villagers were forced to cut down their soon-to-be-harvested fields at threat of major penalties, including imprisonment, which in Laos still carries a powerful image of labour camps. The prohibition was effective. That year there was a major rice shortage in villages unable to trade opium and the development agencies scrambled to provide food. Many Akha villages decided this was a timely, albeit enforced, spur to move unceremoniously out of the hills. And move they did, what had prior been a steady trickle of villagers moving down to the lowlands – in pursuit of a more 'modern' way of life that entailed closer integration with the state, other lowland ethnic groups such as the Tai Lue, the Tai Dam and the Tai Nua and a market-oriented way of life – now became an exodus. A report from GTZ summarizes the snowballing relocation that occurred in 2002/3:

> It is estimated that about 15 villages with about 2000 people from the mountains moved to lowland areas because their poppy fields were cleared. "We knew before the clearing of the poppy fields that villagers would move," the District Vice-Governor informed the team. "On the one hand, it was good that they moved. For many years we had asked them to do so, but they did not. However, on the other hand, it made things more complicated because the district could not carry out the development as planned. Villages were messed up everywhere; it was not according to our plan."

"We have to stop all development activities because of migration: everyday villagers ask the district authorities to find a new place for them to live," the Vice-Governor added.

(GTZ, 2003: 15)

Resettlement has a long and complicated relation to nationalist modes of assimilation in the region. The halting of swidden agriculture and control of land resources (including opium eradication) has been central to the history of minority group integration throughout the Upper Mekong. It is not simply that minority groups seldom negotiate the implicit geographic and economic reconfigurations from a position of advantage. The introduction of new accumulation systems and associated values, themselves attached to externally introduced donor practices, has widespread implications, both for cultural integrity and the very nature of interpersonal relations that take place with people from different ethnic groups. Much of this is leveraged from above. In North Laos, Evrard (2011: 76) notes that "since the 1960s, more than 50 percent of highland villages have disappeared ... Instead, people have gathered in new, bigger, and often multi-ethnic localities, usually on the edges of Laos' main plains or along newly built roads into the highlands." In Muang Sing this relocation occurred more recently. Poppy removal was one key catalyst fuelled by international pressure to conform to the global 'war on drugs'. Donor interventions have also left other footprints. Roads are the next intrusion prefacing the influx of rubber, providing a crucial centre of gravity dragging the movement of villagers alongside these thoroughfares.

Geo-body modifications

The Sing and Long valleys running up from the Mekong river into China have historically been an important route for trade caravans between mountainous areas of what is now the GMS, but it was an arduous journey. As recently as the mid-1990s, it would still take at least two days to travel the roughly 60km between the district towns of Sing and Long. In 1996 the World Bank loaned US$1 million to upgrade the 86km road – Route 17B – from the China border down to the small port of Xieng Kok at the Mekong River. It was completed in 2000 and changes were both profound and dramatic as the road forged a crucible in lowland valleys in which market-based economic and social relations intensified between lowland residents, Chinese labourers and relocating Akha. For a number of years, hundreds of Chinese trucks thundered down to the port on the Mekong and from there goods flowed by cargo boat to and from Thailand. For a brief period, this isolated area bore dreams of rapid consolidation as a key border crossing. But as these things go, China bombed more than 20 troublesome rapids in the Mekong River creating a much more user-friendly conduit for trade items moved by large steamer directly down from Jinhong (capital of the adjoining prefecture of Xishuanbanna, Yunnan) to the Thai port of Chiang Saen. The road is now falling into disrepair. However, even in its fleeting moment as an important highway, Route 17B generated long-term material and social changes in these valleys as increased flows of goods, people and ideas transformed social and demographic structures. Most noticeably, the resulting articulation of social relations, bodies and minds required new subjectivities capable of negotiating new social competencies and ongoing consequences as the 'rubber hits the road'.

Competencies necessitated by transformed livelihoods are an issue for ethnic groups wherever development intrudes. The new roads criss-crossing the Upper Mekong inject mores and social values from outside worlds. This is precisely the rationale behind their construction. As an important precursor and weathervane, the upgrading of Route 17B in many ways mirrored, in microcosm, changes brought about by its far bigger relative the Northern Economic Corridor (NEC), a portion of which runs parallel some 70km away from Muang Sing (Lyttleton et al, 2004: 67). The NEC is longer, wider and channels far more grandiose dreams of growth. The Lao section was finished in 2008 after millions of dollars loaned from ADB. Its humble name, Route 3, belies its portentous future – to be a key section of a corridor that would foster regional market growth. One can now drive from Thailand to China passing 226km of Laos in roughly three hours, give or take. It used to take between eight and nine hours, and that was in the dry season. Thailand, the economic hub of mainland Southeast Asia, is now stitched via efficient and serviceable tarmac to the economic powerhouse of southern China. If economic integration is to take place in the Upper Mekong then this road is its backbone.

Along Route 3's path, the majority ethnic group is Khmu. Here a primary mode of livelihood has not historically been opium but wage labour and out-migration, typically male. But just as Route 17B both facilitated and complicated processes of resettlement and movement into wage labour for the Akha, so too this larger economic corridor has drastically altered the dynamics of access to resources. The Khmu are a minority ethnic group whose lives, like other minorities in the Upper Mekong, have been radically changed by an ethnicized politics of assimilation, modernization and donor-driven development. In Laos, they are the second largest ethnic group after the lowland Lao numbering roughly 10 per cent of the national population. Unlike the Akha, they live throughout large tracts of northern Laos being the majority population in many provinces. Like the Akha they are also resident in neighbouring countries of China, Vietnam and Thailand although in much smaller numbers. At symbolic and political levels, ethnic distinctions continue to resonate in diverse ways in Lao culture even as policies of nationalist unification, akin to neighbouring socialist countries, advocate a country of equal representation. Over many decades the Khmu have played an intermediary and auxiliary, albeit subordinate, role in trajectories of development in Laos, wherein they have constituted a readily accessed resource for lowland labour (including a long history of recruitment into armed forces) and forest trade. For at least 100 years Khmu men have left their villages in search of temporary work in the teak industry and other labour sites as far afield as Thailand and Myanmar. These days many still go, although as Evrard (2011: 94) notes, there is an important difference: "Women are much more involved in migration than before. They started migrating in the 1990s and now account for about 40 percent of Khmu labourers in Thailand." More constrained movement also occurs through resettlement. In

Figure 2.3 Chinese drug control: licence to plant rubber

one district in Luang Namtha Province the number of upland villages, mostly Khmu, was reduced from more than 70 to 16 (ibid: 87). This relocation is mirrored in other locales near the new highway (Thongmanivong et al, 2009). There is also further flow that is pronounced and significant: the movement of young women into commercial sex venues proliferating along Route 3.

Both scenarios that I have been sketching – the upsurge in rubber plantations spurred by the opium prohibition and the changing mobility exacerbated by village relocation – take place near roads and, in a broader sense, resource frontiers. It is not the concrete impact of the roads and their value for frontier capitalism in terms of goods and transport that interest me here. Rather, there is a significant role that roads, and the development interests they serve, play as vehicles to values and creators of new spaces of connection. In both cases we can link forms of commoditization to modernization trajectories anchored by these roads. And we can argue that intimate dimensions are an enduring substrate of ways in which minority groups become connected within these orchestrated transformations.

Roads and rubber(s) – ethnic traditions and intimate opportunism

A graduate student from my university spent an extended time doing fieldwork in the hills of Muang Sing beginning in 2009. The student, herself from the Hani ethnic minority in Yunnan, embedded herself for many months with the Akha, who in many ethnographies are regarded as related to the Hani. She became close friends with a young Akha woman named Midu, who shared details of her life (Li, 2013). Midu made a number of, sometimes quite horrendous, visits from her home in the Muang Sing mountains into Chinese territory across the nearby border. The first time she was nearly raped when she taken into a nearby Chinese town by a Chinese Akha man promising a day of sightseeing. As mentioned, it is not uncommon for men to invite young women to explore the more modern towns just kilometres away. As is also distressingly common, her friends with her at the time were trafficked further into China. In this instance Midu herself managed to escape home that same day. This was not the only time she had to use her wits to find her way back into Lao land. Not long later, she was tricked by her brother-in-law who sold her across the border as a wife to a poor middle-aged Chinese man living further inland in Yunnan, where in her own words she "worked as a servant in his family".[1] After some months she fled and eventually arrived back to her village describing how she drank water from the hollows in buffalo shit to survive. Back home her relations with Chinese men were not over. Despite the hardships already encountered, she teamed up with a young Chinese man who became her business partner and 'husband'. The liaison was seen by both his Chinese employers and her family as a formative link in the burgeoning connections between the village and a Chinese company aiming to negotiate a contract for a rubber seedling nursery and access to many hectares of village land. Midu was, at the time, the sister of the village headman and this was the basis of the company's intent to foster her relationship with a Chinese employee.

When the Shengli Company finalized the contract, the chief investor installed a television (rare in Akha villages at the time) and a satellite telephone connection to Midu's brother's house. He also offered Midu a job as interpreter and plantation supervisor for the company. It was here she met her next 'husband', a relationship encouraged by his boss who invited her to move into the Chinese compound in order to gain a foothold within the Akha community. For her part, even though Xiao Wang was from a poor family, Midu was happy to take him as a partner due to her growing antipathy to Lao Akha men as suitable husbands. The union was strongly endorsed by her family, as Midu describes.

> I think my eldest brother wants more things from the Chinese other than rubber trees. My second brother, who is always interested in doing business, sees Xiao Wang as an ideal liaison for business given [that] Xiao Wang is a Chinese. He even promised that if things worked out, he would buy us a truck to bring goods into our village … My eldest sister also thought it was a good idea to be with a Chinese. But I know that she also wanted to economically tap my future relationship with Xiao Wang since her husband lost [almost all of] their money to drugs [opium].
>
> (Quoted in Li, 2013: 190)

The relationship was not to last however as the company's investment floundered and Midu found time spent in China unappealing. Midu's story, even in nutshell summary, is about how people and relationships are intimate resources that insinuate themselves into economic plans in intricate fashion. The practice of women being an item of exchange in order to facilitate male bonds has diverse precedents in numerous cultures. It also offers a handhold for theorists seeking to locate tales of value creation within human sociality. Graeber (2011: 130) has brought to our attention what he terms "human economies" that employ "social currencies" designed, in his words, "to create, destroy and rearrange human beings". He argues that human economies have predominated human history preceding by millennia the advent of market economies and the accumulation of monetary wealth. Human economies are, according to Graeber, commonly marked by one central mechanism: "important men end up exchanging women, or at least, rights over their fertility" (ibid: 145). This has proved a fertile line of thought (Wynn, n.d.). Rubin (1975), following Levi-Strauss, regards male control of the exchange of women as a primordial form of social networking and/or trafficking of women; or put another way, the history of social connections revolves around a key principle: "the basic aspect of patriarchal power," Giddens reminds us, "was always emotional and sexual" (Giddens and Pierson, 1998: 141). Men so often make the rules and set the terms for intimate exchange leading to a further forthright assertion, "The law that orders our society is the exclusive valorisation of men's needs/desires, of exchanges among men" (Irigaray, 1985: 171). In the hills of Muang Sing, arranged marriages are not typical of Akha society unless the young woman becomes pregnant prior to marriage and then it is hastily organized, but patriarchy is strongly linked to social connection and sexual opportunity. In the past liaisons with village women were, by and large, confined to men within a relatively limited circumference of neighbouring Akha villages. But, as in the case of Midu, relationships with Chinese men are an emerging form of cross-border alliance as transformations in material culture resonate with changes in social relations. Some suggest that *guanxi*, an ideology of reciprocity associated with Chinese interpersonal relations, offers a prime example of an affective economy that has concrete implications in material exchanges. Yang (1994: 6), for instance, notes *guanxi* connections elevate "the primacy and binding power of personal relationships and their importance in meeting the needs and desires of everyday life". In the border areas of Muang Sing many Chinese rubber traders and investors, including Midu's employers, soon learn, however, that what seem familiar expectations require translation as they cross borders. Precisely how affective and personalized expectations fit within new capitalist formations and their transcultural encounters is an ongoing negotiation. Satisfaction is not a given. The burgeoning alliances between Lao villagers and their Chinese counterparts also build out of logics of intimacy internal to Lao Akha society.

Orchestrating relations

Most, but not all, young Akha men and women in Muang Sing and Muang Long become sexually active during adolescence and remain so for several years before marrying. After marriage, women are supposed to have sexual relations only with their husbands. Married men, on the other hand, continue to have sexual relations with unmarried women, who sometimes become second wives, particularly if they become pregnant. The prominent role of multiple-partner premarital sexuality among Lao Akha has recently come under scrutiny for the fact it supposedly differs from Akha in neighbouring countries who, in recent generations, have been taught this liberty is inappropriate to claims on a 'modern' identity. The complex politics of indigeneity in the GMS reminds us that modes of representing sexuality (academic and popular) have the potential to feed into and sometimes exacerbate a context where ethnic groups are simultaneously desired and demeaned for attributed eroticism (Lyttleton and Sayanouso, 2011). Indeed, stereotypes are insidiously reproduced at many turns. Our concerns here are not with engaging debates over representation, but with examining more closely how sexuality and exchange effects social transformations just as modernization impacts on sexuality. One of the most distinctive facets of Lao Akha sexuality is the role of the village youth groups and their facilitation of extended sexual connections.

In most Akha villages in Sing and Long, adolescents form a collective youth group with an elected male head. Not all young women become active members of these peer groups but most do. Premarital relations take place in a range of different contexts that grow out of membership within these groups. The youth group, in particular its male leader, plays a gate-keeping role in structuring sexual liaisons between unmarried women and men from other villages. There are complicated rules and logics governing how this happens that have been described elsewhere (ibid). It is a means by which young men and women become sexually active usually with a number of partners within a broader Akha community. Like numerous societies, it is a means by which the young become intimate with a prospective partner and, while there are cultural distinctions at play, there is nothing unique about the incidence of Akha men and women sleeping together. The important point is that nowadays these peer groups also facilitate the negotiation of broader social alliances and material exchanges that extend to men from China and to a lesser extent the Lao lowlands.

This follows from the particular structuring of introductions and expectations that have coloured village life for many generations. When a Lao Akha male (married or unmarried) visits another village – either with the specific intention of finding a female partner or on unrelated business – he can approach (or be approached by) the youth leader and ask for the company of a young (single or divorced) woman. He must compensate the youth group – usually with whiskey and cigarettes (typically totalling at least $US1.90/15,000 Lao kip). If he does not have a particular woman who he is courting in mind, he will join the gathered youth at the village edge where tiered planks accommodate the evening get-together and if so inclined he is able to make his choice there. After a period of drinking/chatting the arranged or mutually interested couple leaves for an appropriate sleeping place – often a small hut specifically designated for adolescents or, in wake of being told these are not acceptable in a 'modern' village, to a room in a divorced woman's house or simply a mat at the village edge. In the past, women had little choice but to accompany the Akha guest (this mandate does not apply to non-

Akha visitors whose company the woman has always been at liberty to accept or not). But in light of this practice being so easily misunderstood, a significant factor needs further emphasis. While the young woman (in the recent past) must accompany the man to a sleeping area, she is reportedly under no obligation to have sex with him. At times, the couple spends the night together in physical proximity but without sexual relations. If, on the other hand, the suitor is too forceful in his demands the woman can (reportedly) leave his company and is under no further obligation. Men, for their part, supposedly acquiesce to platonic evenings so that they are not publicly recognized as inadequate suitors should the woman decide to leave. In other words, the non-negotiable element of this practice is that the two spend time alone together. The negotiable element is what happens while they are alone. Many women told us that they don't always have sex in these circumstances. Hence, even as women do not relinquish all control over the terms of intimacy, there is a clear hierarchy of male authority in the insistence to spend time together.

Alliances across borders

In recent years, Akha premarital sexual practices have been targeted by government and donor-agency health and gender equality campaigns concerned at the potential for gender violence in these situations. Alongside opium control, supposedly 'promiscuous' sexuality became a core aspect of Akha life slated for moral and social 'rehabilitation'. Alongside top-down moral injunctions that gain little credence, increased educational resources facilitate young women staying at school until late adolescence and play a more significant role in altering these modes of union. But even as orchestrated pairing is being replaced by greater female autonomy in many villages, it hasn't necessarily removed vulnerability to exploitation. As various groups move into closer proximity in the increasingly integrated border areas of Laos and China, cultural difference is opportunistically used by those with advantageous bargaining power. Akha women are increasingly perceived as an approachable commodity in outsiders' imaginations as local sexuality becomes an evocative bargaining chip on the way to modernity and investment in watermelon, sugar and rubber brings a constant stream of Chinese men into the intimate social sphere of village life. Chinese Akha males, aware of premarital sexual networks (remembered from past generations in China), seek out opportunities to engage in liaisons with local women, particularly in villages close to the border. Like Midu's brother, Akha men seek to use access to village women as a means to solidify relations. Many relations are fleeting but a growing number lead to marriage.

Cross-border relations underscore the fact that, only kilometres apart, standards of living vary dramatically. The recent affluence of the Chinese Akha showcases a sense of national superiority. Chinese Akha use their appeal as prospective husbands to exploit sexual access. Playing into these aspirations, in virtually all Lao Akha villages I visited over a period of roughly ten years, locals described the commonplace occurrence of Chinese men seeking sexual liaisons as part of diversifying social and economic relationships. In some villages pursuit of sexual contact repeats the traditional gate-keeping requirement of whiskey and ciga-rettes for the young men. Alternatively, as male youth groups lose their respon-sibility for organizing partners in more modernized villages, young women are approached directly by Chinese suitors. Women are beginning to reject a system in which the youth leader profits from control over their bodies, but this has not led to a simple transformation into a non-material affective economy. Instead, gifts (and money) are now sometimes directly exchanged to facilitate sexual rela-tions between Chinese men and local women. Rubber is a key catalyst in how these relationships take shape. Yang lives in a village 15km into China. His family has more than 1,000 rubber trees in Laos. Yang's father was too busy to manage this plantation so he sent his son over to the Lao side. He described his history with Lao Akha women:

> I had relationships with about five or six young women while working in Laos. I saw one woman more regularly over period of two years and when she got pregnant I asked to marry her. My father was unhappy with this arrange-ment as he felt marrying a Chinese woman was more legitimate due to the requisite marriage papers and birth certificates, both of which are usually lacking in relationships with Lao Akha partners. So my father visited the parents of the Akha woman, but they felt it was their daughter's decision and supported the marriage, so it went ahead and we were married.

Nami, a young Chinese Akha man living in the same village, visits the Lao side frequently and noted the importance rubber is playing in these negotiations.

> If we find a woman to be with on the Lao side we sleep together outside of her home, in the forest or nearby fields. Some men prefer Lao women as they are more honest and diligent, Chinese women only want money these days. But the truth is most men marry Lao (Akha) women who have land for rubber on the Lao side. They can negotiate before marriage how to share the rubber holdings.

Nami used to visit five or six times a month but told us that the Lao Akha women are starting to be far more selective; again based on rubber.

> Recently Lao women avoid me when I visit; I am not so appealing to them. Maybe it is because I am poor. Many Lao Akha want to marry a Chinese man; they see it as something to be proud of. Nowadays Lao girls are getting more wary. They avoid the Chinese man if they think he is not honest, or is already married. They know many men are just interested in playing around. Or if the relationship gets serious, they are also getting smarter. When the family knows a woman has a relationship with a Chinese man, they will come across and find out if he has rubber here.

In the past, a constraint on the pursuit of sexual relations has been language familiarity. Neither the youth group nor young women would accommodate suitors who could not speak Akha. This has not, however, proved an enduring control. Chinese Akha introduce Han Chinese men during their visits. Lowland Lao men, who have worked in the proximity of villages for an extended period of time, have learned a few words of Akha language. In both cases, familiarity facilitates acceptance by local women who might, for their part, desire marriage to a non-Akha. Either way, longstanding courting systems provide ongoing opportunities for Chinese and Lao men to seek leverage through the youth group to request time with young women. By contrast, Lao Akha men carry little appeal for Chinese Akha women and are unable to pursue 'romantic' relations across the border, resorting instead to occasional visits to commercial sex venues when in nearby Chinese towns. Sometimes headmen in the Lao villages seek to prohibit liaisons for fear of losing their women, and thereby a community's grandchildren, to Chinese nationality. But despite occasional stories from returned Akha women concerning the harsh reality of life in China, attempts to curtail the exodus have gained little purchase – many families actively encourage their daughters to marry Chinese men. For their part, Chinese men who marry Lao Akha gain access and family connections with which to further expand their rubber holdings.

Thus, unlike in neighbouring Thailand and Myanmar where longer-term assimilation and economic development have meant that the Akha manage aspects of ethnic culture strategically in ecotourism ventures or even religious conversion, Lao Akha employ social formations in other ways. This is precisely what development ensures. It provides the mechanisms by which culture and ethnicity become integrated within new value systems. In Muang Sing, local men cultivate economic relations with Chinese and Lao men via forms of social accommodation that include introductions to young village women. Alternatively, young women establish relations with outside men regardless of the oversight of young village men. Hence, we might interpret this as a different sort of opening up of Akha culture to outsiders – in this case not just land and labour but also the bodies and emotions of young women.

In Thailand (and Myanmar), development policies and changing value systems led to a pronounced trajectory of Akha and other highland women into urban prostitution. There is also evidence of Akha males entering the sex trade catering to other men (Grieger, 2012). But for the Lao Akha, as affective economies circulate desires for a better life, cultural accommodation of economic change has fostered increased sexual relations in a different manner. Instead of locals out-migrating, outside men seek local partners within the village. To date, these relations are understood as a form of social and interpersonal liaison rather than institutionalized monetary exchange for the provision of sex. This may well change as local cultural interpretations give way to outside frameworks concerning sexual commerce and exploitation. We see this evolution far more clearly and well-established when we turn the manner in which Khmu women are positioned within a changing landscape.

Down the economic corridors – petty investment and ethno-sexual labour

> *Women's bodies and labor are used to consolidate global dreams, desires, and ideologies of success and the good life in unprecedented ways.*
>
> (Mohanty, 2003: 147)

There are many similarities to the manner in which modernization impacts on ethnic groups and their involvement in commercial sex throughout the GMS. At the same time, however, growth in commercial sex venues in Laos has its own characteristics based on historic market trajectories, opportunistic investment and community-based entrepreneurialism, collectively forming a localized expression of neoliberal penetration. It is these specifics that I wish to bring attention to here. Most obviously, commercial sex proliferation in areas of infrastructure development has a simple corollary: it requires women to inhabit these social and economic spaces.

We surveyed drink-shops along the new economic corridor, Route 3, in 2011. In these roadside drink-shops more than 90 per cent of working women are Khmu. In and around larger towns, service provision operates in fancier locales as well with a greater number of women from Tai-speaking groups (Lao and Tai Lue). But in both urban and rural settings throughout Laos, Khmu women heavily dominate this particular service sector, especially in the cheaper and less salubrious settings. In the roadside bars the women range in age from as young as 14 to their mid-20s. They most commonly arrive from rural northern provinces where Khmu are majority populations. In addition to increase in venues, a notable transition is occurring in many of these roadside drink-shops as they provide rooms dedicated to on-site sex. In the past, socialist prohibition of 'social vices' meant commercial sex took place discreetly after prolonged drinking sessions when men would invite their drinking partners to guesthouses in nearby towns. Nowadays, transactional sex is far more overt and numerous small roadside bars have dedicated rooms for women to receive guests. Sex in these drink-shops becomes quicker and cheaper than in larger urban nightclubs where women retain some modicum of choice over whether to accompany their drinking partner for the evening. The owners that we spoke to rationalize the evolution based on a need to protect their employee's wellbeing in face of the increase in Chinese customers who do not speak Lao and pose an uncertain threat of violence or refusal to pay. On the other hand, it also has an undeniable economic logic as the number of clients per day has grown noticeably and some women reported up to six customers per day.

It is more than a demographic curiosity that young Khmu women so substantially fill lower echelons of commercial sex in Laos. While Khmu men and women still have at their disposal certain options that are not subsumed by new rubrics of market exchange, for example, longstanding trade networks and involvement in construction and timber-milling industry in Thailand, networks into commercial sex have emerged more recently from entrenched gender and ethnic hierarchies. The movement of Khmu women into commercial sex is more than men with status

Figure 2.4 Passing time in a drink-shop

and money having minority women's bodies readily available to them, although this is certainly its most immediate expression. Market liberalization and contemporary development programmes are instrumental in defining the terms by which rural poor imagine and experience a changed future through new states of feeling and connection. Given these processes are highly unpredictable, the capacity to aspire carries an implicit ambivalence that Khmu women embody in profound ways. Leaving the village brings broader horizons and, at the same time, blunt confrontation with forces of marginalization that structure capitalist provision of such dreams in the first place. Just one mountain range away from their Akha counterparts, a similar process of catering to sexual desire becomes an affective stepping stone to material transformation as networks facilitating the inflow of young Khmu women play on both cultural connections and the ability to fashion advantage through ethnic exploitation.

Social hierarchy, multi-stranded recruitment networks and changing gender roles are combined elements fostering the predominance of Khmu women in commercial sex. In most sex venues throughout Laos there is a widespread assumption that 'new girls' will get more clients. Young women respond to this rationale of constant movement as the best way of maximizing an income. While some women stay for an extended period in one venue, they more commonly move after two to three months in a given locale, seeking more attention in a different venue.

Catering to this insidious and self-reproducing sense of a short shelf-life, bar owners commonly ask Khmu staff to return home to recruit more women in order to maintain an incoming stream of new staff and cater for growth in client numbers. Occasionally, we heard of money being paid to these pseudo 'agents'. More commonly it was undertaken as an excuse for an all-expenses-paid trip back home. It is also a means of currying favour with the boss. Most drink-shops operate on a style of extended family ethos, where the bar owner becomes a surrogate parent. The owners/managers typically provide food and board, they eat together with staff and more importantly they play the role of family caretaker, looking out for the young woman's wellbeing (taking her to the hospital when she is ill, taking her to the bus station when she returns home, etc.). This sits next to an overt assertion of control when the owner locks away the young woman's possessions, refuses to pay her, insists on a minimum number of customers or amount of beer consumed, etc. We heard of one example of the owner giving staff amphetamines, widespread throughout Southeast Asia, to keep them indebted. But even in these more oppressive scenarios, an overriding ethos of a family operation is still maintained. A second means of recruitment takes place when beer-shop owners visit, or make contact with, village communities usually through connections made with women working for them. The owners target poor families with daughters who have quit school at an early age and make promises of a robust and affluent future. This too is a strong conduit of market values into local communities, values that suggest material gain from mobile and transient female labour can benefit families and communities. A third mechanism is self-generating and further expands affective economies that gird recruitment into the sexual service industry. In many Khmu villages there is now a cohort of young women who have been away from the village for a number of years and who provide persuasive evidence of money to be accrued through outside employment. As recruitment becomes more widespread, an increasing number of single (and divorced) Khmu women follow these examples and leave rural homes to work in the service sector.

To facilitate these processes, a careful deception is maintained. During recruitment, work is usually described as serving food and drink, which fits closely with female obligations during village ceremonies and in this sense is not perceived as a radical departure from existing duties. Not surprisingly, it is not mentioned that women will also be obliged to sell sex. At times, this deception results in young women being pressured into prostitution once they arrive at the beer-shop. They are obligated to repay travel costs and sometimes an agent's fee, first through having to drink copious amounts of beer with clients, and subsequently to accompany them for sex. This acculturation process might be rapid – over the space of several days or even hours – or it might be more subtle and take weeks as the young woman is gradually socialized into a world that validates comparatively large amounts of money to be made for sex. In most instances, the young woman either promptly returns home (giving up all dreams of an income) or begins to engage in sex herself. For example La told us:

> I left home in Luang Prabang at 16 without telling my parents where I was going. I went with three friends who had contacts in a beer-shop in Bokeo. I

stayed there for five days. The owner made me leave after I refused to sleep with customers. I was taken to a second shop after I met the owner at the bus stop of a nearby town. I was made to drink with guests. I got very drunk with a Lao construction engineer. He offered me 900,000 kip [roughly US$110] for being the first man to have sex with me. I was so drunk I went with him. I was too scared to drink with anyone for days after that.

While similar descriptions of personal distress at entry into selling sex are not uncommon, for a majority of women that we met during our research sexual obligation came as no surprise and, however uneasily, it was more often than not accepted as the means by which one's income can be maximized. On the other hand, recruitment relying on false promises and occasional coercion raises the complicated issue of trafficking, sometimes involving the young women as victims/agents themselves, to which interventions have only awkwardly been applied (Molland, 2010).

Inter-ethnic service economies

Snowballing recruitment in the beer-shops can only be sustained if it takes root in accommodating state and community structures. It relies in the first instance on forest-management policies that radically transform rural livelihoods and income streams. Highland rice cultivation is increasingly prohibited by forest protection and village consolidation schemes and more recently by large-scale concessions awarded to Chinese investors that collectively deprive local communities of access to land. Out-migration becomes an inevitable response as marginalization and ensuing social disjunctions affect resettled ethnic groups (Rigg, 2005). In one roadside village, the headman's wife summarized how changing circumstances galvanize new strategies:

> In the past, we lived in the forest. It didn't matter that we lived in small huts. But now we live near the road where many people pass by and see our house. We feel embarrassed with just a small house. Therefore, we want to have a new beautiful house to show our wealth to other people. So most of the men go out to work as construction labourers in towns or for Chinese business-men; most unmarried women work in drink-shops.

But while the political economy of agrarian transition, poverty and/or relocation is a significant underpinning to high levels of Khmu sex workers, it is only part of a set of nested variables. In aggregate, other ethnic groups in Laos, the Akha for example, are at least as poor as the Khmu and many have also been resettled. Just as we considered how rubber was a prominent vehicle of change for the Akha, we must also look to how social relations articulate with changing patterns of modernization for the Khmu. The Khmu in general have had a longer and more closely entwined relationship with lowland Lao than most other ethnic minority groups. Desire (and pressure) to socially assimilate – most Khmu dress as lowlanders and speak Lao – has afforded long-term integration as a labouring class

(Simana, 1998). Together, the impact of historical engagements and contemporary recruitment strategies targeting young women are combining to fundamentally reconfigure local value systems in rural villages.

Significantly, Khmu women's growing prominence in drink-shops is gaining self-reproducing profile as it becomes accepted both in source communities and at a larger level of Lao society that young Khmu women are successful wage-earners within the sex industry. They are perceived as an ever-available and, thereby, desired resource. This imputed 'cultural' willingness to inhabit a low social and economic niche in the service industry gains market value and is used to leverage ongoing sexual commodification of young Khmu women. It is a tool for bar owners (usually lowland Lao, Lue or sometimes Khmu women themselves) wishing to expand their mercantile enterprises based on one simple fact – drink-shops with young women sell more beer. Over time, it becomes a generative facet of capital growth that Khmu women are perceived as an optimal and flexible labour source for a growing commercial industry based on saleable youth and cheap recruitment. One central tenet holds true here as much as anywhere: the line between outside exploitation and self-exploitation can easily become blurred in contexts of neoliberal capitalist expansion. So too the widespread recognition of Khmu women as a resource in the sex industry becomes internalized by young women themselves, as they are conditioned to see sex work as a logical means of capital accumulation.

As in the case of the Akha (and elsewhere in the GMS), 'proletarianization' is changing the landscape of options in Khmu village life and impacting significantly on gender relations. When production was largely geared to subsistence and forest access, women played an essential role in household economies. A Khmu saying, "to have a daughter is to have rice, to have son is to have money", confirms that in the past migrant Khmu labour was almost exclusively male (Tayanin, 2005: 141). As domestic agricultural requirements alter in sync with changing land-use patterns and a rise in wage labour, there has been a consequent shift in migration trends. More recently, young women constitute a far greater proportion of labour migrants, and many go into the service industry. We conducted a survey in 2011 in four Khmu villages in Luang Prabang. Of the 437 men (roughly 30 per cent) who out-migrated for work, the majority (238) did so for wage labour in nearby towns. Of the 215 (roughly 20 per cent) women who out-migrated nearly half (91) worked in bars and/or restaurants and 47 worked in factories in other provinces. Most women do not assume they leave behind domestic responsibilities indefinitely. Leaving the village not only allows exposure to men with money, but also stems from the desire to postpone becoming a 'daughter-in-law'. Pin (18 years old) explains:

> My parents think I work in a factory in Vientiane, they don't know I work in this beer-shop. I will return home when I am 20. Then I will have to get married. When that happens I will have to work in the fields. But I would rather play around first [Lao: *lor len*].

Figure 2.5 Drink-shop adjoining the Northern Economic Corridor

Against a backdrop of few work options due to minimal education (girls often leave school after only a few years' primary education), exposure to commodity culture hastens changes in village work relations. Khmu men who work outside the village contribute to domestic economies (and there are anecdotal tales of Khmu men also joining the sex industry in Thailand), but women are increasingly seen as a more reliable means of increasing family wealth or providing everyday support. Not all women accumulate ostentatious amounts of cash, but a notably visible number return home with modern clothes and, increasingly, the capital to renovate houses for their parents, a responsibility nowadays unevenly allocated to female children. As part of this display, it is incumbent to come back with at least some evidence of accrued wealth. Few are willing to acknowledge hard-luck stories or personal distress: these are buried under showcase tales of 'city fun'. Those who make little money seldom return home, waiting until they at least have new clothes to show off when they do.

In numerous Khmu villages across Laos, new houses, tin roofs and new shopfronts contribute to a growing sense that money can successfully be made in the service industry. Noi described her engagement in this economy:

I married when I was 14. My husband was 34. I didn't love him but my parents chose him because they thought that he was good person. He became involved in drug-use and didn't contribute money to the household. I decided to divorce him. After divorce, I worried about how to take care of my children. One day, I visited drink-shops in a nearby town with my three friends who were also divorced. There, I saw how young Khmu women could earn money by being sex workers. At that time, I was amazed that they could earn so much. I wanted to make money too so I decided to be a sex worker.

In addition to family support, the desire for consumer goods is a powerful motivation spurring more and more women to enter this mode of wage labour. Aoi, a 17-year-old student, told us how Khmu girls from her secondary school go to work in drink-shops during summer because "their parents can't afford to buy them mobile phones or motorcycles. Some save some money and return to study but some girls don't return." This mode of acquisition employed by female students is found in many parts of the region. In the border casino of Dok Ngiew Kham, described in the next chapter, Thai tertiary students make weekend trips from across the river in search of short and lucrative liaisons with itinerant gamblers.

Further to this trend of visible accumulation, some women accrue enough money to begin small business ventures, usually small shops, when they return home. This has become the aspirational template in an environment where rural married life involves backbreaking work in sun-baked fields. Previous research has shown that beer and local whiskey are the most popular commodities in small stores in village settings (Lyttleton, 2009). But, so too when Khmu women return home to open stores and employ assistants in service and sales, this style of capital penetration has direct links to the drink-shops outside of the village wherein men request more than just provision of alcohol. Thus, the structural networks, and the values associated with commodification of female labour, uneasily perpetuate in Khmu villages in ways not (yet) seen among other ethnic groups in Laos. This process was detected in earlier stages of modernization across north Thailand in the 1970s and 1980s as young women in rural villages became (in)vested with new forms of use value as migrant (often trafficked) wage-earners amid the advance of mechanized agriculture and growing debt. The resonant refrain is now echoing its siren tune throughout Khmu communities in Laos.

Sexuality, marginalization and health

In the cases above, concepts of symbolic and everyday violence help us gain a conceptual grasp of the implicit social inequality by showing how individuals are persuaded "that their own actions are the cause of their own predicament and that their subordination is the logical outcome of the natural order of things" (Bourgois, 2002: 223). But, even as oppression is part of the everyday, so too, resilience is obvious. Far too little attention has been given to marginalized people's ability to dream of a better future and the role of economies of desire in promoting these dreams. For, as Appadurai (2004: 66) argues, even though the poor are pressured to "subscribe to norms whose social effect is to further diminish their dignity, exacerbate their inequality and deepen their lack of access to material goods and services", nonetheless, hopes for something better always surface. As such, aspirations, just like other cultural formations implicit to a sense of identity, are not readily excised. At the same time, while they might be pan-human – the point I made earlier: who doesn't dream of a better life? – they are unevenly distributed and grounded in the complex politics of modernization and contingent array of affects they produce.

Land redistribution, agrarian transformation and nascent commercial enterprises represent the orchestrated intrusion of a market economy in local communities throughout rural Laos. The combination of relocation to lowlands and a decline in alternative forms of livelihood has led to an uptake in wage labour for many ethnic men and women. However, the 'culture' of neoliberalism doesn't arrive *sui generis*. It must integrate with local production styles and social traditions. As Taylor (2010: 570) explains, "the arising of global capital is not merely the expansion of dispersed structures of exchange, but the shifting relationships through which labouring bodies are formed, reproduced and differentially incorporated within the circuits of capital". Nowadays, financial accumulation is becoming a central value for Lao ethnic groups in a climate of growing consumerism and has profound impacts on gender roles and social relations. Hall et al (2011) accurately point to the key role families and kin play in creating exclusions. But, so too, there are processes under way throughout developing countries where market expansion and competition over resources prompts men and women to use affective relations as a means of making new connections, what we might term 'intimate inclusions'. This can take a range of forms from using one's family as a bargaining chip through to more 'voluntary' decisions to actively sell sex on a short-term basis as part of a family-oriented mode of accumulation. Household improvements afforded by immaterial labour of Khmu women are a case in point.

In contrast, for the Akha, this process of accumulation is far less advanced. Akha women are not (yet) snared in specifically commercial sexual interactions. For their part, Akha women in the Sing and Long districts turn to Chinese suitors in the hope of a more affluent life in China. This seems a logical choice given, as Midu describes, a growing aversion to life in local communities.

> You have to work and work day after day and year after year. We Lao Akha know nothing but to plant rice and eat rice day after day and the same thing year, in year out. We do not know how to plan or manage the family life. Husbands play with other women, leaving their wives and families at home without enough food to eat.
>
> (Quoted in Li, 2013: 74)

But, while nowhere near as overt as work in bars, relationships between Chinese and Lao Akha are, nonetheless, orchestrated through the interplay of material exchange and affective practices. On the one hand, young males in the village gain money and whiskey for regular introductions. So too, family aspirations hinge on these relationships. For example, in Midu's case, after she and Xiao Wang subcontracted the rubber seedling production, her eldest brother immediately asked to be given seedlings free of charge. Given she was not legally married, her brother had customary right to claim her possessions, in this case any rubber trees she and Xiao Wang would produce (ibid: 68).

These examples show that as commodity capitalism forms the bridge to the modern, development-born transformations have multiple benefits and equally diverse damages. The uneasy interpenetration of cultural systems fosters optimistic imaginings as well as processes of ethnic 'minoritization' and marginalization. And, along the way, new forms of subjective experience both good and bad. In turn, neoliberal processes of inclusion/exclusion that shape people's choices implicate sexual possibilities and their commodification. Everyday lives of the Khmu and Akha in northwest Laos are embedded in this space of negotiated intimacy through the burgeoning opportunities (rubber or road-based) for both entrepreneurism and exploitation. Just as in previous epochs of imperial intrusion all over the world, sexuality remains central to the complex politics of indigeneity throughout the Upper Mekong. At the same time it proffers a sometimes poisoned chalice. In almost all cases where sexuality becomes entangled in manoeuvres to better one's life, women's choices are shaped by a difficult combination of hope and subordination. Despite obvious yearnings for a better life, when young women place their bodies at the front-line of economic expansion, the outcomes are multi-faceted, introducing material gain as well as emotional hardship and disease. In these circumstances, the intersection of intimate and material economies is never isolated from cultural frameworks, nor unfortunately from violence or disease threats.

As I have been describing, large numbers of Khmu women follow relatives, friends or village acquaintances into work in the service industry. The downside is that beer-shop owners and clients also play on ethnic and gender subordination in order to maintain an ongoing flow of young women into situations where they can readily be exploited. In all accounts, women suffer the work they do, not exalt in it. At an embodied level, transformed income choices harbinger growing disease threats emerging from the combination of marginalized gender and ethnicity. Men have a ready source of young female partners whom they can either persuade through their appeal as potential long-term partners or pressure through their age, wealth and status into unsafe sex. In this instance, the ghettoization of ethnic labour in sex work highlights individual vulnerability emerging from changing community attitudes to female migrant labour. Leveraging ethnic and social marginality is a powerful means of subordinating the ability to negotiate sexual safety. Young women in these drink-shops report that men remove condoms during sex, or play on rank and status, offering more money to insist on their lack of use. Others profess to be potential husbands and as such offer an additional enticement to have sex without condoms. Thus, in the small drink-shops along Route 3 there remains ongoing evidence of STIs (sexually transmitted infections) and occasional pregnancies as women are either coerced or persuaded into not using protection (Lyttleton, 2009). Female sex workers, many of whom are Khmu, remain at the forefront of detected HIV in Laos. While HIV detected in sex workers has declined recently, according to the Lao Center for HIV/AIDS/STIs, one of the provinces (Bokeo) through which Route 3 runs ranked highest in HIV sentinel surveys among sex workers through the 2000s (3.9 per cent in 2005 and 2.1 per cent in 2008). Likewise, service women working in areas near Routes 3 and 17B showed high levels of chlamydia and/or gonorrhoea. A survey from the Lao Center for HIV/AIDS/STIs (CHAS, 2009) revealed that 53 per cent of service women reported having had a client who refused to use a condom in the previous month, while 39 per cent had a client offering money for unprotected sex. Women working in bars also suffer pronounced stigma from the very health service personnel who could ideally help (Phrasisombath et al, 2012).

Turning to the Akha, the picture is less epidemiologically transparent but there is ample evidence of mobility, sexual contact and gender violence that create the probability of recurrent health problems. As sexual networks expand within Laos, and as non-Akha men seek to take advantage of cultural systems that support multi-partner relationships, in all likelihood single Akha women will be pressured into a greater number of short-term compensated relationships. With this comes the spectre not just of male abuse, both within and beyond local communities, and increasing cases of trafficked women, but also of infectious disease. In the past, aid agencies offered basic primary health care services, but only since 2005 have these targeted reproductive or sexual health. There has been no HIV surveillance among Akha groups in Laos. But there are many anecdotal details from health workers of explosive gonorrhoea outbreaks popping up in different Akha villages over the past decade and increasing evidence of endemic STIs. To date, capacity of district hospitals for clinical diagnosis of STIs is virtually non-existent anywhere in rural Laos and, until recently, no state-based health services capable of assessing or treating STIs reached local Akha communities. Between 2005 and 2008, an NGO-funded HIV intervention was conducted in 60 Akha villages in Sing and Long. Based on syndromic management protocols entailing physical examination and description of symptoms, 5.25 per cent (637 men and women) of those attending outreach activities (the percentage would have been notably higher if only adults were counted in the total attending the events) were treated for STIs, including chlamydia and gonorrhoea (NCA, 2008).

Conclusion

The connective tissues of everyday social life I have been laying out, the intimate pleasures, the wilful hopes, the demeaning subjugation, the perilous choices some are forced to make, all take especial vibrancy in frontier zones. It is here that we discern most clearly how development processes structure the particular contours of life.

> The space in which we live, which draws us out of ourselves, in which the erosion of our lives, our time and our history occurs, the space that claws and gnaws at us, is also, in itself, a heterogeneous space. In other words, we do not live in a kind of void, inside of which we could place individuals and

things. We do not live inside a void that could be colored with diverse shades of light, *we live inside a set of relations* that delineates sites which are irreducible to one another and absolutely not superimposable on one another.

(Foucault, 1986: 23, emphasis added)

In the spaces I have been describing, living inside a set of relations means being part of affective practices that structure desires and promote multi-partner sexuality as the means to social and material gain. Akha women are subject to rules central to the reproduction of sociality wherein Akha men still largely control the terms of sexual negotiation. At the same time, they find themselves confronted by ruptures in this cultural system that allow outsiders increasing access to local forms of sexual partnering. Mobile men, most commonly Chinese Akha market gardeners and agricultural traders, make their presence felt through infective consumer consciousness and capitalize on loosening cultural systems to become sexually involved with young Akha women. They use material persuasion such as gifts, money or the promise of marriage to effect this. For their part, some Akha women embrace broadened social horizons that allow increased access to concrete material improvement through (cross-border) relationships that include marriage. For other young women, the benefits are more obscure as local male youth receive payment for facilitating short-term connections between visitors and local women. Just as Akha cultural knowledge represents a pragmatic resource base for everyday life, so too cultural capital is used to maximize aspirations in other ways. Where men sign land deals, women respond to the contagious pull of independence and entrepreneurship and utilize an alternative set of affective practices to increase personal opportunities, and as we have seen actively choose to seek alliances, fleeting or otherwise, across the border.

Meanwhile, the contours of commercial sex in contemporary Laos are significantly shaped by forces facilitating Khmu women's predominance in this service niche. As in many forms of market expansion, social relations become a form of social capital. Development projects and modernization trends have elevated women as significant contributors to capital accumulation in changing village economies. For Khmu women it has created opportunities for – or leveraged – the sale of sexuality and, in turn, upped the value of female migrant labour. In Khmu communities, modernization is heavily gendered through circuits of value that stimulate social and cultural expectations that women will provide sexual services as part of their (and their families') aspirations to a better future and promote networks that usher (or coerce) young women into this exchange. In these frontier zones, under pressure to engage in a market economy and commodity culture, the marriage of material pursuits and affective practices – in this case sexual endeavour – has become a logical strategy for many women. Dynamics underlying this union demonstrate once more that development never takes place in purely material terms. Subjective engagement in modernization and its more recently encouraged entrepreneurship inevitably implicates emotional strategies. Khmu women increasingly out-migrate as traditional lifestyles give way to fractured livelihood pursuits. Even as the labour opportunities affording exposure to a broader world are themselves highly constrained, they nurture (promised) dreams of a better future. Sometimes women accrue enough wealth to allow them to pursue economic strategies at home based on commercial enterprise rather than physical or immaterial labour. Sometimes they marry non-village men. Others have less hopeful stories as relentless dreams lead only to physical and subjective distress.

To suggest economic growth leads to the rise in forms of commercialized sexuality (and its mixed bag of gain and depredations) is nothing new and hardly radical. But what I wish to emphasize is that the interpenetration of economic figurations and social relations ensures that sexuality becomes a core element of a broader spread of market values and desires as the productive and reproductive merge. This process is obvious in both Akha and Khmu communities and, as we shall see, also commonplace in other places in the GMS where rapid change is taking place. It is wrong to consider negotiated sexual relations as a discrete component of social change wherein they are typically typecast as 'prostitution' and thereby some sort of anomalous negative consequence that gets silenced or hidden from discussion. Rather, it is more important to recognize that affective practices are an ever-present dimension in the modes by which 'intimate inclusions' are used to create new connections and networks of accumulation. Taken together the above examples demonstrate the intersection of material and intimate economies to be a fraught process in which material achievements oftentimes sit alongside damaging personal and physical compromise. The difficulty, therefore, for donor and state agencies seeking to assist the assimilation of ethnic groups, and provide safeguards implicit in this nationalized belonging, is to not advocate a new set of 'sanitizing' morals, as if this were the essential substrate of modernization, or to further inculcate prejudice as is also an unfortunately common outcome, but rather to ensure that adequate social and sexual safety accompanies material change.

For, as Garcia and Parker (2006) stress, it is far easier for outside agencies to practise negative sanctions regarding sexual rights – that is, to mandate strictures that make sexuality conform to generic (mainstream) rules – than to find alternative ways to allow safe practices. Disease, prostitution and human trafficking might be readily termed negative externalities by planners and policymakers intent on remapping the region. But there is nothing external about how change is embodied within the intimate connections that are part and parcel of development. Some trends, such as the proliferation of bars on new roads, create self-evident connections to marginal groups caught in the cut and thrust of frontier self-making. Discordant changes affect many other groups in other parts of the GMS in more diverse fashion. Hekou, on the China/Vietnam border, has its own version of itinerant and embodied sexual commerce in what Zhang (2012) terms a "not-spot" due to the tandem recognition of the economic value of Vietnamese women who come to sell sex to Chinese tourists alongside the equally tacit unwillingness to act on trafficking and coercion that accompanies its presence. Feigned or actual ignorance to the complex ways that capital structures intimacies occurs not just at the policy level, it is found in many border locales where a productive amalgam of special zones, veiled pleasures, and the rhizomatic connections support a contagious spread of affective practices as a means to wealth.

Note

1 Feingold (2013: 213) reminds us that despite being readily typecast not all brokered marriages across borders are examples of trafficking and that "marriage brokers have a recognized traditional function that is valued by the community".

3 Special zones – anomalous spaces

What is new, on the other hand, is the extent to which this affective immaterial labour is now directly productive of capital and the extent to which it has become generalised through wide sectors of the economy ... which is in turn highly gendered.

(Hardt, 1999: 97–8)

How we experience material worlds, be they frontier zones or urban ghettoes or anything in between, is always inflected by the social, which is to say, physical

Figure 3.1 Chinese god of fortune in residence at Dok Ngiew Kham Casino

places are also social spaces. De Certeau made a widely-employed distinction describing space as "place plus bodies"; or, as Augé explains, place is best thought of as "an assembly of elements coexisting in a certain order" and space is "an animation of these places by the motion of a moving body" (Augé, 1995: 80). When modernization policies and development programmes seek to usher change through reconfiguring physical terrain, and thereby the means by which people animate spaces, they inevitably restructure relationships and interpersonal connections. The preceding chapter showed how intimacy and money become conjoined within aspirational endeavours embedded in larger fields of economic diversification, infrastructure development, ethnic hierarchies and competing social competencies. In this chapter I wish to focus on the way in which border zones physically structure social and intimate relations, and thereby animate these spaces in 'special' ways. Modernization policies and development programmes foster investment and channel mobility through peripheral zones making the intense and often anomalous nature of life in these spaces a crucial element of regional economic growth.

I mentioned earlier the ripe pleasures on offer to the gamblers in Dok Ngiew Kham casino (literally: golden kapok flower – named after an exuberant tree common in the area) – a package of sensual enticements beckoning men from a large regional orbit into its halls. The large sign near the casino's international immigration checkpoint – looking for all the world like an old British train station replete with clock-tower reading Beijing time – makes a different claim on our attention. 'Golden Triangle Special Economic Zone' is carved into the riverbank's edge. This, too, is the image the owner wishes to cultivate, based on the assumption that special economic zones (SEZs) are places that kick-start local economies. Indeed, SEZs are expanding throughout the GMS, where they are benignly framed on policy fronts as 'experimental'. The most common are mini industrial enclaves in frontier zones relying on export-driven commodity production feeding global supply chains. They are spaces marked by their difference, as Arnold and Pickles (2011: 1598) remind us: "These are not regions in the conventional juridico-political sense … and they are not governed in a conventional territorial sense." Alongside the more bona fide SEZs (to which I return in the next chapter), casinos are also multiplying as a form of special zone geared to high-profile and high-cash turnover businesses in border areas. The products they market are far more ephemeral than manufactured goods but in many ways more economically efficient as they sheet home the link between commodity desire and money in dead-eye fashion. In the past, large-scale gambling venues have been associated with transient and often illicit economic investment along the Myanmar/Yunnan border. Most of these pleasure palaces now no longer operate. But in more recent years, the presence of casinos in border areas of Laos and Cambodia has been officially sanctioned as a means to draw investment capital into local economies from their larger neighbours China and Thailand, which prohibit casinos on their own territory (excepting Hong Kong and Macau), and Vietnam which only selectively does. In 2013, Cambodia had 27 casinos mostly in border areas; Laos has four although more are planned (MMN, 2013: 302).

Given it is wide-open as to what is exactly produced in these spaces, SEZs are commonly described as 'exceptional' because of flexible and diverse modes of governance they deploy in the neoliberal goal of "accumulating values in spaces within and beyond national territory" (Ong, 2008: 121). At the same time, others suggest that they are mundanely unexceptional as the state chooses to judiciously apply or withdraw oversight (Walker, 2009). For our purposes, this is a somewhat barren debate as exceptional and unexceptional can be found side by side in the GMS depending entirely on what one wishes to focus on. What remains more relevant is the ways that certain border zones seek to capitalize on some form of 'specialness' as they create eddies and whirlpools on the edges of neoliberal expansion and its accompanying migrant and capital flows.

Out-of-place spaces

Export-processing zones, border markets and gambling palaces each have their own strategies for accumulating value that rely on space-specific behaviours and practices. In this chapter I wish to show that their specialness has very specific implications for those drawn into these places. For example, in the case of SEZs such as Dok Ngiew Kham, the casino space creates diametrically opposed experiences for gamblers and local employees through its management of time and space. For local staff, new and stringent rules become the defining parameters of a 'modern life', whereas, for the cross-border visitors it is precisely a release from restrictive norms in their home locales that generates the appeal. At the same time, like other special economic zones, the casino does this through an enabling legitimacy born of development rhetoric and policy. A thousand miles away, the tiny settlement of Dan Nork, a border market in the south of Thailand, also accumulates value through flexible and specialized commodity production. Its booming micro-economy closely fits the GMS mould of integration and growth through road networks that promote 'connections' – and a large 'Welcome to ASEAN Community' billboard greets arrivals from Malaysia. Like the casinos, Dan Nork generates market appeal through management of space and non-conventional practices that typify special zones. Experiences cultivated in both these places, however, are decidedly not of your normal prescriptive aid interventions.

Talking about out-of-place spaces at a lecture in 1967, Foucault conjures an unexpected postscript:

> you will understand why the boat has not only been for our civilization, from the sixteenth century until the present, the great instrument of economic development ... but has been simultaneously the greatest reserve of the imagination. The ship is the heterotopia par excellence. In civilizations without boats, dreams dry up, espionage takes the place of adventure, and the police take the place of pirates.
>
> (Foucault, 1986: 27)

One may or may not agree that civilizations need boats as ferries of free-floating imagination. But, if one does follow Foucault's line of thought, then we could also suggest that as boats decline in passengers' preferences but transnational mobility continues to soar, there remain plenty of border zones that share a ship's potential to prosper dreams in their role as a bridge between different worlds. Likewise, one might argue that piracy remains not far below the surface in many demarcated zones that dot peripheral regions of the GMS as illicit goods stake their centrality within border economies. These zones too might be thought of as heterotopias made up of particular sorts of enticements, commodities and sets of relations that create their own realities for people called to inhabit these spaces.

As one indication, far removed from any official recounting of flexible governance at national peripheries, let me relay something as mundane as turning on a television in two border enclaves through which I was passing. On an earlier visit when I stayed for the first time at Dok Ngiew Kham it was recently unveiled and loomed like a shimmering mirage in the midst of seasonally desiccated rice fields with its vaunted gold domes reminiscent of a misplaced Coleridge verse and its garden of Greek and Roman gods looking forever askance. As I flicked the channels in my hotel, in-your-face graphic and heavily grunting hard-core porn came on the screen. No warning, no alerts, these videos were offered, I assume, as part of the hotel service. Cut to Dan Nork, the small dense market ghetto at the Thai/Malay border – a special zone in a very unofficial sense. The enclave thrives almost entirely through illicit economies of sex and drugs, promoted and sold in numerous ways. No Greek gods in Dan Nork, except perhaps Dionysus slumming it as thousands of day-tripping Malaysian men seek service from thousands of women hustled here from throughout the GMS. The hotel where I stayed was, at the time, one of the more up-market options replete with a massage parlour staffed by hundreds of Tai Yai and Dai women from Myanmar and China. Despite the more overt offerings of women as service providers, the rooms were very similar to the hotel in the rural Lao casino complex. Except here there were two channels showing porn movies.

In my years of travel in the region, these are the only two spots where I have encountered porn piped through the television 24/7. Sure, other parts of the world offer pay-per-view and internet porn is everywhere, but in both Laos and Thailand pornography is illegal, and the notion of it being freely available to whoever turns on the TV flies in the face of the conventional moral codes the governments publicly proclaim in most of the national territory. A trivial example no doubt, but one that shows 'specialness' can take on numerous dimensions within the confines of border zones: special in very specific ways that link to desires and their excitation, to the ways bodies are integrated within broader economic aspirations, to the way affect and sentiment takes on value as a strategic resource. Different rules, different conventions.

Curtain towns and the value of border bodies

I used the term 'heterotopic' in a previous chapter as a preface to the juxtaposition of social norms and expectations constellating in the crucible-like Muang Sing valley; or the relations occurring in makeshift bars along the new roads where sex and money and ethnicity collide in northern Laos. The Greek statues and biblical murals at the casino similarly evoke markedly incongruous but juxtaposed worlds. Here, I wish to expand on the more general point that border zones are fundamentally and often glaringly obvious sites where the prosecution of rules and their 'experimental' transgression defines who does what and how. Following Foucault's descriptions, heterotopias subvert or contradict norms governing interactions for a purpose. Typically they are spaces walled off or isolated from conventional surrounds – boarding schools, prisons, brothels. Hence, comparisons with SEZs become immediately apparent. As described by World Bank, SEZs are commonly characterized by "geographically delimited areas, frequently physically secured, that are usually but not always, outside customs territory of the host country" (quoted in Arnold, 2012: 741). And then there are alternatives where what is controlled within the space, rather than right of entry, is paramount:

> This type of heterotopia, which has practically disappeared from our civiliza-
> tions, could perhaps be found in the famous American motel rooms where
> a man goes with his car and his mistress and where illicit sex is both abso-
> lutely sheltered and absolutely hidden, kept isolated without, however, being
> allowed out in the open.
>
> (Foucault, 1986: 27)

Such venues might have indeed retreated from the American landscape but hardly from our civilizations. 'Curtain' and other short-time hotels (in Thai, *rongraem marnrut*) can still be readily found in many Asian cities. In fact, we might suggest that Dan Nork is in effect simply a 'curtain hotel' expanded to small town scale. The free-wheeling border market is in no way cloistered but it operates with different norms. Here the mornings are quiet – as people sleep – and 'productive' life begins in the late afternoon. Sex is its raison d'être and a large part of its economy operates 'behind the curtain' via illegal labour, brokered movement of women and clandestine kick-backs. Thousands upon thousands of Malaysian men come for one express purpose, and crossing the border for a day or so on a temporary transit pass with no records, is exactly like parking one's car behind the curtain, leaving behind (Islamic) moral strictures for a space with far different sensual figurations. As Askew (2006: 192) notes, this is a permissive zone, which for Malaysian men represents "an escape, albeit briefly, from the daily round of life in their countries. The cathartic nature of the experience – which essentially involves drinking, involvement with sex workers, and often gambling – was succinctly expressed by Manu … 'When we come to Thailand we forget everything'." The women who gravitate here also cross borders: Dan Nork is a decidedly anomalous space within Thai territory in that women from neighbouring countries to the north, east and west of Thailand come to serve men from countries to its south. Far fewer Thai women and men engage in such service here. The casinos at the northern borders share a similar trait: Lao soil, Chinese investors, Chinese and Thai patrons. Factories in a number of Thai border zones are similar: international investors, Chinese managers, Burmese and Cambodian labour sending goods to

Figure 3.2 Affective labour in Dan Nork – available for a song

overseas markets. These zones are marked by their geographic presence in one country but inhabited primarily by cross-border workers and itinerants.

Perhaps, even more pertinent than its ability to keep certain things hidden is a further variation of heterotopias whose "role is to create a space that is other, another real space, as perfect, as meticulous, as well arranged as ours is messy, ill constructed, and jumbled" (Foucault, 1986: 27). Foucault was thinking that colonies might fit this latter example: spaces organized by the separated, controlled and militated superimposition of meaning on the local. Some of the bona fide special economic zones, such as factory enclaves, fit this depiction, given their tight policing of enclosed space and regulated time. So too, one might add, do the casinos in their careful manufacture of enclosures dedicated to pursuit of dreams. These heterotopias are spaces created for specific purposes, geared to producing material as well as non-material commodities – factory-based woven goods in some sites, or site-specific experiences in other places that mimic but exaggerate the desires of the more conventional environment.

These spaces exist in direct contradiction to their neighbouring world, operating with different rules, different modes of time regulation, different conventions for producing and consuming even as they loudly assert they are promoting development. It is not just economic flexibility but also the divergent ways bodies animate these places that makes them special. It was notable that when the Golden

Boten City (GBC) casino opened at the Lao/China border in 2007 it unveiled a city alien to the rest of Laos. So too, Dok Ngiew Kham was a complex the likes of which was absolutely new to disoriented locals. Nothing in Laos (at time of writing at least) short of the occasional hospital emergency ward, operates 24 hours a day. In glaring contrast, night and day have little meaning for the thousands inhabiting these gambling palaces, as sequential 'shifts' over 24-hour cycles have become part of the local lexicon and a new mode of 'being in the world'. The working rhythms and lifestyle management fall under the watchful eyes of marching cadres of security guards in Chinese uniform. Orchestration of the modern within these bounds – people, time, food, smells, money, duties, values – are all definitively non-Lao.

Head-shaking in a border disco

Development programmes – and the factories, the casinos, the brothels they promote in these border zones – do not ostensibly intend to radically subvert local norms. But, they are premised on more flexible ways of operating. Given their special status, they have varying degrees of liberty to operate with their own rules and regulations as they aim to attract investment and, as the World Bank notes, build on their capacity for "acting as experimental sites for the application of new policies and approaches" (Farole, 2011: 1). The juxtaposition of different sorts of spaces – experimental within, conventional without – reminds us starkly that the physical world is not just an inert backdrop to everyday life. People invigorate the material just as the space shapes their experience. So too, spaces inform intimate connections as much as they do styles of material production or labour relations or leisure time. Freud might have famously noted that the sexual explains everything, but to repeat that simple line is to avoid making certain connections explicit, even the seemingly incongruous ones. As mentioned, development planning – be it related to physical space or expanding market economies – seldom considers non-material dimensions to life, as if this is the part of life that is somehow best kept undisclosed, unexamined, unimportant even. This is not surprising. Intimacy, for example, is something typically considered best bound within the private sphere and commonly expected to be curtained (and curtailed) within the spaces of domesticity: "in the western tradition it [intimacy] reflects the colonization of the world by a private individual" so much so that in some cases to be involved in an intimate sphere is seen as a "retreat from worldliness" (Boym, 1998: 500). But, on the contrary, both public spaces and the intrusion of capitalist formations carry strong implications for intimacy and its expression and, in turn, the workings of localized affective economies.

Think for a moment of how people of 'minority' sexuality are usually expected to behave differently in public spaces than those who are hetero-normative in sexual inclination. In much of the world, gay men and women are pressured not to display affection, intimacy or desire in the same way as heterosexual couples can, often for fear of scorn and at times physical violence. Space governs behaviour through the implicit visibility that goes with its public use. That is to say, some groups of people have to behave differently than others in all but the most private places. It is not that all intimacy must be private; rather only certain forms of intimacy can be public. This enforced 'closeting' is not just about avoiding scrutiny: it has an analogy within legal frameworks defining appropriate citizenry and nationalist belonging. Social and economic entitlements are structured by normative versions of domestic sexuality and reproduction. Those who live publicly registered heterosexual lives have different rights, – marriage, adoption, inheritance, etc. – than those who don't. Thus, it follows, at least in most Western societies, that the organization and experience of one's surrounds also 'naturalizes' heterosexuality (Hubbard, 2001: 54). Different rights create different spaces in which one can be intimate.

Physical geography and management of space also structures the ways in which 'deviant' or dissident forms of heterosexuality are able to be expressed. For example, prostitution is often regulated and there are multiple pressures to keep it physically hidden. All over the world, commercial sex is contained and often restricted to out-of-sight and/or policed venues: thus the longevity of 'curtain hotels'. Hubbard makes a point that is applicable almost everywhere:

> notions of morality – what is right and wrong in the eyes of the state and its citizens – create sexual geographies at a variety of spatial scales. Notions of morality are thus branded onto the spaces of the body, the city, the region and the nation in constantly shifting and complex ways that, nonetheless, serve to order flows of desire.

> (ibid: 58–9)

That the spaces we colonize, construct and inhabit should have a concrete effect on our experiences, and the flows of our desires, is hardly a novel thought. Precisely how the production of specific spaces is central to development trajectories is less often explored.

This becomes even more obvious when we consider particular types of locale that emerge as part of attempts to fast-track modernization. Certain spaces, such as SEZs, frequently start as frontier enterprises premised on opportunity and exploitation but, over time, leave indelible fingerprints on the social landscape and in turn strongly colour the trajectories of development in and around these zones. Supply chain factories in many border zones might struggle with economic vicissitudes but Dan Nork and Dok Ngiew Kham are booming as centres where catering directly to on-site desires manages to short-circuit other drags on their growth. And while it is obvious that service economies are a global growth sector, becoming part of these economies changes people in less transparent but nonetheless profound ways.

Take another example from Dan Nork, which from every angle resembles a frontier zone built on a marketplace for visceral pleasure. One night I am in a disco invited by a colleague and her Chinese Dai friends who work in Dan Nork, initially as masseuses but now as freelance companions to Malay men. One Chinese-Malay man joining us that evening routinely travels from his home just

Figure 3.3 A 24-hour STI clinic and shoe shop in Dan Nork

outside Penang to visit his girlfriend whom he has ensconced in an apartment so she can be free of other work obligations. These extraterritorial and extramarital unions are set up commonly by married Dai women who arrive from one particular border county in Yunnan. Judging by their stories of accumulation, they are relatively successful at this form of companionate coupling, seemingly more so than the Shan women who do massage or the Lao, Burmese and Han Chinese women who work the short-time bars. There are specific reasons for this to which we will return in a later chapter. In the meantime, this particular night, the Malaysian man has brought a friend from Australia. He and another Dai woman make up the partying foursome. Up-market pubs and discos provide a venue for visiting men to hang out with their girlfriends as the closest thing to more conventional domesticity – there is nothing else in this small little town. We join them for a while. The music is loud and talk is difficult. It doesn't matter. These men are more interested in standing and rocking to the beat. Their heads move back and forth in trance-like fashion. Here disco patrons commonly take what in Chinese is referred to as the head-shaking drug (Chinese: *yao tao wang*), a form of amphetamine commonly available in Dan Nork. And indeed their heads shake. Ketamine (Chinese: *k-fen*) is also widely taken as a spur to more indolent intimacy. And, like Foucault's floating ocean liners, if one needed any further confirmation, it becomes obvious that Dan Nork is deeply a place-out-of-place, where men and women suspend other realities and forge intimacy of a special kind as wave-like rhythms and shaking heads beat time. My point is that dreams and adventure remain common currency in this place for both men and women, and piracy is all too present.

In the lift on my way to my hotel room, I overhear three women talking in Lao. I can speak Lao so I ask them where they are from and where they work. The next day I visit their bar (in effect a brothel). They are eating lunch and preparing for afternoon and evening's clients. One has startlingly blond hair and blue contact lenses that seem bizarrely incongruous when she tells me her home is in Huaphan – one of the more remote Lao provinces where village life has little in the way of modern trappings, much still without electricity, a far remove from the levels of cosmetic adornment this 18-year-old had taken on. She has been working in Dan Nork for about six weeks. A friend brought her here she tells me, noting at first it was miserable but now she loves the work: "It is fun (Lao: *muan*)." While we spoke, a black van pulled up and a large Chinese man corralled three young women from the back seat into the bar. They sat at the other end. They were also from Huaphan, I was told. They looked young, small, out-of-place, with none of the cosmetic or behavioural adornments displayed by the women I was speaking with. They also looked terrified. They had arrived two days earlier. Several potential clients walked in and the overbearing pimp made two of them stand and turn around. He spoke Chinese to the clients. He told two of the girls to prepare themselves. The remaining girl was instructed to give condoms to the two who were leaving. She took one condom out of her small handbag, saying this was all she had. One girl took it. The other looked too dispirited to say anything. They left. Several weeks later, 70 trafficked Lao women were rescued by the Thai police in a raid in Dan Nork.

Distress is a prominent part of the affective economies of life at border zones such as Dan Nork and it is not something I wish to trivialize even as my focus in this chapter is elsewhere. Dan Nork serves as a key transit zone for women coerced further into Malaysia and as such its economy has a gruesome underbelly even if only a small percent of the overall numbers of women who come to work do so under coercion. Voluntarily or under duress, overwhelmingly Dan Nork is a space geared to the sexual. Spaces in Dan Nork are carefully organized and controlled. Occasional Thai newspaper reports highlight the lawlessness and corruption required to keep Dan Nork the curtain town it is.

> It is common knowledge that legitimate business in Dan Nork is not more than 30%, the rest are illicit operations, that is, drugs, gambling and prostitution. Dan Nork is a centre for the trade of all types of drugs, from cocaine, ice (Thai: *Ya-I*), ecstasy (*Ya-E*), speed (*Yaba*), opium and marijuana – both for use and for trade … It is heaven for drug users from Malaysia and Thailand because all those in charge of the law have no interest in policing this zone. Apart from drugs, the sex trade here is huge … It is no surprise that the public health call Dan Nork the hot spot for HIV in Songkhla Province. Whatever, this town relies on illegal business, and has its own mafia to control these enterprises … more than this almost every public sector official gets

kickbacks from the trade in Dan Nork ... even the most senior official will celebrate his birthday in the pubs run by the mafia. Together, it all makes this town run completely outside the law and entertainment businesses operate 24 hours a day without permission.

(*Daily News*, 13 May 2009)[1]

Academic studies similarly describe Dan Nork as a legal abyss, with lawless establishments run by Chinese gangs:

And if it is true that they are pragmatic, rather than really evil, and fully take advantage of this manna from the Muslim Malays, they in their turn operate without any respect for public morals, serving solely their own financial interests, thus placing themselves in a vast shady zone with which they are associated in the popular imagery but from which they can easily extricate themselves by changing their field of work.

(Dialma and Le Roux, 2007: 112)

Even though the settlement only extends about 800 metres into Thai territory, the anything-goes atmosphere and its pulsing rhythms generate a phenomenal number of connections. I am unsure how many men arrive from as far afield as Australia as my head-shaking chum from Melbourne did to pursue a weekend's frivolity, but every weekend literally thousands of men cross the border on short-term passes.

On a basic cartographic level, Dan Nork is divided up between numerous sex-specific venues. In 2011, a public health survey counted 40 massage shops, 165 karaoke bars (including what are called in Thai '*bar book*' that on the outside advertise karaoke but function simply as a booking site for men to pick up women and take them to their hotel paying by the hour) and 34 nightclubs, up from a total of 146 venues in 2008 (Sadao AIDS Committee, 2011: 14). These sex shops are crowded into a space less than 1km^2 in size. Venues draw different clientele as about 15 lanes radiate in either direction from the main artery into Thailand from Malaysia. Sites to one side of the road are oriented to Indian/Malays as Hindi songs boom from the karaoke bars: on the other side, most signs and songs are in Chinese. Ethnic Malay men wander both.

Dan Nork's allure extends across transnational borders to the north through a constant and growing stream of women. Local health authorities suggest up to 10,000 women work in these venues – a majority from Myanmar (Tai Yai from Shan State), China (Dai from Yunnan) and various ethnicities from Laos. As its reputation spreads, more young women are now coming from other parts of China. Only a relatively few women from Thailand, usually the northeast (Isan), sell sex in Dan Nork. Source country matters, as Dai and Tai Yai mainly take Chinese/ Malay customers: Lao and Thai Isan primarily service the Indian Malays. So too worksite varies. Lao, Han Chinese and a few Vietnamese women work primarily in the karaoke bars while the Shan women from Myanmar and Dai women from China mainly work in the massage parlours. Bao, a 29-year-old Dai woman who was given ownership of a karaoke bar in Dan Nork as a gift from a well-heeled Chinese-Malay lover, explained further:

> Dai women cannot sing Chinese songs as well as the Han Chinese, they are too shy. They make no money if they work in karaokes. So they work in massage shops. Han Chinese are much more 'hungry' for money, they will do anything and bluntly ask for bigger tips. Young Lao women with no working papers are usually found in the *bar-book* where they are kept under constant watch by pimps. Some women get pregnant, usually single women or those with regular boyfriends. Married Dai women seldom do as they have IUDs or have had hysterectomies.

The commodity outlets in this market-town cater to demand. Clothes shops specialize in female underwear, short skirts and high-heeled shoes for those arriving from less well-stocked outlets in their home villages. Gold shops cater to the need for gifts for girlfriends. There are more than 15 pharmacies and one high profile STI clinic runs 24 hours a day. Condoms are sold in large quantities, but are not always deployed. Pharmacists tell us that each day they sell STI antibiotics to anxious women who self-treat, as well as substantial numbers of the morning-after pill. Surrounding the skeletal set of lanes with bars one finds proliferating dorms where women live independently or are kept by patrons or pimps. Unlike most marketplaces, mornings are eerily quiet as nearly everyone sleeps. While the scale of the operations at Dan Nork is an eye-opener, the fact that border zones operate as thriving sex markets is hardly a unique phenomenon. Illicit economies are much more likely to be found in border regions. While this is sometimes subject to flights of fancy – such as a brief internet frenzy a few years ago over unverified descriptions of a weekend market in Northwest Laos apparently selling ethnic women like slaves at a Byzantine bazaar to the highest bidder from China – there is no doubt that borders profit from the sale of bodies alongside other commodities. If Foucault can suggest brothels are prime examples of heterotopias inside of which everyday conventions of intimacy are suspended and subverted (although one might add that there are many examples where these distinctions are not as watertight as he would have us believe), then Dan Nork is heterotopia elevated to hyper-level. And if we are to suggest that space matters, and that heterotopias mirror and reconstitute outside relations for their own purposes, we see this most clearly through the way transformations – sexual and otherwise – are supported within these spaces.

Border and frontier appeal is, therefore, often analysed in terms of liminality where transformation based on crossings and contravention is expected and celebrated. It is a psychoanalytic truism that non-standard intimacies take on value precisely for the transgression. "Affective life," Berlant tells us, "slops over into work and political life; people have key self-constitutive relations with strangers and acquaintances; and they have eroticism, if not sex, outside of the couple form. These border intimacies give people tremendous pleasure" (Berlant and Warner, 1998: 560). Following this line of thought, Sacramento (2011) describes a Spanish zone where clubs proliferate and the women come from Brazil to service large numbers of Portuguese men crossing the nearby border, noting a key element of the geography of these sites is to both encourage patronage through privacy and appeal of identity transformations taking place in a new 'cultural space' where normal assumptions and routines are suspended. Crossing borders allows a divesting of domestic moral constraints. Sacramento quotes a Portuguese client:

> It's that feeling of passing from one world to another! For example, it's like going from a small village to a city … you enjoy life, you have got no worries, there are women all around, and it seems like a different world. All you see is women and you forget everything else.
>
> (ibid: 372)

Likewise, Askew (2006: 198) describes Dan Nork as a "pleasure periphery" whose appeal relies on both familiarity, a "virtual colony of Malaysian men", and difference where "Thailand permits behaviours that are illicit and illegal in Malaysia".

But there is more than the transiently liminal to this picture. Market forces spurring entrepreneurialism and sale of human capital mean there are various sorts of relationships on offer in these locales, from the quick sex charged by the hour through to relationships valued in quite different senses. Dan Nork offers all varieties. For example, in contrast to younger Lao or Han Chinese women, many migrant Dai women from Yunnan are married, they market affective dimensions of human capital – care-taking, solicitude, patience and so forth – understood as skills honed by familiarity with married life. Men, as it turns out, respond enthusiastically to Dai women's immaterial labour as these aspects of self are turned into capital in ways that, as Hardt indicated at the start of the chapter, are more and more central to economic expansion. One Chinese male from Malaysia told us in Dan Nork: "I don't like young girls because they are childish in terms of taking care of a man." Another (56-year-old) man from Malaysia offers his thoughts on broadened service economies.

> Many wives in Malaysia hire domestic staff and free themselves from housework to participate in social and political activities after their husband becomes rich. They dress themselves gorgeously every day for going out, and pay little attention to their husbands. Facing a lack of love and care, men of course look for someone else. It is normal for men who have been successful in public life to have extramarital relationships. Dai women are 'good' and they are diligent, working hard for their family and children. They never ask for luxury gifts, just assistance for their family … Having a relationship with them is not just for sex, otherwise we could go to visit a prostitute whenever. They dress up properly and understand how to take care of men so we are willing to take them out to walk around and meet our friends. We will not lose 'face' … Actually, I don't like young girls. They look just like my daughters, and always dream to have romantic event with handsome boys. They cannot sincerely fall in love with an older man like me.

It should be clear that in these intersections of bodies and yearnings space matters. Who can meet whom, and with what assumptions, allowing which range of expressive relations, are defined, for those that come here, by the spaces of Dan Nork. So, in answer to the query, can affective practices be a means to accumulating other forms of value? Then the answer – at least when one visits Dai women's hometowns and observes the material benefits they gain from 'immaterial labour' with cross-border men in Dan Nork, be they gold amulets, or gleaming houses back home in China, and/or support for children and husbands – is resoundingly yes. So too, there are other more subtle speculative and affectionate dimensions to these relationships that I will return to in a later chapter. Meanwhile, there is more to the specialness of border zones than the red-light sale of sex and the flickering glimmer of emotional connections. Casinos offer a more complex reading of how bodies and affective practices take on new value in border zone work-sites.

Gambolling along Kapok Avenue

The letterhead on the stationery at the main hotel in Dok Ngiew Kham reads 'Kapok Garden Hotel: Development of Integrated ASEAN Economic and Tourism Areas at Sam Liam Thong Kham (Golden Triangle)'. There is no mistaking the casino investor's intentions, both in branding and internet publicity, to be a key player in local development. This nod to a leg up for Lao modernization was also heavily apparent in the advance publicity for Golden Boten City, at the point of the Northern Economic Corridor where Laos meets China, built some years prior to Dok Ngiew Kham. While it was still just hills and a forest with several inconvenient old Tai Lue villages in its midst (the land for GBC was leased from the Lao government in December 2003), the 48-page publicity booklet produced by Golden Boten City Management Company pitched the wonders of its vision to prospective investors. It described (in English and Chinese), in euphoric prose and glossy pictures, a 1,640ha complex as the core of an ambitious programme to transform the region. It imagined foreign investment in this tax-free zone and pleasure domain as only a matter of time and pitched its appeal to both an Asian and a Western audience. The language in the brochure is not short on hyperbole (and decidedly awkward English) aiming to entice investors unsure of its tourist appeal.

> Golden Boten City, a golden place hiding in the luxuriant jungles, just like Peter Pan's city of never falling down, just like mysterious treasure island … tempts the deepest desire in each tourist's mind. As a golden port, her convenience, tolerance, prosperity and elegance will conquer every person who arrives at here. Traffic convenience will endow her with advantaged tourism, and Laos's attractive natural landscape together with advantage of Boten will draw in numbers of international tourists.

These borderland casino zones might be anomalous in terms of territory and sovereignty, but, ripe prose aside, they remain steadfast in advertising their intent to introduce modernity to backward populations. As Nyíri suggests:

They cast themselves as doubly modern by simultaneously deploying the regalia of the Chinese State, which stands in the region for the strong, successful modernizing state, and a pioneer discourse of economic and social freedom from the strictures of that very state, also in the name of modernity.

(Nyíri, 2012: 535)

The question is, of course, what precisely is being developed in these pioneer enclaves given this dual agenda of mimicry and freedom? And what is it that modernity is delivering to the locals? Specific deliverables were listed for the Dok Ngiew Kham site on the contract (shown to us by local district authorities) between the Lao government and the Myanmar Macao Lundun Co. Ltd., the investment company as it was called at the time (nowadays known as Kings Roman Group). It itemized: economic development infrastructure; agriculture and livestock assistance; multiple processing industries; hotels, tourism and entertainment venues; education and health facilities; international trade and business including tax-free zones, banks and insurance services; postal and other communication services; transport. In short, a mini-metropolis, a hive of modernity to be delivered to the Lao people replete with grandiose dreams, watched over by the pantheon of Greco-Roman divinities and Chinese gods of good fortune even as the huge casino entrance has biblical frescos depicting what looks suspiciously like Jesus expelling locals from Gomorrah. Development with a mission. Closer to home, an administrative assistant told us glowingly that Dok Ngiew Kham would be "like a mini-Hong Kong, with Zhao Wei [the Chinese owner] as its president!"

While casino visions rely on geographic efficiencies for tourists (customers could walk across the Chinese border to GBC – a helicopter drops VIP international passengers directly into Dok Ngiew Kham, others cross the river in from Thailand in a matter of seconds); so too, the two casinos pitch themselves as free-trade zones intended to create business hubs for trade from other countries in the region. Perfectly in line with GMS rhetoric, the advance publicity brochure talks about creating a new community where there was very little:

> Although now there are just 1500 people living in 3 villages in Golden Boten City, you should believe that thousands of people will gather here in a beautiful setting of an autumn evening. They live and develop here with various occupations and identities, to form a huge community and a new modern society.

That was in 2004. The booklet didn't mention the word casino or gambling once. And yet it was the casino that first opened in early 2007 and the casino that functioned as the luminous drawcard for many thousands of Chinese visitors to GBC. It was the lynchpin of GBC's growth and, however dubious, the supposed vehicle of local Lao development and the "new modern society". Gradually the site expanded to include some of the entertainment venues referred to in the brochure – short-lived transgender shows, golf courses that were never quite completed, new hotels – but nothing replaced gambling as its core operation. And,

Figure 3.4 Biblical warnings at the gates of Dok Ngiew Kham gambling hall

as these things go, the vision of a perpetually golden sunset was short-lived. As the radical 'otherness' of this zone fed euphoric publicity as well as habituated appetites for short-term gain from thousands of daily visitors to the gambling halls, so too it raised major concerns over rule of law and control of behaviour. The Lao government relocated its immigration point to the Chinese edge of the complex in order to control incoming visitors (prior to this they could come and go unmonitored by the Lao authorities) and its customs control point to the Lao side of the leasehold. Ongoing discussions of jurisdiction centred on how to handle the often quite violent crimes that took place with seeming regularity. Most Chinese offenders were sent back to China; those of Lao citizenry were handled by Lao authorities. But this was not enough. In mid-2011, only four years after its opening, the Chinese authorities unceremoniously closed the border for anyone without visas – that is to say, the thousands of day-trippers were no longer able to access the casino on border passes. A short while later, phone networks and electricity sourced from China were blocked from the complex. Within several months, what had been a thriving frontier town revolving around the casino economy with more than 20,000 residents became a ghost town with only a handful of shopkeepers or traders remaining who had paid advance leases and had no idea where to go. Tellingly, the sex shops were the only businesses that stayed open for passers-by to gain some token of the city's quickly faded fantasies.

This highly effective cease and desist order was undertaken due to growing concerns over violence and lawlessness. A television documentary had aired in China telling the tale of a woman who had been tempted to Golden Boten City with advance cash and promises of free accommodation. Upon losing the advance and then some, she had supposedly been kept captive until her family could pay. During our visits we heard many stories of stand-over tactics like this. My colleague spent a few days staying in the casino's private health clinic after she befriended the Chinese nurse; every day or evening there were a stream of incongruous injuries: fingers cut off in 'construction' accidents, legs broken having 'slipped' from a roof-top and so forth; the most gruesome being a sex worker who was found with no hands and her throat cut. As I write, the Golden City casino remains a hollow shell of weeds and empty buildings, even as company public relations staff suggest it will reappear more successful than ever (after a required gambling-removal makeover). Peter Pan's Never Never Land, indeed.

Meanwhile, Dok Ngiew Kham, some distance from the China border, continues to parlay a more salubrious image since its opening on 9 September 2009 (9/9/09 – nine is a lucky number to many Asians) – with a race course for miniature horses, a promenade by the river and a kids' play area in the main casino building. Overall, as the casino diversifies its client base into Thailand as well as China and its staff recruitment into Laos and Myanmar as well as China, it appears, to date, to be standing on more stable ground. This is not to say violence is not present – staff mention 'accidents' alongside regular tales of corpses found floating in the river and continued stand-over tactics for those who cannot pay. One local staff member told me she had accompanied a security officer to a small holding cell in the forest well away from the complex where about 20 or so men were crowded in a prison-like atmosphere waiting for their relatives to send money from China. A woman working in a massage shop mentioned a number of inveterate gamblers she had met who were missing fingers. Nor are selective affective economies any different than in other casino sites. Just like the banana packers I mentioned in the introduction, Chinese staff described to us the casino's appeal. One young tour guide noted that he thought "virtually all men will avail themselves of other sensual pursuits while they are here, because the casino offers the 'liberty' to pursue sex, drugs and money in ways that are a far remove from the experience of life at home". Not quite what neoliberal proponents had in mind with the experiments and freedoms they relentlessly promote – but on the other hand, perhaps at its most basic level of self-appreciation amid wishful fantasies, not that different.

The combination of bodily pleasures and aspirational addictions should be unsurprising given that gambling so often relies on persistent unleashing of fantasy, wherein the evergreen 'I might win' prompts one to lay down more money. It has been documented in the US that people who visit casinos are more likely to pay for sex than patrons of other entertainments (Walker et al, 2010). Wants and desires, as we know, are often remarkably pliable and can, in specific circumstances, spread to related targets quite easily. Desires for money, desires for visceral pleasure, desires for excitement and the out-of-ordinary, desires for bodies;

all are common bedfellows in the casino complexes. Given heightened interest in the sensual, it is equally no surprise to find gambling venues trade in the sale of bodies and affective stimulations. This is common in most parts of the world. In Las Vegas, for example, casinos secure legitimation as family entertainment by being formally opposed to prostitution but, in practice, encourage it as part of the tourist package (West and Austrin, 2002: 495). Reichl (2005: 34–5) observes further that the "success of Las Vegas depends, however, on the ability to manufacture desire itself", visceral and sexualized desires inspired through the "semiotics of pleasure-zone architecture" and the publicity campaigns that emphasize the casino's promise of "freedom to do what you want, when you want … freedom from inhibitions, freedom to indulge, freedom to go nuts". These enticements find remarkable consonance with appeals reverberating around the Lao casinos. Zhao Wei himself wants Dok Ngiew Kham "to expand it so it's like Las Vegas" (Hilgers, 2012).

Despite being so deeply lodged in these carnal realities, the special zones hoist a wholesome and optimistic veneer of being about development and newfound respectability for their chief investors, even as their resources are beholden to a persistent 'vice economy' (Nyíri, 2012). Chairmen of both special economic sites have had previous experience in running casinos in Myanmar borderlands where local economies are heavily reliant on illicit drug production and trade. They (seemingly without a hint of irony) tout their current initiatives as part of China's assistance to rid the region of a dreaded scourge under its state-assisted opium substitution programme. Despite such rhetoric and the common presence of anti-drug posters, drugs are widely described to be prevalent in both casino sites. A Thai woman, Daeng, who works as a masseuse at Dok Ngiew Kham, described how smoking amphetamines (Thai/Lao: *yaba*) is almost de rigueur whenever she is called to attend to Chinese men in their hotel rooms. She described its impact on long-term gamblers: "Some men come here for months, they start out as healthy and normal-looking but over time end up skin and bones from so much drug use." Others receive more abrupt sentences – on earlier visits I met several inhabitants who subsequently 'disappeared' over suspected drug trafficking.

More visibly than drugs, sex is part of service economies and the casino atmosphere at every turn. Prior to its ignominious closure, many hundreds of Chinese women worked selling sex at Golden Boten City, at certain times of day forming a veritable conga line that men had to wend their way past to access the casino. At Dok Ngiew Kham soliciting is similar. The Chinese women give out name cards with mobile numbers to male passers-by and billboards advertising their services are everywhere. As mentioned, Thai students from across the river are known to haunt the casino halls on weekends looking for short-time gain. Thai, Lao and Myanmar women work in massage shops within the complex, while Lao women mainly work the periphery in small drink-shops. This is a logical outcome. Casinos are magnets for those wishing to gamble and for those wishing to make money from these gamblers, including through the sale of intimacy. Like Dan Nork, the networks are broad and, occasionally, brutal. On one visit, we met three young women who had just arrived that day from Phongsaly, a remote northeastern Laos province. They had been brought to work in a Chinese bar within the casino: one young woman had never left her village before and when I spoke with her was absolutely dismayed at the sight of the river, let alone the huge statues. The short skirt she was made to wear for the first time in her life also clearly added to her visceral discomfort.

Just like the economic corridors that feed these sites, the footprint of the casino is immediate in the types of economic enterprises and social relations it generates. And following the manner that frontiers are often heavily masculinized, just as in Dan Nork, in the casino in-your-face sex becomes a central commodity and key vehicle of connection in these affect-saturated zones. Alongside the porn movies, there is a high profile sale of stimulants. Sex shops showcasing a huge range of sex accoutrements were one of the first (and only surviving) displays to greet the traveller crossing into Golden Boten City. According to sales staff in Dok Ngiew Kham, visiting men commonly purchase sex drugs at the on-site pharmacies. They come in many forms, including candies that can be passed around as a treat to enhance female desires. Perhaps the men wish to assert fleeting control over their environment: would-be winners at the card table, would-be winners in the bedroom. Working women also, apparently, give men Viagra or its equivalent in order to enhance his experience and thereby the connection he will feel with her (and the money he might give her).

Catering to demand, drink-shops and small bars have quickly expanded around the casino as well in spaces that felt more familiar to the Lao women than those inside. Bars that had been run in desultory fashion for many years were suddenly made-over. So too, the modalities of the trade are evolving. No longer do men pay a bar-fine as a source of income to the bar owners, women are not beholden to the owners in the type of pseudo-family I described earlier. Rather, serving women are in such demand they have become an even more casualized and flexible labour source and simply use the bars as a meeting place. They can come and go as they choose. However, the owners know that proximity to the casino offers one concrete advantage that will hold women there. One sex worker near Dok Ngiew Kham told us with absolute clarity: "You make much more money from the casino clients here than customers elsewhere." This boom started during the construction phase as thousands of labourers were employed from Myanmar, China and Thailand but is now mainly fed by gamblers. Noy, a 30-year-old divorcee from south Laos who manages one of the nearby drink-shops, tells us that Chinese men arrive at any hour of the night in one of the casino's fleet of limousines and take women back to the casino. Sometimes they go for several days with a client.

Women selling sex in these bars are attracted to the Chinese clients' money but at the same more than a little cautious about entering the casino hotels. We heard from a number of women they will not go into the casino with clients for fear of violence. Others are willing to take the risk, but word spreads of difficulties they confront. As Ji, working in a nearby bar, notes: "Some girls went to casino with clients, I heard from other girls that some Chinese clients hit girls." This theme of violence is often repeated as Ji described: "The Chinese man brought a woman from the bar to the casino and when she entered the room she found that there

Figure 3.5 'Self'-entrepreneurs: women awaiting customers at Golden Boten City

were two men waiting. She had to have sex with both for fear they would beat her." Daeng the masseuse told us she had encountered the same thing; several men in a room having sex with a woman, or even the reverse, one man with several women hired to 'take care of him'. All part of the package. Ging, another Thai woman working in a massage-shop that was transplanted to the casino from the Thai side of the river, was astute enough to teach herself basic Chinese in the three months she has worked there. She said this gives her an edge in attracting clients but, more importantly, it allows her to control the moods of the Chinese gamblers that seek her company, noting "they are often bad-tempered: other girls get into trouble with the men because they cannot speak to them, to calm them down". She reasoned that she gets more clients than the Chinese women working as sex workers in the casino because she is Thai and, as such, is regarded by the Chinese men as more convivial and warm with the men. She makes an effort to promote this image, making sure she is hyper-deferent to her customer, in her words treating him like a 'lord' (Thai: *prajaow*).

Jun, a 19-year-old from Udomxai, working in a small cluster of bars some distance from Golden Boten City, added a different perspective. When asked why a Chinese man might bother to travel 25km to pick her up when there were numerous women on site, Jun answered simply: "He wants to sleep with a Lao woman." This is a crucial point. The advertising for these casinos talks about the exotic beauty of Laos. Part of the experience of coming to Laos to gamble is also to experience local 'flavour'; this is not an uncommon attitude for men who travel in Asia (or for that matter other parts of the world). According to male opinion, one has not adequately visited a place or culture until one has 'tasted' its (female) flesh. There is however a hierarchy. While Lao women might represent local exoticism, culture cannot be separated from economic adjudications. Thai and Chinese women command higher prices: economically and socially deprived (that is to say more primitive in the Chinese male eyes) Lao and Burmese (Tai Yai) women get less. Thus, the few Lao and Tai Yai women selling sex in the complex pretend to be Thai, just as Han Chinese pretend to be Dai north of the border (Hyde, 2007). Ethnicity has its price. Lao women, so men tell us, offer more time in order to get paid as much as the Chinese women. Self-making processes extend to embodied identification: the casino market is able exert pressure on which national body has most value. To counter this competition in the name of equity, one sex worker told us the casino has attempted to standardize prices regardless of nationality: just like other forms of production, here too rules apply.

Ambivalent space, supplanted values

As evidenced by the growing appeal of concessionary land leases, one might argue these special zones offer valuable regional economic assistance through the high level of investment they represent. While mores, rosters and work-styles are all Chinese, visions of success echo core tenets of the GMS programme. Cooperation, harmony and, above all, economic growth are predicated on competitiveness and commonality, which is to say creating a niche market and employing ethnic exoticism and geographic proximity as the key selling points. Certainly, the Lao government receives financial compensation for the leaseholds, but the economic and cultural impact these zones will have on local communities and to what extent they will achieve the grandiose dreams they tout is still very much an open question. Despite the allusions to agricultural innovations and educational assistance, what is being produced here is far more amorphous. The casino complex is geared to producing immaterial goods: a leisure experience and an economy of affect. This is no export-driven SEZ, but an import-driven development model that brings men with money into these environs. Most significantly, gambling is a growth engine that markets a very particular sort of circumscribed pleasure. The staff working here learn how to assist in the exploitation of a customer's habituated desires. In turn, they gradually internalize the values associated with this model of compulsive accumulation. This then seems a far more complex notion of development than normally imagined under the guise of foreign assistance, although, at heart, it shares in the unadulterated mission of spreading opportunities to 'take a chance'. More aptly, it fits with the generalized characteristic that Chinese development assistance is oriented to teach by example, rather than lecture and train as Western development tries to do. The important question is of course: precisely what aspects of human quality (Chinese: *suzhi*) and values are being transmitted in these environments.

One characteristic becomes apparent. This rapid insertion of modernity into rural and undeveloped parts of the GMS relies on a set of contradictory but highly fertile and repetitive imperatives. Dan Nork's masculinized appeal, according to Askew (2006), relies on familiarity and difference, close to home but with new moral codes. Nyíri (2012: 554–5) notes that the casinos simultaneously affirm contrasting modes of Chinese paternalism and militant order alongside economic and social freedoms. Thus, it is also no surprise that the experiences of those drawn into these zones will be fired by a profound and ambivalent sense of transgression and/or alienation. This inflected sense of difference – wherein Laos represents the exotic, the 'primitive', the undeveloped, at so many levels – seeds affective economies radiating throughout the casino complexes with powerful and infectious images: compulsion as freedom, hedonism recuperated as poverty alleviation and drug substitution, the erotic appeal of the exotic woman, the fear of the Chinese man. These are the contagious examples of what a 'better' life comprises that are most available to those being sucked into this development enclave. In more concrete terms, the service economies in these casino complexes – chancing one's hand/taking a risk, sexual enticement, drug-assisted relations and even fear of orchestrated stand-over tactics – highlight how intense states of being take on heightened value in these venues. In short, all who enter these zones confront the heavy saturation of affect and cannot avoid its interpenetration with market value.

This is a ploy not just for the gamblers who buy into the package often to the point of visceral excess (as the regular need for finger removal would imply), but is sold as crucial for the development of the local economy and livelihoods of those around these spaces. Even as the internet allows one to enter the gambling halls via web cameras and avatars who prowl the floors with headphones, so too the casino's tendrils extend beyond the bodies of gamblers and sex workers and beyond the walls of this zone. The casino space alters how people experience life as it clinically inserts a model of 'the modern' with a new set of customary rules and practices. The casino's success relies on a heightened sense of freedom for the men coming to gamble and equally on the imposition of an opposing set of management constraints targeting local workers. The workplace conventions and emotional connections might not be the ones envisaged in the GMS publicity but they are remarkably immediate for the local men and women impacted by the casino's presence.

Overwhelmingly, it is an alien space in terms of cultural norms that requires both subjective and objective adjustment. Despite allusions to global trade, there is no mistaking both casinos are primarily Chinese operations capable of potent conjuring tricks the most obvious being that, by crossing into these zones, Laos becomes China. Given that all clocks are locked in sync with Beijing, as soon as one enters it is one hour in advance of local Lao time. Return to your village and you gain an hour. Default currency is Chinese yuan. One local calmly noted to us: "This is not Laos anymore it is China." Lao staff are required to quickly adopt new rhythms and mores as they become part of the Chinese management structures. The investment companies stipulated at the outset that they would diligently hire

Figure 3.6 Watchful gods adorn Dok Ngiew Kham

Lao staff in the hotel/casino complexes. Chinese staff outnumber the Lao signifi-cantly but many hundreds of Lao (and workers from Myanmar) have indeed been employed as croupiers and hotel staff. There is, however, a steady drop-off, even despite high pay rates, as Lao staff find the atmosphere unbearably alien.

Lao employees told us it is the unfamiliar work environment they found most difficult, with the Chinese next-in-command sometimes quite abusive in han-dling subordinates. One Lao hotel worker mentioned how she had been severely rebuked for not greeting guests with a friendly hello (in Chinese) every time she passed someone in the hallway. Another spoke of the perceived discrimination in the food hall, where she felt the Lao staff received smaller portions of food than the Chinese. Others mentioned the difficult and unfamiliar work hours, or the public bathrooms where Chinese were more comfortable than the Lao bathing semi-naked. Lao staff who leave are generally replaced by Chinese. Likewise, to get a promotion, Chinese language is required. Thus, what started out as being a nod to support Lao employment is gradually reverting to an institution of Chinese employers, Chinese customers and Chinese staff. Within this amalgam of cultural value and circulating capital, time and space take on new meaning. Staff must offer sharp attention to customer pleasure and perform the same tasks hour-in hour-out – counting, distributing, collecting, smiling. They clock in for eight- or 12-hour shifts. There is no designated day-off. In the construction phase it was the 12-hour shifts that posed the biggest obstacle to Lao staff being hired as construction workers. They could not accustom themselves to this pacing: Chinese and Myanmar workers soon took their place. Nowadays, as gambling employs a majority of staff (around 3,000 at Dok Ngiew Kham in 2011), shift work becomes part of a fundamental transformation of life within casino walls. Croupiers and other service staff work for 1.5 hours and then break for 30 minutes as concentration and acuity is paramount. Failure to count correctly as they distribute cards and collect chips means loss of wages and maybe employment. So too, physical space is organized like nowhere else familiar to these, often rural, recruits. Similar to the gambling halls where staff work, with their carefully arranged tables alongside each other, young men and women are crowded into large on-site dormitories regardless of where they are from and grouped into separate but adjoining male and female rooms.

Workplace sites and rhythms are geared to producing a solitary product: customer mood and, more specifically, satisfaction with the risks he (and occasionally she) is taking. The opulent surrounds are not casual whimsy. Staff and patrons respond to the trappings and they soon begin to aspire to this hyper-fantasized world. Most of the largely poor and relatively uneducated staff choose to work in the casino precisely because it is a high-paying job offering reminders of visceral pleasures at every turn, the plush panels, faux-European artworks, fine marble, baroque staircases, boutique shops, exotic women and so forth. They sacrifice familiar aspects of a threadbare life for the sensory overload of consumer fantasy. But an accompanying anxiety at the alienating degree of immersion is commonplace. This too infiltrates all aspects of life and prompts a constant question for the workers: "How long before I leave?"

Time and a state of being

I suggested earlier that, these days, as service economies gain prominence within global production regimes, the productive and reproductive are no longer neatly separated. For a sense of self being remade under neoliberal structures the sensation of where work and non-work stop and start is not clear-cut. This collapse is central to our understanding of the specialness of border zones. Under global circuits of value, the elevation of immaterial labour breaks down the separation of work and other aspects of life. "Living labour oriented to producing immaterial goods, such as cognitive or intellectual labour, always exceeds the bounds set on it and poses forms of desire that are not consumed and forms of life that accumulate" (Hardt and Negri, 2009: 25). Just as the spread of supply chain capitalism has generated forms of production where the worker/producer self-exploits in the interests of postulated profit, so too in the spread of the service industry and its affect-laden provisions, the division between work and non-work life becomes muddied. Changing understandings of time are crucial in this transition. Whereas previously 'capitalist time' could be concretely linked to material production and the measure of time needed to make a profit, the link between labour time and exchange-value is not so clear within service economies that foster an overlap "of

Figure 3.7 Opulence untrammelled in the gambling halls

production and exploitation, of work and life" (ibid: 242). The point to emphasize is that affective labour is less easily bounded within Fordist forms of time and space management than manual labour simply because it is hard to define where work and other aspects of life, emotional service and emotional satisfaction, start and stop. Subjective responses prompted by duties and pleasures in these surrounds are not readily contained for those either working or gambling. This becomes obvious in the conflicting feelings staff have about being part of these pleasure complexes, and in the new pursuits many take up while so employed.

As one Lao croupier bluntly put it, "here, time is everything" – a fact of life that also structures how intimacy inevitably makes itself felt. Staff might move out of their work shift to other spaces, but they still operate with rules and conventions established within the gambling hall. The values and affects that they are hired to produce – customer mood and satisfaction at taking a chance – subtly inflect self-making processes provoked within these spaces. Affective pursuits (sexual relations, gambling and drugs) are strongly intrusive in these zones for both gamblers and, in a more gradual but no less potent sense, for the staff. A sense of self gradually changes. Putting to one side the compulsive need for intimacy that gamblers feel as a counterpoint to their intense concentration on making money, working in the casinos creates radically new forms of relating to the world for Lao staff as well. Money-making might be productive in a material sense based on relatively high salaries, but so too desires and anxieties born in these out-of-place spaces spread into the reproductive, the intimate, the need for sentient creatures to have sensual contact.

Hence, fleeting sexual relations become common under the new regime of piecemeal life. Male staff spend pockets of free time playing cards in their room, drinking or visiting nearby villages looking for female company. Some female staff begin relations with regular customers cum 'sugar daddies'. More commonly, given the tight and foreign environment, young Lao, Chinese and Myanmar staff pair up as transient couples. At GBC a small disco, pool room and gambling hall for staff were heavily patronized. Short-time hotels and guest houses hosted the growing number of young couples from the casino staff who wanted down-time liaisons. Dorm rooms, not strictly policed, offer ready alternatives. With constant shift rotations there is no way of knowing where an individual is at a given time, and couples often find time to be together. Meanwhile, the local Chinese clinics offer related services. According to the Chinese nurse, prior to the GBC closing, she was performing an average of 20 abortions a month. At Dok Ngiew Kham, one evening stroll indicated less clinically based interventions – I could see used wrappers of the morning-after pill lying on the concourse.

There is another dimension to affective economies (beyond the desire for satisfactions) that infiltrate life in this zone. Anxiety is widespread. Highlighting the radical newness in time, space and pursuits, Lao staff in the casino, as well as the residents in the villages around it, talk constantly about the uncertainty of life that accompanies the new icon of modernity. Peung, a 20-year-old Lao from a nearby village, speaks to the 'bareness' of life as a casino employee, not in Agamben's sense of governance and sovereign rights, but in terms of conflicting impulses – life in the casino is uncomfortable and shallow.

> This is all our life is. Work and sleep, we can't go anywhere. Actually, life outside the casino is better. Being at home is better. There is too much pressure here. We can't be ourselves even in our room, there is no private time in the dorm or in workplace. With three shifts, there is always somebody going to work while somebody is going to bed. I can't sleep. Too much noise. And sometimes it is too hot to sleep during the day. We have an electricity quota in our room so if we overuse we have to pay. Work schedules are changed every ten days. Hard to fall asleep during the day. Working here makes you look old quickly. In one room there are eight people, often strangers. Chinese stay with Chinese and Lao stay together. But working here, where I make 7,000–8,000 baht a month, is better than working in the rice fields. Actually, I would have nothing to do if I stayed at home now. I'm not rich like other people. So this is good enough for me. If I could save money, I would like to be shop-owner in my village.
>
> People in dorms always play cards, some of my friends take their boyfriends to our room. Each bed has a curtain, so there is some privacy. In the past the dorm supervisor would come and check for this. But not these days.

Some men have a lot of girlfriends. Sometimes couples arrive together, but the man soon gets a second girlfriend, a '*kik*' or '*E-nu*'. During work breaks it is easy to meet and chat. It takes just a short time to start going out together and people soon cheat on their partners without caring. But couples soon split up, too. Not so easy for Lao to have a Chinese or Thai partner, but it does happen. I had a Chinese man interested in me, but I didn't like him. Now he has another girlfriend. I worry that if I hang out with someone, how do I know if he is single or not? I don't want to be abused by his girlfriend. Actually, I have many guys who are interested in me but I don't like anybody yet. I'm scared because things are so uncertain here, if I decide to be with someone you never know when he will quit to go back home and maybe never come back. What can I do if that happened? It is different from having a relationship with a boy in our village that everybody knows and we just hang out together for three to four months before getting serious.

I've been to Thailand before. But now I can't go anywhere. If I don't go to work they will cut my money 700 baht for each day. They pay staff a salary for working full-time, every day. Extra money is 100 yuan a month (nearly 500 baht) for no days off. And every day I get a tip of 10 yuan. But the casino is always cheating too. Sometime they gave us a salary that is not correct. And they always calculate from the lowest exchange rate. Once an outsider asked me why this casino only employs young people compared with other places. It's true that mostly teenagers work here, although the rules say they have to be over 18. Those who are not 18 feel nervous. But actually, the casino does nothing about this. They welcome them to work here.

Jao is from Tachilek, just across the border in Myanmar. He runs a small restaurant. Unlike Peung, he is a classic example of flexible labour in the region as he moves from place to place but he too is uncertain how long he will stay. Jao has ID cards from China and Myanmar and worker registration cards for Thailand and Laos, allowing him a security that not many of his co-staff have.

I don't know how long I will work here. For now it is still good. But if it doesn't work out, one day I will go back to Tachilek. I don't want to go back to Thailand where I worked as a chef for 6,000 baht a month. Here I can earn 10,000 baht a month. To stay here I have to pay 800 baht a year for a Lao ID card. The owner organized it for me. I can go everywhere with it. Even if you don't have an ID card you still can stay here. There are all types of people here, many are illegal. Actually it is dangerous, if you have a lot of money – you can be killed for money. The police have no idea. In situations like this, Chinese and Lao security are supposed to take charge but I haven't seen them cope with the problem.

Some years ago, Lefebvre noted that an expanding leisure industry embeds class-based modes of production in its conquest of new spaces as people are increasingly persuaded to seek respite from everyday lives:

Thus leisure enters into the division of social labour – not simply because leisure permits labour power to recuperate but because there is a leisure industry, a large scale commercialization of specialized spaces … In this way, the country takes on a new profile, a new face and new landscapes.

(Lefebvre, 1976: 84)

The casinos are parachuting new forms of social hierarchy directly into what was previously dominated by peasant production systems, as they too carve out new profiles and new landscapes offering an irresistible invite to villagers to participate as peons in the blossoming service industry. If to be modern is to live in a world that is different from yesterday and that requires new skills and competencies (Benko, 1997: 5–6), then these SEZs are enforcing a particularly abrupt transition in their hyper-efficient injection of modernity. For many staff being outside or somewhere else may be better in sense of a more familiar lifestyle, but even within the enclave-like workings of the casino the outside is coming in. This combination makes these casinos such a potent blend of heterotopia and frontier. One cannot resist the enticement to explore even as the marked differences, as Lefebvre has reminded us, make it almost inevitable that one will end up as the exploited party. Inside the casino, visiting Lao villagers are unfamiliar with these parlour games but follow what they observe others doing. If someone is winning they copy him or her. Likewise, changing tables is seen as a way to conjure good fortune. Everyone watches for the winning table. We observed one woman avidly followed her son's (maybe 11 years old) directives – she won even though it appeared he was just guessing. One middle-aged Lao woman reiterated how casinos have infiltrated local rhythms:

Nowadays, going to the casino is a way of life, just like the temple. Things have changed here, gambling is an everyday thing, no longer something to be kept secret from the family. Tomorrow I won't come to the casino. I'm going to the temple.

Likewise, owners of the Lao bars and drink-shops that surround the complex also see the chance to enter the new space as an everyday practice as they use money they earn from sex to gamble. In an insidious recycling of the casino dollar, both bar owners and the women who work in the bars repatriate the profits made from patrons back into the casino economy. Some women in the bars suggested they entertained more clients precisely so they could have more to gamble with.

Anxiety: it is gone but what is lost?

Huean is a Khmu woman living in a village that was resettled here during the upheaval of the Indochina war. As the casino began to be built she sold most of her land to urban speculators (at 20,000 baht per *rai* or 0.4 acre) fearing she would be pressured to sell to the casino for a cheaper price. Like Peung, she defers to the labour regime at the casino as something tangible in its imposed structures and rhythms.

I have five children, one is married, leaving two daughters and two sons living with me. One son and one daughter do nothing, just work in field with me. My youngest boy is still at school and my youngest girl, Nok, works in the casino. She is just 14. But she looks like an adult. She is the youngest one employed in the casino. They know her age but they still chose her. Only those who are good at maths are wanted at the casino. Low formal education doesn't matter. You need to prepare for your ID documents and your picture. Then you can work for them. Another daughter is 22. She still works with me. Actually, she does nothing. She does her mother's job. At first, she planned to apply for work at casino as well but now they have enough staff.

For me my life is getting better since my daughter works in the casino. She can earn 7,000 baht a month. Women are better suited for work there than men. They have more discipline. Male staff take drugs and they drink, which the casino doesn't like. In the casino you have to be on time, not late. If we have a festival, those who work in casino can't join. They just work, that's all. My daughter left school at the start of secondary year. Going to school doesn't make money. Going to work does. In the casino there are many people who left school, so they could work. My other daughter Ning works with me in the fields – we share the work together. She gives me all the money, although working in the cornfields doesn't get much – only 20,000–30,000 baht per year. But never mind, she is with me.

Hardt and Negri (2009: ix) have intoned in heady brush strokes that through globalization "capital not only brings together all of the earth under its command, but also creates, invests and exploits social life in its entirety, ordering life according to the hierarchies of economic value". The transformation of time and its regulation within this particular social space in northwest Laos is a pronounced marker of this pervasive reach and stratification of social existence (just like the recalibration of relations in the Akha rubber fields or Khmu villages). Life in and around Dok Ngiew Kham is ordered through the appeal to modernity and the market value of leisure. Except here, the leisure experiences for the gamblers are compulsive and almost entirely driven by affect-intensive stimulation: the enticement of endless amounts of money (the casino), endless choice of men and women (from all countries surrounding the space), endless energy (amphetamines), endless eroticism (sex-drugs). This excess is contagious and staff begin to internalize the free-floating sentiments and emulate these behaviours.

But, as mentioned, these pioneer transformations provoke an insistent anxiety. This is evident in the descriptions of fear, boredom and tension alongside aspirations of prosperity and better life. Local people begin to problematize 'free time' as wasteful and recast working in the fields as 'doing nothing'. People are worried about losing their land to egregious land-grabs and the insecurity this implies. Young women are unsure how trustworthy men they meet are. This combination of rapid change and incipient concerns should not be surprising. Nor should there be difficulty in recognizing that for young men and women new to this world, fledgling desires will overflow the parameters of work and material gain. What we also need to recognize is that the intrusions made by this casino space take place alongside resonances from life before its arrival. "Nothing disappears completely," Lefebvre tells us. "Nor can what subsists be defined solely in terms of traces, memories or relics. In space, what came earlier continues to underpin what follows. The preconditions of social space have their own particular way of enduring and remaining actual within that space" (quoted in Gregory, 1997: 227). Nothing comes from nothing and everyday life, as modernized as it is becoming, carries strong sentiments of what went before. This double loop ensures an often uncomfortable ambivalence for locals supposedly benefitting from the casino's presence.

For example, for those who were resettled by the casino's presence resonances from the past ring loud and jarringly clear. A 100-year-old Tai Lue village was moved from its home on the riverbank because it was undesirably located within casino territory. There are ongoing battles over adequate compensation. In place of large old low-slung wood houses, a new village has been constructed out of modern cookie-cutter concrete houses at the back edge of the casino well away from their pristine riverside location. It is in fact intended to be one of the model ethnic demonstration villages, and in the casino itself a huge electronic billboard shows a repeating loop of Lao officials and Zhao Wei making great currency out of its official opening. One woman we spoke with seeks her own access to capital with a small *somtam* (papaya salad) shop she opened in the casino grounds since her land was lost to the casino. For her the past is all too present and present-day suffering palpably real.

> We can't bring our old temple to the new village. Instead the Chinese will build a new temple for us. But actually, our old temple has many holy relics. They will be lost. I still grow rice, as before, but now our new house doesn't have any storage facilities for keeping it. It is much harder than in the past because too much water is being used by the ice factory built for the casino. The area was called 'watershed forest'. In the past two to three years, there has been a constant water shortage. Even raising fish is too hard. The small lake near the new village belongs to the government. At first, our leaders told us they would move our village and give us that pool for feeding fish and for rice field. But now Chinese control it. They cancelled the agreement. They just lied! The government said they won't let us become poor. They can say it so easily. But now we are already poor. If you don't believe you can come and look in our village. Now we have nothing to do. In the past we have land to do agriculture. In one year we can grow the corn twice and make a profit of roughly 100,000 baht. But now life is much worse. I received a little compensation for the land they took. But now we have nothing left.
>
> My son works as a card dealer so he gives me money. People working in the casino often quit. They complain it is exhausting with too many rules. If they don't have customers, they can't leave their posts. They have to put their hand on the table to show they are not doing anything. My son complains it is too tiring, constantly changing shifts between day and night. I've told him to be patient. We need money from him. In the casino, going to work

late, even five minutes, is a problem. My son used to sleep in the dorm. But now he moved out. He couldn't sleep. Some others play cards or drink very often. And also there are problems with women. My daughter had a Chinese man who wanted to marry her. But we don't think he wanted to have serious relationship because if Chinese people encounter problems they can run away from here anytime. Children who have lost their Chinese father are increasing. Chinese can be very rich. But if they are broke they can sell even their wife.

Now murders are increasing around here. Usually Chinese. It is awful. At night, dogs are always barking. I'm so scared, I can't go outside. It means strangers are coming into the village. They are looking for people who owe them money. In the past our village wasn't awful like this. It was fun. We were close with nature. But now when evening comes people prefer to stay in their home. And it is so silent. I don't hear gunshots. But I have found people who are dead. This situation is happening both in and outside the casino. It is because of debt and gambling addictions. Yes, I'm scared; I'm scared of being robbed. Lao police always come too late. Here there are a lot of car accidents as well. Casino takes no responsibility. I teach my child every day we have to be careful. Even though we follow traffic laws but when the cars come by we stop our motorbikes and let them go first. If not we might die for free. Licence plates here are special, Golden Triangle, special economic zone models that have no number. Somebody said with this plate you can go anywhere. But actually it doesn't help anything because we can't identify which car is responsible in an accident. So being here, everything is awful. We have to take care of ourselves. Nobody can protect us.

People in my village usually don't gamble in the casino but other villagers or people from the south do. Some people sell their land and house because of gambling. In the past I saw on TV that people can get killed from gambling. But now I see it for real. In the market I saw men just talking for a few minutes and then trying to kill each other with knives. My heart was shaking. It is the same as TV. There are a lot of amphetamines (*yaba*) here also. I can't talk about this. If you would like to know you have to ask drug-users to buy drugs for you. But one has to wonder why there is so much *yaba* and the policemen do nothing.

I have suggested elsewhere, along with Pal Nyíri, that these casinos offer an eerily similar silhouette to the shadow cast by the treaty ports run by the English on Chinese territory in colonial days where illicit economies of gambling and prostitution operated with impunity (Lyttleton and Nyíri, 2011). It is perhaps inaccurate to suggest casino leaseholds in Laos represent Chinese attempts to run their own version of extraterritoriality in an imperial sense, that is to say, insistently stamp their authority through insisting on legal jurisdiction. But, at the same time, the absolute dominance of all facets of life in these off-shore spaces by (ex-) Chinese overlords, coupled with an unstated but ever-present underbelly of illicit economies, is remarkably reminiscent of the ways the British went about controlling life in Shanghai and Macau. Perhaps, in this instance, there is a more appropriate comparison to be made with the extrajudicial claims of the British East India conglomerate in colonial days. Either way, the fact that local Lao find it hard to adjust to these jurisdictional ambiguities, lawlessness and worksite demands is an unsurprising and ever-present reality that redefines the parameters of life in these places.

It has been a commonplace post-modern descriptor to see time as one of the key means by which contemporary capitalism alters subjectivity. For instance, Connor suggests that a contemporary discourse of economics

> expresses itself in terms of an instrumentalization which not only requires the medium of time in which to operate, but actually makes time a commodity ... this is to say that the economic movement which produces pleasure not only takes place in time, but is also a rhythm which binds and unbinds, accumulates and expands, concentrates and diffuses time itself, in short which economises with and on time.
>
> (Connor, 1992: 93, 95)

Peung describes much more succinctly the combined impact of immersion in this form of modernity: "Working here, you get old quickly." She means, of course, that the rigours of no sleep and worry age one prematurely. But she also made clear that it was, in fact, a new sensation of time that ensured this accelerated senescence. The casino is a space where an intrusive logic of experience defines processes of modernization and fosters deeply seated anxieties. Resonances from the past conjure sentiments of the loss of secure and familiar community, which add to an uneasy accommodation of new terms of living. Into this unsettled condition, the casino provides singular examples of how its service industry operates through an economy of affect that makes life and work inseparable for the Lao staff, while it makes freedom from everyday life its selling point for the patrons. The combination creates a fractured and synthetic experience of life in these special zones.

It is the supposed freedoms that the casinos symbolize that make this experience of space most deeply felt: the ostentatious trappings, the 'miracle' of modernity in this remote 'no-man's-land', the smell of winning, all together prompt visitors and locals to the heady pleasures of aspiring to something new, to the good life. This is no accident. Zhao Wei has repeated this utopian vision:

> The casino offers people an alternative to working in the drug trade. We want to expand it so it's like Las Vegas in the US ... Some people here can care for vegetables, some people can drive cars. Everyone can have work that fits his age and abilities if they want it. We have to be responsible to Laos, we have to be responsible to history.
>
> (Hilgers, 2012)

One wonders which precise version of history he means. Even as anti-drug messages are posted throughout the complex, they are mere window dressing as locals attest that drugs are everywhere. Nyíri (2012: 555) confirms that the "prominence of gambling, drugs and sex is arguably not just a product of short-term profit seeking, but also a functional element of this discourse of freedom". Indeed! But with all freedoms come risks. Gamblers know this inherently and try to ignore it or calculate their way around it. So too, entrepreneurs do their best to hedge against undesirable outcomes even as they have little ultimate control. Beck has famously told us that reflexive modernity produces risk consciousness as we embody modernization's inherent contradictions: "The individual is removed from traditional commitments and support relationships, but exchanges them for constraints of existence in the labour market and as a consumer. An increasingly individualised private existence is dependent on conditions and situations beyond its reach" (1992: 132). This is the new and uncomfortable logic of modernity that is underplayed at every turn in this environment. Compulsive and affective practices spreading throughout the complex ensure the sensations of doubt and anxiety cannot be avoided. Something not quite right could be emerging here. As Beck adds: "In the individualised society, risks do not just increase quantitatively, qualitatively new types of personal risk arise, the risk of the chosen and changed personal identity. Things going wrong become a 'personal failure'" (ibid: 136). I cannot suggest the casinos or sites such as Dan Nork are the equivalent of industrial modernity, but the alienation and contradictions they evoke make the individual feel they are very much on their own, in ways often deemed characteristic of being modernized.

Conclusion

In Dan Nork, thousands of women in bars and massage venues work for no pay, that is to say, no salary short of the tips and direct payments for services they deliver night-tripping men. They are a flexible and precarious labour force in most elemental fashion. No customers and working women receive no money. This is not to say the owners run no risk: no customers and the staff soon leave for elsewhere. But 'easy money', as it is so readily and egregiously described, is a huge draw. Dan Nork and the casinos are magnets for women and men who see value in the experiences that these heterotopic place/spaces offer although, or even because, crossing the bounds to these new zones makes the itinerant feel divorced and estranged from his/her home terrain. New rules, new conventions, new frameworks of understanding take shape even as there are residual emotional connections with other spaces/other times. This in turn prompts the pursuit of new forms of connection that are the core to how these zones accumulate vice-driven value: sex, drugs and gambling. As mentioned, this is at times ruthlessly abusive: one bar I visited in Dan Nork had recently been deposited with two migrant women from Myanmar by their mothers who sold them and their virginity for a sum the girls were still paying off some months later. Bao told us she had a number of women aged between 14 and 20 come to her karaoke bar asking for prospective buyers of their virginity at a price of 100,000 baht or roughly US$3,000. What pressure these girls/women were under one can only surmise. NGO staff told us that murders happen regularly in Dan Nork and no one is apprehended as people move back and forth across the border with little surveillance and practical impunity. Meanwhile at the Lao frontier, gamblers literally become prisoners of their desires and are tortured if they cannot recompense the owners. Special places, these economic zones.

The casinos, as seen by locals, might be new and different in almost every dimension. But they are situated in their underdeveloped and capital-poor homeland; this is never forgotten. Hence, the constant sentiment of ambivalence within the narratives told to us. There is money everywhere; this drawcard and its seductive embrace are insinuated into all who enter. But at the same time, people are uncertain and scared. Threats circulate. Women who work in casinos can't trust romantic relations – they lack all the hallmarks of security provided by social life in the village where kinship is perceived to still guarantee a degree of permanence for intimacy. The owner of the *somtam* shop is sure that Chinese men will desert their Lao partners at any moment: clear evidence, as far as she is concerned, of this intransigence is the increasing number of children left to local single mothers. She anguishes over the increasing exposure to murders and accidents over which the government and casino take little action. Just the warnings: stay at home – don't go out at night (even as home does not feel like home anymore).

Women working in Dan Nork know that their everyday life is a gamble, if they find the right man they win, the wrong man and there are other repercussions as sales of STI drugs and the morning-after pill testify. HIV data from Dan Nork is not routinely collected nor aggregated by ethnic group, although local health authorities are convinced it is significant based on observable risk. As I will describe further, Dai women returning to China from Dan Nork are routinely tested and some are indeed HIV infected, although it is not clear whether transmission originates in Thailand or at home. Other forms of violence also leave their fingerprints as mafia and corruption in Dan Nork mean trafficking and murders are common. As Feingold (2010: 49) notes, most trafficking does not start out as such, "although some trafficking victims are kidnapped, for most in the Mekong region, trafficking is migration gone terribly wrong". In places like Dan Nork it certainly can go wrong.

Emotional outlines of fears and desires that proliferate throughout these zones become the templates by which development is understood and experienced in a much larger sense. The practices I have described as central to the processes of self-making conjure a modern identity but do so in ways that cannot help but reproduce uneasy immersion into the new. The subjective response thus mirrors the larger political response. So when Arnold (2012) suggests that SEZs in border areas exist through a combination of restrictions and enablings, and Nyíri (2012) describes the casinos as a mixture of orders and freedoms, these contrary pulses are internalized by people animating these places as anxious desires for the values on display. I suggested earlier that moral silhouettes that define social spaces leave their imprints on individual bodies and subjectivities. Border zones show this process in absolute clarity. This is not to suggest policies alone determine the experiences, but that the experiences and desires also create the spaces that take shape around them. Casinos would not exist without gamblers: Dan Nork would not exist without desires for exotic experimentation. Policies accommodate as much as create these experiences. They rest firmly on the logic that free-market entrepreneurialism – the right to experiment, the right to take a risk – makes the risks, the violence and the moral ambiguities all supposedly appropriate and acceptable.

At a more general level, if we are to take seriously that special spaces offer something different, then development policies need to be highly cognisant of the fact that flexibility touted as a recognized and advertised marker for economic innovation also creates refined modes of exploitation. For the ways in which hopes and dreams are channelled in these spaces is not a trivial matter. To simply see economic growth as being born on a sex commerce or gambling addiction is to miss the incongruities that affective dimensions of these zones generate for the many that move through them. This is in fact the core warp and weave of development in the border areas. Mitigation and health impacts will never be understood if these affect-drawn impacts are ignored. A subject I develop further in the next chapter through the rubric of precariats.

Note

1 www.backtohome.org/autopagev4/show_page.php?topic_id=2708&auto_id=4& TopicPk= (accessed 24 July 2013).

4 Intimate safeguards and affective politics of the precariat

Intimacy builds worlds; it creates space and usurps places meant for other kinds of relation. Its potential failure to stabilise closeness always haunts its persistent activity, making the very attachments deemed to buttress 'a life' seem in a state of constant if latent vulnerability.

(Berlant, 1998: 282)

People have many partners because the situation here is so fragile, there is no security. People find lovers where and when they can, so they can find some comfort.

(Ex-factory worker, Mae Sot, Thailand, 2009)

Figure 4.1 Cross-border passage between Myawaddy and Mae Sot

My arguments, thus far, reveal that borders ringing the GMS foster numerous crossings – licit and illicit, conventional and unorthodox – as they channel the dreams of millions of migrants and itinerant travellers. Selected border locales also anchor enterprises and conglomerates that profit from proximity to national boundaries and the application of different rules than elsewhere. As we have seen, casinos and sex zones are common outposts whose high-cash turnovers are embraced enthusiastically as spurs to rapid local development. So too, brokers and traders use cross-border networks to maximize personal gain as regional and politicized demands and displacements impinge on the value of migrant bodies. For their part, state actors and institutions seek to monitor and regulate myriad flows and thereby accrue benefits in their own fashion. Operating in a broader terrain than borders, frontiers generate different sorts of edges with broader social significance than more linear geo-political demarcations. They, too, define what belongs and what doesn't, determine who is 'other', and what is entailed in, and by, gaining entry. Modes of 'frontier capitalism' act as a bridge between disparate modernities that beckon newcomers to cross bounds and embrace what difference offers. Meanwhile, national strategies of governance and scrutiny abut awkwardly against such burgeoning aspirations. Moreover, the experience of frontier itself is being constantly reproduced and reframed by ongoing social and economic change. Hirsch suggests that forest/farmland areas, peri-urban zones and national boundaries in the GMS are each characterized by frontier-like temporal and spatial dynamics as permeable and shifting boundaries open up new opportunities for capital:

> Relative to capital-rich and increasingly natural resource-constrained Thailand, then, a new and seemingly boundless frontier has opened up through improved relations with neighbouring countries on the Southeast Asian mainland … Thai border towns have achieved a new vibrancy because of, rather than despite, their frontier location.
>
> (Hirsch, 2009: 129)

I described in the previous chapters how something akin to this vibrancy was central to modes of accumulation that capitalize on sexual networking in rubber zones, ethnic subservience along economic corridors and visceral and intoxicating satisfactions in brothel towns and casinos. I indicated also that, even as intimacy is fundamental to these relations, there is ongoing vulnerability built into its unstable formations. In this chapter, I wish to focus on another dimension central to accumulation in peripheral zones increasingly connected by development architecture. It should be clear from earlier examples that the attributes of exploration and exploitation persist in frontier zones bounding national polities of the GMS. In line with policies targeting investment, these spaces also rely on experimentation and exception as they drive the proliferating wants and needs generating capitalism's spread. This has immediate and concrete implications for migrants in these zones. Factory enclaves in border areas, just like more opaque special zones, thrive on opportunity's appeal even as they exploit its ready-made reservoir of cheap labour. Hundreds of thousands of migrants from throughout the GMS are drawn to production sites flanking Thai borders. These migrants are part of what is now increasingly described as a precarious labour force: precarious in the sense of being unstable, surplus and subject to the whims of market and/or policy with little in the way of social or economic capital providing physical or emotional security. It is the affective dimensions of bare life characterizing migrant populations that I wish to explore in this chapter, in particular in terms of health and other subjective dilemmas that face these millions, who en masse form a central pillar of visions of progress in the region.

In 2011, a survey of more than 160,000 British residents broadened discussion of social hierarchy in provocative ways. Transplanting the familiar three-layer class model, the study derived a new framework by which to rank social forma-tions along with British people's quality of life. At the bottom of a now seven-rung ladder lies a group termed the 'precariat'. This is the poorest group, marked by significant lack of economic, cultural or social capital: "This is clearly the most deprived of the classes that we have identified, on all measures, yet they form a relatively large social class ... a significant group characterised by high amounts of insecurity on all of our measures of capital" (Savage et al, 2013: 25). One of the measures used to determine levels of social capital was the number of contacts an individual has in different sectors. Those in the precariat were shown to have the most limited range: "Their social range is small with an average of seven contacts whose mean status is the lowest of any of the classes" (ibid), lead-ing to the widely publicized conclusion that this group is the least 'connected'. Certainly, lack of social capital has concrete ramifications. So too, the precariat is an apt descriptor for groups of people who end up suffering due to the uneven impacts of globalization. But it is inaccurate to suggest individuals classed in this way are somehow less connected in meaningful ways. "The poor, migrants, and 'precarious' workers (that is those without stable employment) are often con-ceived as excluded," Hardt and Negri (2009: xi) remind us, "but really, though subordinated, they are completely within the global rhythms of bio-political pro-duction ... Economic statistics can grasp the condition of poverty in negative terms but not the forms of life, languages, movements, or capacities for innov-ation they produce."

Following this line of thought, I wish to show that, while social and material suffering indeed characterizes life for precariat populations in the GMS, we can usefully broaden our perspective on the types of connections that exist in these environments. It is certainly not the case that lack of social capital equates to lack of relationships. We should be on the lookout not to further marginalize those lumped into this category by portraying them as somehow having less meaning-ful connections. Let's be clear: people in a precariat have multiple connections at numerous levels, ranging a wide gamut from supportive through to damaging and detrimental. Such connections are full of meaning, including those wherein people are shoehorned into risky relations not anticipated by the workplace or policy-related environment. This is development's constant bugbear – unfore-seen outcomes – and it is here, within the nitty-gritty of modernization's impacts, that we can observe intimate engagements once again become a clear-cut and instrumental means to secure forms of emotional and material wellbeing, even as relations begun in the name of 'safety' and attempts to buttress life add additional and unexpected dimensions to physical and subjective risk.

Producing precariat

The productive, albeit minimally rewarded, role of migrant labourers throughout the world makes the term 'precariat' a timely appellate. At a global level, it is easy to point to connections between short-term migration and neoliberal capital structures. On the one hand, receiving countries' demand for an ever more controllable and flexible workforce embeds the dehumanization of labour in short-term contracts justified by the logic that these migrants will return home as 'model' development agents. On the other hand, privatization and lack of subsidies in home countries conspicuously bring about the need for migration in the first place (Glick Schiller, 2009: 28). Despite the profile of these machinations, it remains much harder to disentangle equivocal conditions that the 'new transnational agents' embody as they become valued commodities in ever expanding modes of circulation. So too, there are many questions to be asked of how migrants operate as change agents, especially given the range of so-called modern values they internalize as they are exposed to trickle-down aspirations. Thus, more recent approaches to migration reject notions of "homogeneous cross-border social formations", citing in their place dynamic 'fields and spaces' that might allow us to identify "spatial dimensions of social life" and "inner logic of social action" (Faist, 2009: 44).

Bringing our attention closer to Asia, Hall (2012: 1202) cautions us to avoid romantic notions of 'traditional' rural peoples who resolutely wish to maintain subsistence-oriented and market-avoiding lifestyles, thereby ignoring "the enthusiasm with which they have embraced certain types of commodity relations". No doubt this historical enthusiasm Hall is describing for a market-based lifestyle is at least partially behind the increased presence of mobility in the GMS. It also stems from factors beyond their control. People move as they are shunted out of previous, largely agricultural, livelihoods. They move in response to economic deprivation or political oppression. What is less clear is how these contrary dimensions are negotiated, and, to whatever extent, reconciled, which is to say, there is more to uncover concerning the 'inner logic of social action' within the fields and spaces of precarious migrant lifestyles as they seek a better life. In this chapter we will focus on labour migrants in Thailand and turn to a factory zone at the Thai/ Myanmar border to look more closely at impulses that animate these spaces.

Clearly, at one level, the institutionalization of mobility has become a major element of political manoeuvring as ASEAN 2015 economic unification takes shape. This is in line with global development trends. For example, the 2009 *Human Development Report* advocated legalizing labour migration in order to contribute to both the wellbeing of migrants via reduced risk of trafficking as well as promoting economic distribution from wealthy to less wealthy areas (UNDP, 2009). Thailand, due to its export-driven economy and well-established industrial base, has been the centre of gravity for migration in the GMS for some years now. Over the past two decades it has initiated different regimes of registration and regulation aimed to formalize and manage the millions of workers that are widely acknowledged as crucial to the economy even as they are seen as an archly destabilizing intrusion. But registration systems miss just as many mobile bodies as those they manage to corral and total numbers remain rough approximations at best. Huguet et al (2012) estimate that there are around 3.5 million migrants living in Thailand, of whom perhaps the majority remain unregistered. A huge number are in low-skilled and labour-intensive worksites such as manufacturing, construction, agriculture, processing and domestic sectors, where they make up possibly 10 per cent of the Thai labour force (Arnold and Pickles, 2011: 1608). Many have been in Thailand for a significant period. For example, a survey of 3,387 migrant workers found they had stayed an average of 5.3 years, some of them considerably longer (Huguet et al, 2012: 6).

Guy Standing popularized the term 'precariat' when he labelled a "new dangerous class" or more specifically "denizens" as those having some but not all rights of citizens and who thereby endure unstable and uncertain residency, labour and social protection. Migrants fit this picture closely and constitute a high proportion of the global precariat class: "They are the cause of its growth and in danger of becoming its primary victims, demonised and made the scapegoats of problems not of their making. Yet, with few exceptions, all they are doing is trying to improve their lives" (Standing, 2011: 90). The GMS has huge numbers of migrant denizens, millions to be precise, with limited social or economic rights or claims to assistance and services. They are a cheap, flexible and readily dispensable labour force. They are also the families of mobile workers, who are themselves rendered vulnerable through their partner's or parent's precariousness. One study showed that among a sample of married female migrants from Myanmar over 75 per cent had given birth while in Thailand (Huguet et al, 2012: 6). Indeed, the lives of migrant children themselves is often one of desperate compromise. As one example of the hostility their presence can generate, a Thai police officer reportedly suggested:

> Having migrant children studying in the town centre is also not appropriate, due to potential security problems. For safety, the migrant population should be in a restricted zone under state control. Also, if they want to study, their older peers should do the teaching, not our people. I cannot see how educating these children can benefit our country in any way. We have to think about the burden society must shoulder if these children decide to stay on.
>
> (Quoted in Kusakabe and Pearson, 2010: 32)

Standing (2011: 113) reminds us that none of this is accidental as the system of global capital is premised on a growing sub-class who are demonized as 'dirty, dangerous and damned' even as they are crucial to the requirements of a flexible and docile labour force. Tellingly, people living precarious lives find trust in short supply. With little stability on which to build a more secure sense of self and one's place in the world, what trust does exist becomes "contingent and fragile" (ibid: 22). We saw this fragility among the staff in the casino who in the new work conditions were not trusted by the employers (croupiers must keep hands on the table at all times) even as workers themselves felt they could not trust those around them (potential intimate partners promising fidelity, authorities promising wealth and security). We see similar lack of trust hugely exacerbated in the industrial fields in Thai border spaces.

Cross-border bodies and disease

Given prominent precariousness, health is one dimension that is often raised when considering migrant experience and its management. It is a central facet in the perception that migrants are valuable but feared; a crucial import but exhaustive drag on social and economic wellbeing. Policymakers in the GMS are contending with the vexed issue of how to provide adequate health services for regional migrants under ASEAN integration policies but, at the same time, preserve the sovereign sense that intruders are less deserving than citizens. Despite their long-term presence, migrants are never quite the same as locals. The harrowing narratives of beleaguered mobile groups attest that limited and prejudicial access to services is one overt litmus test of this difference. Examples are easy to find. In this chapter they come from Mae Sot, Thailand, a border zone that is famous for its industries built on the sweat of Myanmar migrants. A report on work conditions here offers the following vignette:

> Nu is 22 years old. She comes from Pa-an, the capital city of Kayin State [Myanmar]. At the age of 14, she began work in a garment factory. She returned to Burma but then came back to the factory at the age of 16 in 2000 to work at an export garment factory. At that factory, Nu typically worked from 8 am to 10 pm making two dozen sweaters in order to earn 70 Baht per day. "My employer will deduct Baht 300 monthly for permission to work, but we have to run and hide every time the police or even a visitor is here." Nu had to play hide and seek with the police and her work was extremely insecure. "The supervisor told me – The police are here. You've got to run." But I didn't listen. 'Let them come, I'm not going away. Those on the ground floor would stay, so will I.' So 16 people, including me, were arrested. Before we were arrested some of us had hidden underneath the clothes piles, but were pricked with sharp iron sticks by the police." Nu ended up having to sleep in jail for 15 nights. She and the other migrant workers arrested at the factory that day contracted food poisoning from the prison rations. Nu's father and brother raised 700 Baht to pay for non-prison food and to pay for her transportation when the police deported her. Nu explained that being forced to pay the police bribes is a part of all Burmese migrant workers' lives. "When we meet the police in Mae Sot, we have to prepare at least 200 to 300 Baht in bribes to keep out of trouble." This is a huge amount of money for workers who sometimes earn less than 60 Baht per month after their employers make various deductions from their wage of 1,500 Baht per month. Thai authorities and Thai people often look the other way when such abuses of Burmese

migrant workers occur. "I want Thai people to look at us as equal human beings. We want to get the same respect and the same rights. When a Thai person is killed, the Thais say that it is a Burmese who killed them. But when a Burmese is killed by a Thai, the Thais just say: 'This is our country, killing Burmese is alright.'"

(Yimprasert and Hveem, 2005: 32)

Such examples remind us how easy it is to think of transnational migrants under the sway of state controls that treat migrants as manipulable objects and seek to transform them into a well-behaved labour resource. Denizens such as Nu endure long-term and deliberate sacrifice of citizenship and social familiarity in order to access economic opportunities. Typically, this means acquiescing to reduced civil rights and sometimes severely punitive work environments where abuse is prevalent and dangerous working conditions are too often the norm. Numerous migrants in Thailand are forced into low-skilled sectors referred to in this part of the world as the '3D sectors': dangerous, difficult and dirty. The fishing industry, for example, employs large numbers in gruelling and sometimes perilous conditions, provoking a situation where coerced labour is needed to maintain an adequate labour force on deep-sea boats. Anti-people-trafficking programmes in the South of Thailand find their primary target group is young men forced to work at sea for many months without hope of escape.

Even the ADB, not known for its advocacy of workers' rights, notes that migrants employed in the above sectors typically "work in substandard conditions because enforcement of labour standards is generally weak even for protection of local labour" (ADB, 2009: 24). This, in turn, has over the years led to a pervasive disincentive for migrants to formalize work registration, given that even for documented workers recourse to assistance or employment rights is limited. While there is a general lack of coordinated information concerning health status of migrants in the GMS, there is plenty of anecdotal evidence of dilemmas. Abuse of workers' rights in special economic zones is commonplace as "former agricultural workers, unable to find jobs in the newly oversaturated industrial labour markets, toil on the fringes of the subregion's capitalist transformation, struggling to maintain precarious employment in growing informal economies" (MMN, 2013: 175). Table 4.1 shows the scale of registered migrant labour in designated occupational sectors in Thailand.

Violations that migrants face include any combination of excessive work hours, low or non-payment of wages, confinement and forced labour, no legal status, employer and police harassment, sexual abuse and other workplace injustices, uncompensated workplace injuries and/or layoffs, child labour, trafficking and so forth. Reproductive health problems abound including infectious diseases and unwanted pregnancies. An estimated 6,000 babies are born to migrant workers every year in Thailand (Dunlop, 2011: 17). They receive no birth documents as their parents are considered to have left Myanmar illegally, and as stateless children they are ineligible to any benefits such as schooling and are at heightened risk of being coerced into hazardous employment (CPPCR, 2009: 51). As a

Table 4.1 Numbers of registered immigrant workers from Myanmar, Laos and Cambodia, as of December 2011

Permitted sectors for migrant labour	worksites	Total workers	Myanmar			Laos			Cambodia		
			Total	Male	Female	Total	Male	Female	Total	Male	Female
Total	261,804	1,248,064	905,573	504,171	401,402	106,970	53,164	53,806	235,521	145,384	90,137
Manual labour	197,405	1,163,002	844,390	492,080	352,310	90,518	50,216	40,302	228,094	143,400	84,694
1. Fishing	5,530	41,128	24,902	22,192	2,710	1,153	880	273	15,073	13,068	2,005
2. Fishery related	8,778	106,851	96,882	46,193	50,689	820	446	374	9,149	4,450	4,699
3. Agriculture	57,750	228,041	174,422	106,756	67,666	17,737	10,983	6,754	35,882	21,470	14,412
4. Construction	28,326	232,162	135,473	85,306	50,167	12,321	7,722	4,599	84,368	54,883	29,485
5. Agriculture related	7,942	81,882	68,054	42,514	25,540	3,493	2,131	1,362	10,335	6,067	4,268
6. Abattoirs animal processing	4,370	42,037	36,726	21,131	15,595	1,767	1,019	748	3,544	2,278	1,266
7. Recycling	3,490	18,331	11,981	7,737	4,244	1,395	903	492	4,955	3,016	1,939
8. Mining	344	2,724	2,245	1,559	686	190	145	45	289	200	89
9. Metals	3,741	24,437	17,772	12,122	5,650	2,978	1,934	1,044	3,687	2,465	1,222
10. Food and drink	18,084	61,598	38,759	19,949	18,810	13,499	4,915	8,584	9,340	4,740	4,600
11. Earth products	1,419	9,842	8,168	4,647	3,521	718	425	293	956	574	382
12. Construction materials	3,963	17,010	12,922	8,921	4,001	1,435	1,009	426	2,653	1,821	832
13. Cutting rock	411	3,272	2,732	1,731	1,001	174	114	60	366	278	88
14. Garments	7,760	74,681	63,973	21,995	41,978	6,285	2,682	3,603	4,423	2,078	2,345
15. Plastics	3,020	24,135	18,251	10,990	7,261	2,670	1,496	1,174	3,214	1,839	1,375
16. Paper	755	5,282	3,572	2,268	1,304	457	237	220	1,253	755	498
17. Electronics	1,000	6,893	5,080	3,195	1,885	461	312	149	1,352	839	513
18. Transport	1,850	10,765	7,664	5,262	2,402	513	323	190	2,588	1,706	882
19. Import/export/vending	16,786	55,595	37,439	22,854	14,585	8,067	4,363	3,704	10,089	6,011	4,078
20. Auto repair	2,649	8,769	5,902	4,241	1,661	1,646	1,164	482	1,221	856	365

Table 4.1 (cont.)

Permitted sectors for migrant labour	worksites	Total workers	Myanmar			Laos			Cambodia		
			Total	Male	Female	Total	Male	Female	Total	Male	Female
Total	261,804	1,248,064	905,573	504,171	401,402	106,970	53,164	53,806	235,521	145,384	90,137
21. Petrol stations	1,254	4,910	3,115	2,016	1,099	1,103	742	361	692	403	289
22. Educational institutions	458	2,103	1,714	864	850	141	68	73	248	144	104
23. Other services	17,725	100,554	66,642	37,637	29,005	11,495	6,203	5,292	22,417	13,459	8,958
24. Domestic work	64,399	85,062	61,183	12,091	49,092	16,452	2,948	13,504	7,427	1,984	5,443

Source: Department of Employment, Ministry of Labour (DOE, 2011: 40)

result child labour remains obstinately present in migrant worksites. It has been estimated that there are roughly 200,000 Myanmar children living in Thailand, and that 20 per cent of the migrant workforce is made up of children aged 15 to 17 years of age (ibid: 37). In Mae Sot, where many of these children reside, factory workers are told to say they are 18 on their registration forms when in fact many are under this age.

In some sites, local government services have been mobilized to target migrant health, but low awareness of health and social needs as well as lack of language and cultural familiarity only add to insecurity and social isolation. Even when covered by insurance as part of the registration process many migrants are unaware of the services this provides. Another study notes:

> Routine information systems for health centres and hospitals do not generate useful data on migrants and despite attempts to develop a practical migration health information system; there are still problems in operating it. Moreover, many migrants with illnesses and injuries never get to see Thai medical staff due to problems of access and thus the extent of these health concerns remain unknown. Finally, there is little understanding of the social determinants of the health of migrants which, if addressed, may possibly have the greatest effect on migrant health and well-being.
>
> (Baker et al, 2010: 9)

Registering movements

Indeed, this lack of profile is a central element of the condition of precariousness. Collectively, migrants form a recognized but wilfully ignored group that falls outside the radar of most government health programmes. This is acknowledged at a regional and policy planning level, but the difficulty persists in precisely how to assist national governments in targeting adequate resources for individuals that local lawmakers feel ultimately do not belong. For instance, the ADB, aiming to underscore the importance of regional initiatives on safe migration, acknowledges the combined dilemmas:

> The dynamism of the border mobility, and the related difficulty in estimating its magnitude and legal status, also raises issues concerning the vulnerability of both the daily and international migrants. The rapid expansion of the border towns results in the creation of slums with the related problems; irregular daily border crossing through smaller checkpoints implies the use of brokers and increases the risk of trafficking.
>
> (ADB, 2013)

But precisely what to do about the unrelenting problems is effectively left up to each sovereign state, which in turn seeks to develop (or not) internal policies. Largely, in Thailand at least, this has revolved around registration as a means to formalize the migrant presence and provide a form of social safeguarding in the provision of insurance schemes for health services.

During the 1990s, a number of Thai Cabinet resolutions allowed temporary employment of migrants in certain unskilled sectors of the Thai economy. A formal registration system seeking to regularize migrant labour was begun in 1996 delivering work permits and a temporary 13-digit ID card (Tor Ror 38/1). This ID restricts migrant labour to a two-year period in specific worksites, allowing little if any movement between jobs or locales. The migrant is required to pay 3,800 baht to register (usually paid up-front by the employer and then deducted from wages over time) covering the work permit (1,800 baht); health insurance (1,300 baht); health examination (600 baht); and an administration cost (100 baht). Employers, in charge of whom and how many they support for registration, have the means to control the labour force in restrictive and sometimes punitive ways. Subsequent rounds of registration up until 2010 were driven by fears over the sheer number of migrants versus ongoing requirements for labourers and vacillated between allowing new registrations and insisting only prior registered workers could extend their stays. By December 2011, a total of 1,248,064 migrants were registered for temporary ID cards (see Table 4.1); of these 905,573 were from Myanmar, 235,521 from Cambodia and 106,970 from Lao PDR. But, as noted before, in all likelihood even greater numbers remain unregistered. Moreover, while numbers are far fewer, nationals from China and Vietnam are not eligible for registration; thus, in Dan Nork, for example, when asked about work status Chinese Dai women quickly say they are from Myanmar so they can be regarded as legitimate 'alien labour'.

The protocols for registration have evolved as ASEAN economic integration draws closer. Since 2009 labour migrants in Thailand have been required to undergo a 'national verification' process following bilateral agreements between Thailand and Myanmar, Cambodia and Lao PDR. Designed to replace the ID card system, verification requires passports issued from the worker's home country allowing them to stay in Thailand on work visas rather than temporary permits. While facilitating offices have been set up at key border locations the process has, to date, been costly and complicated and many fall through the cracks. Once completed this system is said to have certain advantages. The migrant is no longer bound to one worksite, visas can be extended to four years allowing, in theory, time and location flexibility although, as the policy currently insists, the migrant must return to his/her home country once the visa expires. Migrants under this form of verification supposedly gain certain civil rights such as the ability to gain birth certificates for their children born in Thailand.

A further advantage of the verification process is access to more comprehensive health coverage provided under the national social security scheme (SSS), although this does not apply to workers in all sectors – those employed in fisheries, domestic labour and agriculture/livestock are excluded. Currently, many thousands on temporary work permits are covered by compulsory health insurance paid for at registration, which only provides limited services through the Thai universal coverage scheme. As of December 2012, 630,185 Myanmar migrants had completed the passport verification process (MMN, 2013: 135). The presence of two overlapping systems and constantly shifting deadlines has not helped clarity. Not everyone has been able to apply for passports, due to bureaucratic obstacles or concerns over security and identity. For the hundreds of thousands of migrants not registered in either scheme, little in the way of social safeguards exist. In short:

> [T]he sheer numbers involved, the complexity of the procedures, and the costs imposed on migrants have left large numbers unable to register. The result for the Thai economy has been severe shortages of unskilled labour, while undocumented migrants continue to live precariously in the country, unable to access basic human and labour rights.
>
> (ibid: 141)

Mae Sot: an archetypical frontier market

Mae Sot is a bustling border town in Tak Province in northern Thailand earmarked for some years as a special zone and a locale where issues of governance and regulation and expanding economic sensibilities come together in stark profile. It is on a key node of the East–West Economic Corridor connecting Vietnam's sea port on the Pacific with Mawlamyaine on Myanmar's Andaman coast. It is joined across the Moei River with Myawaddy, an important market town in its own right (elevated in 2011 as a special zone), by the Thai-Myanmar Friendship Bridge. The town and its surrounds have been host to years of outside investment in industries and agriculture relying on migrant labour. It has huge numbers of registered and unregistered migrant residents. It has a persistent underbelly of illicit trade in people, drugs, timber and precious stones. It is the target zone of numerous investments in human capital geared to profit-making and taking. They sit next to a large range of interventions with humanitarian objectives linked to political upheaval in Myanmar including programmes targeting nearby refugee camps, the large labour market in Mae Sot town or the detritus left by various smuggling economies. Its location at the edge of periodic civil war zones across the nearby border and its function as a major gateway into Myanmar has cultivated an ongoing frontier atmosphere with its characteristic combination of dire need and infectious desire, tireless mobility and resilient aspiration, steady assistance and hard-edged opportunism.

For decades Mae Sot has received a constant stream of beleaguered migrants forced across the adjoining border by political or economic necessity. It is also the newfound home to many who see their options as being better here than elsewhere. Any brief walk through this town makes immediately obvious the number of Myanmar residents that support its economy; thousands of young women and men flood out of hundreds of factories at closing time, strolling in search of food, marked as migrants by the *longyiis* (a Burmese wrap) they wear and the *tanaka* (a Burmese face cream) they apply. The market is staffed by migrants lugging goods, the shops tended by Myanmar workers, and the houses and gardens cleaned by Myanmar staff. All of whom have decided this town is the best place to pursue a claim to a better life. Mae Sot's official population was, according to provincial authorities in 2009, 72,657 Thai and 86,318 non-Thai registered migrants, making official what everyone knows by sight, the town is more Myanmar than Thai. Estimates from local factory owners, hospital workers and NGO staff put the number of migrants residing in Mae Sot as well over 200,000. Up-to-date figures are unreliable for labourers in the industrial sector but most sources suggest it is around 100,000 or more. A majority are employed in garment and textile factories, although this can vary depending on season and changes in the political and economic climate.

Mae Sot has also been the centre of operations for services to nearby refugee camps. About 140,000 refugees from Myanmar have lived in nine official camps dotting the Thai border for several decades seeking legal status as 'displaced peoples'. Several, including Mae La which, at time of writing, was home to nearly 40,000 refugees, are situated in districts adjoining Mae Sot (TBBC, 2009). While Mae Sot town is more likely to be made up of Burmese and Mon, nearby camps are largely home to Karen or Karenni ethnic groups, although this has changed over time. Their presence contributes to the zone's frontier dynamics in complex ways as the injection of outside assistance and scrutiny creates a dual economy within/without the camps and those in the town. The borders of the camps are in fact extremely porous and camp residents can seek local employment, usually in the agricultural settings around the camps. As Brees reports:

> Local people in the border regions have been hiring Burmese people for centuries, seasonally for agriculture or the whole year through in domestic work and the services industry, such as laundry and cleaning. They can even contact the camp committee about the number of camp refugee workers that they need for farming or infrastructure projects. This large demand for labour thus drives employers to sidestep the formal regulations.
>
> (Brees, 2008: 387)

These mobile populations form a quite different precariat as they find ways to be part of the diverse economies in the surrounding areas – agricultural workers, itinerant labour and sometimes sex workers.

Recent changes in Myanmar signal the imminent closure (anticipated for 2015) of the refugee camps and relocation of their residents back across the border. How the prosecution of these agreements will play itself out remains to be seen. Central to anticipated changes is a tighter union of officially endorsed economic and social interests joined rather than separated by the border. It seems unlikely, however, that the vibrancy and vicissitudes of this frontier zone will diminish. In 2003, led by the Thai government under Prime Minister Thaksin, the Ayeyawaddy-Chao Phraya-Mekong Economic Cooperation Strategy (ACMECS) created the structural framework whereby cross-border cooperation could take place between its five country-members of Myanmar, Thailand, Cambodia, Laos and Vietnam. It had key objectives to generate growth and to relocate agriculture and industry to border areas with comparative advantage based on tax breaks and the availability of cheap labour. While there is ongoing national and provincial political prevarication around the degree of special status it should receive, Mae Sot remains the predominant conduit of goods into Myanmar (accounting for 55 per cent of exports from Thailand to Myanmar[1]) and, as the beneficiary of huge numbers of migrant labour, a vibrant industrial sector continues to fuel its connection to global supply chain networks.

Based on its strategic location, cheap labour and tax breaks, Mae Sot's economy is centred on a large number of export factories, many of which have relocated from other parts of Thailand. According to provincial data,[2] the total number of factories in Tak Province in 2011 was 591 with 331 of these in Mae Sot. In 2009, these comprised 57 textile factories, 90 garment factories, 89 agro-industries, 41 food factories and others such as woods and handicraft. There are also small, informal and unregistered factories, meaning the industry sector in Mae Sot probably totals somewhere above 400 locales in all (Arnold and Pickles, 2011: 1610). The workforce in these factories ranges from a few dozen workers in small 'house factories' to upwards of 2,000 in several sites. Most of the factories are Thai-owned subcontractors to East Asian or Western supply chain companies (Kusakabe and Pearson, 2010: 16). Language and culture are, of course, an issue. "The Chinese management and supervisors cannot speak Thai or Burmese; Thai office staff do not speak Burmese; and the Burmese workers cannot speak any of the management languages. If they communicate at all, it is in poor English – allowing great potential for the management to manipulate the workers" (ibid: 38). The number of factories increases and decreases in sync with the economic climate and there is more recent talk that some will relocate to the Myanmar side as the political climate has improved and labour remains cheaper. In 2012, Aung San Suu Kyi made a noteworthy visit to labour sites and camps in Mae Sot during her first trip abroad in 24 years, telling migrant workers and refugees "they would become a valuable resource for their country once they return home" (*The Nation*, 31 May 2012). The most prominent of these resources is found in garment factories – where young women make up the bulk of the employees stitching clothing for global brands – and textile factories where men work alongside women manually operating the heavy cloth-making machines. It is a highly volatile work environment where connections gain the meanings that define a precariat class, running from the most macro level of national policy and provincial power politics, through to the micro level of owner interactions with workers and interpersonal relations between workers themselves.

Precariat in practice

Pay scales are generally lower than elsewhere in Thailand, and lower than the minimum wage mandated by Thai law. In Mae Sot migrant workers usually are paid around 2,500 baht per month for domestic work and between 1,500 and 4,000 baht per month as a shop assistant, while construction or market labourers earn around 100 baht a day. On average, employees in garment and textile factories receive anywhere between 1,500 baht and 4,000 baht a month depending on overtime and seasonal workloads. In some factories they are provided a ration of rice and free board, but they must purchase additional food (usually curry or other foods from stalls outside the factories) and their own bedding, etc. In other places even accommodation costs are deducted from wages. Jammed into the workplace shed, conditions are gruelling, hot and asphyxiating. Long hours and few breaks deliver a litany of physical stresses and ailments. Attached accommodation is equally inhospitable: 20 or 30 workers crammed into sleeping rooms with minimal toilet facilities. Some workers, seeking respite, rent rooms next to factory sites. The entire town and its surrounds are governed by overbearing scrutiny and surveillance where a worker's liberty to move beyond the factory confines hinges significantly on whether s/he is registered or not.

Quotas for documented workers are supposed to be based on a factory's production capacity, but actual numbers are left largely to the discretion of the factory owners or managers. Usually around 50 per cent are registered, leaving the owner a sizeable group who can be more readily jettisoned depending on the state of the market. Sometimes unregistered workers have to pay an additional fee (up to 200 baht per month) to their employers for supposed security (warnings that raids are about to happen, agreements to intervene should they be arrested) but this amount does little to defray the myriad threats they face. One textile factory owner told us bluntly that he didn't register his workers because he was concerned they would then agitate for the legal 'minimum wage'. So too in some instances, the workers opt to remain unregistered not wanting to forfeit the fee and allowing them more freedom to move between worksites. Making light of the oppressive environment, a textile worker told us "if we are not registered the owners have to speak more softly with us because they will be scared we will leave to work elsewhere". Warnings of raids are a regular occurrence and undocumented staff are told to flee and sleep in the fields/woods during the several days of surveillance. Despite such evasions, workers are constantly arrested and there is a regular stream of hundreds of unregistered migrants sent back across the river each day. A border police official told us in 2009 that roughly 200 are sent back across the border each day, more men than women as they are the ones that tend to be out in public more. He noted "they come back within a day or two with no further repercussions as no records are kept". Sometimes they are held for days in the local holding cells to see if relatives or employers will pay for their release (1,500–3,000 baht) and during this time abuses are commonplace. This border officer indicated candidly that corruption is normal, and that to get along one accepts paybacks (in his words, "to do good here is to do the wrong thing"). Those security personnel that don't play by frontier rules don't remain for long; we heard of examples of police reporting illicit timber shipments who were soon relocated. The implications, of course, fall most heavily on migrants. One Myanmar man who was detained for having no papers told of us how he witnessed a young woman in the same cell beaten when she refused to leave the room with the police – she told him afterwards, "they can hit me as much as they like, but I won't go as I know what will happen if I do".

Figure 4.2 Supply chain labour in Mae Sot garment sector

On the other hand, being registered has its own downsides. Registration is only valid for one worksite, and if they leave they will be blacklisted from employment elsewhere. If a worker is dismissed or chooses to quit, his or her documented status expires, leaving very little room for negotiation. Many factory owners retain ID cards and working papers, meaning workers are subject to police harassment anywhere outside the factory compound just as the undocumented employees are. Increased public scrutiny leveraged by NGOs is bringing more cases of workplace violations to court, in particular regarding compensation for summary dismissal, but factories find many ways to avoid legal repercussions. Hence, having an ID card or not impacts on all aspects of life in Mae Sot, including where and how far you travel in public, and of what happens when you do. Much of the abuse is physical, sexual and degrading. For example, Gaew, a Thai female motorcycle taxi driver, told us:

I will charge 50 baht per trip to those with cards, 150 baht to those without which means I will make sure we don't run into problems with the police. They make the choice how much to pay. Some sex workers choose 50 baht even without cards because they have their own ways of dealing with the authorities. It is a great job because there is so much opportunity to get extra money … If the taxi-driver is male he can grope the Burmese women as much as he likes.

Given the profile of this zone and the indignities facing migrants at every turn, well-rehearsed analyses focus on labour relations in Mae Sot, which, as Arnold and Pickles (2011: 1599) note, raise questions about "the ways in which 'surplus' is being produced, ordered, segmented and racialized in nearly every Asian labour receiving country". These authors argue that as workers' rights and workplace standards are more effectively monitored in urban settings in the GMS, borders are areas where pressure to lower wages and oppressive workplace conditions become a competitive tool for regional industry. Just as we saw the combination of order and freedoms characterizing the casinos and border brothel towns, so too, in peripheral industrial zones, "institutions of national cross-border governance and development infrastructure have emerged in ways that combine authoritarian and liberal economic features to manage the ways in which different production systems are able to compete in the global economy" (ibid: 1605). This quest to compete ensures what the earlier described report (Yimprasert and Hveem, 2005) calls a "race to the bottom" and is made possible by the constant supply of Myanmar migrants, facilitated by Thai investment privileges and sustained by the fact that insufficient migrant labour protections means companies can flaunt non-compliance with codes of conduct.

Mobile affect

At multiple levels then, we can suggest that workers' lives are structured by insecurity with a profound impact on both physical as well as emotional vulnerability. Migrants experience a combination of various sentiments, strategic opportunism, official regulation and hostile attention that collectively impact on their health and wellbeing. This is not to say there are no benefits in being here. Many thousand migrants choose Mae Sot rather than Myanmar or further infield in Thailand. Strong links are kept with family members at home or in the nearby refugee camps. Subjective responses to oppressive but selected conditions are a necessary part of an analysis that seeks to uncover the 'logic of social action'. But we need to trace our steps carefully to uncover specific affective practices that are part and parcel of accumulation in these zones. To shed light on these processes, Ahmed focuses our attention on antipathy towards migrants revealing, first and foremost, that "emotions *do things,* and they align individuals with communities – or bodily space with social space – through the very intensity of their attachments" (2004: 119, emphasis in original). Her argument centres on fear and hatred targeted on migrants and terrorists in the US and UK. These emotions circulate, both unifying (those who do the fearing) and distancing (those who are feared). Thus, Ahmed notes: "the impossibility of reducing hate to a particular body allows hate to circulate in an economic sense, working to differentiate some others from other others, a differentiation that is never 'over' as it waits for others who have not yet arrived" (ibid: 123). In this sense, feelings generated by the presence of migrants are, as Deleuze and Guattari (1987: 400) assert, highly strategic: "affect is the active discharge of emotion, the counterattack … Weapons are affects and affects are weapons."

One can easily discern this type of fear of 'otherness' in the GMS: in long-term antagonism towards certain ethnic groups as stateless highlanders who are perceived as drug traffickers and forest destroyers, and towards migrant populations who are perceived as political dissidents, burdens on the state, harbingers of disease spread and so forth. Thus, in pointed rhetoric concerning the ethnic or migrant 'other', the same words appear the world over as fears of being 'swamped by dirty, diseased, uneducated masses' ratchets up the emotional investment in preserving distance. Heart-rending demonstration of how such sentiments propagate violence are easy to find: Buddhist extremists burning the homes of Muslims in Myanmar, Thai authorities turning boats of starving Rohingya back to sea, migrants suffocating to death in the back of an airtight Thai truck, uncounted homeless beggars sent back to Cambodia lest they sully the tourist image in Bangkok. The media perpetrate images of insistent waves of unwanted migrants arriving at all borders. Locals fear, disdain and distrust – and migrants suffer – as economies of affect spread these sentiments with efficient cruelty. This process can be traced clearly within Mae Sot worksites as Arnold and Pickles (2011: 1613–4) describe: "The Burmese in Thailand are subject to deeply embedded historical perceptions of them as an evil and aggressive neighbour ... one consequence has been the easy justification of intolerable work conditions for migrants." Likewise the prevalence of these affective economies are felt at deeply embodied levels for migrants as violence takes place at ground level with harrowing consequences. One Thai woman who rented a house to migrant workers on the periphery of Mae Sot recalled incidents of local violence: "They robbed the migrant workers. Some tied the hands of a brother and raped his sister and forced him to see." So too structures of oppression reproduce themselves within families as stories of domestic violence and community tensions are commonplace (CPPCR, 2009).

Clearly, circulation of fear underpins instances of structural violence impacting minority groups and mobile peoples throughout the GMS. But there is a further element to this argument that brings us back to development processes more generally. Mechanisms of marginalization persist because they operate through rubrics of uncertainty, in the sense that they are never fixed, and because the circulation of these signs is ongoing, the 'other' becomes perpetually threatening. This is the insidious productivity of networks of hate:

> fear works as an affective economy, despite how it seems directed toward an object. Fear does not reside in a particular object or sign, and it is this lack of residence that allows fear to slide across signs, and between bodies. The sliding becomes stuck only temporarily ... whereby a sign sticks to a body by constituting it as an object of fear.
>
> (Ahmed, 2004: 127)

Furthermore, it is the instability of affect that delivers its emotional clout. Given it is never contained within a specific body, dread lurches forever into the future directed towards the mobile and illegal body who is always about to arrive. And as fear remains contagious it becomes a more generalized anxiety over that

Figure 4.3 A break from work

which might yet happen – our worry of the future, a threat ever-looming. The very promise of increased migration through economic integration levers up the persistent concern and distrust of the outsider overriding any purported benefits derived by resident populations. Thus, as much as the GMS rhetoric trades on the euphemistic notions of community and connection, it is more specifically the implications of competition that do their damage because the work of defending oneself is never over: "That is why the politics of fear as well as hate is narrated as a border anxiety: fear speaks the language of 'floods' and 'swamps'" (ibid: 132).

The sensation of ever-present threats of border transgression, and the work this does in provoking the imperative for securing boundaries, is relevant at numerous levels in the GMS still coming to terms with its new architecture. Anxiety underpins attempts to regulate movements of trade goods in areas famous for flows of illicit substances (the Golden Triangle), it fuels panics over viral vectors of animal diseases (Asia as the purported petri dish of new infectious diseases), it generates paranoia over the millions of undocumented labour migrants regularly crisscrossing the region. Hence, Arnold and Pickles (2011) are able to suggest that the border zones are politically constituted and strategically located as sanitizing locales to act as a buffer absorbing these 'floods'.

At the same time, it is important to follow the argument that emotions circulate a step further. Affective economies do more than inflict damage or promote 'protective' distancing, that is to say, Deleuze and Guattari's counterattack. At times, they also operate in more solicitous ways for migrant communities under sway of these discourses. Looked at closely, we see that circuits of emotion animate social spaces inhabited by migrants as much as those around them, and prompt subjective responses that radiate in diverse directions. Thus, even as fear proliferates, there emerges an insistent need for counterbalancing emotional connections. Kusakabe and Pearson (2010: 14) maintain that insecurity intrudes deeply into intimate realms of female migrants as they are "involved simultaneously in reproductive as well as productive work … but who still retain the responsibility to resource, organize and often deliver care work for their own families, including their parents and siblings as well as their own children". This is true. But there is more to the intersection of the reproductive and productive than the struggle to discharge familial obligations. Social relationships and the ways young migrant men and women derive personal pleasures and emotional satisfactions, however fleeting, within the factory confines are a deeply embodied response to the dilemmas of everyday life in Mae Sot. Here affect is not a weapon, it is a salve; its practices are not based on distancing but on the embrace. One pressing characteristic of life for migrants in Mae Sot is the volatile, enticing and very transient nature of intimate relations that are an attempt to stave off insecurity but that, in turn, create their own forms of vulnerability.

Sex and the social life of migrants

I argued in the previous chapter that place matters. In Mae Sot, just like other border zones I described earlier, the town and worksites are particular sorts of social spaces that generate particular sorts of experiences. Firstly, there is the overwhelming physicality of proximity. Hundreds of thousands of young men and women live and work in close quarters. Come factory closing time, or the monthly day off, the lanes and food markets are thronged with young Myanmar men and women in clusters paying acute attention to whom is nearby or to when they might meet up with others in their circle. At every turn within the few square kilometres of Mae Sot they are reminded of the massive number of young people in similar circumstances, sharing similar depredations, who could be potential friends, partners or competitors for attention. At the same time, there is the fact that a majority are single, giving the prospect of a 'mate' acute meaning in otherwise uncertain conditions. The presence of gruelling life well away from family familiarity leads to a hyper-sensitized quest for emotional connection. Thus, one doesn't have to probe too deeply to feel the tenor of social interest in this town. Absolutely every person we asked about the nature of young people's lives in Mae Sot – migrants, factory workers, owners and supervisors, security guards, health staff, NGO personnel – all echoed one common theme. There is a vibrant and constantly shifting kaleidoscope of intimate relations in this town.

Sometimes, relationships in Mae Sot become overtly commodified in the quest for money. There is a high profile landscape of sleazy bars staffed by a constant turnover of women from across the border. Apart from language distinctions these are not fundamentally different from the brothels found in any low-end sector throughout Thailand (and nowhere near the scale, density or variety found in Dan Nork). Trafficking fuels a constant supply of these women. For most Mae Sot is not the final destination. The town is a marketplace, a conduit and a stop-over as women (and men) are sent to internal and less easily discovered zones within Thailand. There are ready-made and easily accessed networks of agents that service both migrants and would-be employers of trafficking victims. If one has no papers, a migrant can easily pay an agent for passage further into Thailand. Payment is said to range from 3,000 to 15,000 baht. Sometimes, payment in cash is not required. Maem, a young 18-year-old Mon woman, grew up in the nearby refugee camp, moved into Mae Sot town as a teenager, worked for several years in factories before deciding to freelance as a sex worker. She described to me how she had travelled throughout central and north Thailand as the companion of a local police officer: "I didn't need papers – I speak Thai and my friend took care of everything else." No questions asked.

There are numerous ways that sex is commercialized in Mae Sot. In addition to freelance migrant women (and men) who rent abodes and then canvas clients through mobile phone networks and local agents, there are also migrant women who maintain 'day jobs' and moonlight as sexual partners at night. At other times, the very act of being a domestic worker from across the border opens opportunities to sexual abuse from employers, compensated financially or not. At other times, some domestic workers connect with outside clients for casual sex through networks operating out of massage parlours. Or there is the generation of young women who, like Maem, have now grown up in Thailand; they speak Thai fluently and are equally conversant in fashion and mores. Without any form of permanent status, they typically work as shop-front assistants where they are prey to stereotypes that portray them as being in constant search for a Thai husband, but who, in practice, more often end up being a 'kept' wife (*mia gep*) or mistress of Thai traders or businessmen. Myanmar men also sell sex to Thai male clients, reproducing a further version of the eroticization and embodied value that allows exploitation of cross-border bodies.

At a more opaque level, commodified relations also take place from within the multitude of factory workers. A-bert, a young Burmese man who has lived in Mae Sot for many years, told us candidly:

> Some women in factories will sleep with male staff for money, 250–500 baht. You have to get to know them first. Others are more like sex workers who use phones to set up liaisons. About 10 per cent of girls in factories will sell sex to other guys in the factory or to outsiders if someone introduces them (it costs about 800–900 baht). It mostly happens if a guy in the factory is not yet having sex with his girlfriend and wants it badly, an alternative to a sex worker from outside. Most will go to Myawaddy to stay in a hotel as it is cheaper.

Female workers described an identical picture, as Aye Aye Moe notes: "In factories there is sex for money, some girls do it for gifts or for cash. In this instance, it doesn't matter if the guy is married or not. Married guys have other girlfriends, gifts or money is all it will take." Occasionally men sell sex for extra money. Maung Oo, a staff officer at a local clinic, told us that factory men will also offer services, leaving their contacts with beauty and salon shops to set up meetings with Thai or Myanmar males (or sometimes older Thai women). That some of the 100,000-plus male and female migrants in Mae Sot will seek financial return from sex should come as no surprise as it fits perfectly within the type of frontier sensibilities we have been examining in earlier chapters. However, it is the prevalence of relations that come together without direct monetary exchange that I wish to focus on. How to begin or support existing families is an ever-present issue that intrudes deeply into reproductive and economic strategies. Even more prominently, there are levels of intimate negotiations that fleetingly form and then destabilize the bonds of domestic security.

Mae Sot love lasts ten minutes

Romantic relationships are almost universally depicted as the most vibrant threads of everyday life for factory workers in Mae Sot. Myint Thu, born and raised in Mae Sot by Myanmar parents, tells us simply: "Work in the factories is so monotonous, there is no escape from routine. Changing partners is one of the few things that offers variety." This dimension was captured in a common catchphrase, spoken, in this case, with both pride and resignation, by a Myanmar health worker who had been in Mae Sot for many years – "Mae Sot love lasts ten minutes". Nearly everyone else we spoke with embellished this notion of fleeting and ephemeral intimacy.

> In Mae Sot, everything is easy [Thai: *ngai*], girls are *ngai* – they change partners often. No one knows here, go back to Burma no one will know the women are no longer '*saaw*' [virgins]. Here there is no family oversight,

some guys are married back in Burma but they get new girlfriends here, like-wise women ditch guys quickly if they think he is no good. (Lha, a married woman who left her husband behind in Myanmar, has worked in Mae Sot for more than ten years)

Here it is perfectly normal that people take lovers – it is their only pleasure in life. (Jammu, a boat driver)

So many comings and goings, so many intersections, so many girls and guys. There are maybe 300 factories, 700–800 men and women in one worksite – at the factories anything goes. So much choice! (A-bert, a young man of around 22, who has worked in Bangkok as well as Mae Sot)

Here the change is too rapid! The people come here from Burma for money but suddenly find so much freedom, everything from the past dissolves. It is a huge shock, and all cultural constraints are gone in this environment. No fam-ily. It is all too exciting. The workers here are even more daring than the Thai who modernized more slowly. They take whatever chance they can to have partners or sex. Those that are good looking can use this and have numerous lovers. Older, unmarried Burmese women take all comers, as they want to get married. Guys can be more choosey. In fact, there is pressure to take advan-tage of the freedom. Here there are no family controls. Only the legal codes, but this doesn't stop anyone. In addition to some women taking money for sex, there also lots of *kathoeys* [male transgenders] and *toms* [lesbians] in this environment – these relationships are also much easier here than in Burma. (Somchai, an ex-factory worker who now volunteers as an outreach worker for a health programme)

The picture is unambiguous: lack of constraints, peer pressure and desire for an appealing partner that might provide some fixity in Mae Sot's unstable terrain prompt ongoing serial relationships. The ways in which unions come together are in turn heavily controlled by the environment in which the young people work. Joshee, a middle-aged Myanmar man in charge of security at a factory with 800 males and females living on-site, tells how he tries to maintain control.

There are factory rules but they get broken. Guys drink and fight, women have hygiene problems – sanitary pads left lying around. In both cases we have to embarrass them to make them behave better. But there are always good and bad young women and men. It is because they are away from their parents and relatives and there are no controls that work here. In the past, one could only speak to a woman in the company of others but, nowadays, they just send everyone else away so they can be alone together. Culture has changed here tremendously, young women wear short skirts, trousers, let their hair out, sleeveless shirts, shoes in the temple. If anyone tries to say anything they say "you are not my parent, why should I listen to you?" They come here to make money; this is why all the old ways are disappearing. How can you control them? They want to emulate Thai styles, porn movies are also a big issue, they all have clips on their mobiles, women and men, and they all look at them. If they were still in Burma none of this would be like this.

Importantly, these depictions highlight that there is far more than just an affective economy of fear that infiltrates the experiences of migrant workers. Desires are shared between young men and women that might emerge, in part, from the environment of fear but are never subsumed by it. The desire for partners, the desire for a break from the monotony and the desire for something new collectively create an economy of aesthetics and an economy of desirable partners. Formation of these desires, and how to act on them, is reproduced throughout the factory compounds and Mae Sot more generally. Moreover, the ways in which these sentiments move within the migrant communities is central to the ways they accumulate value. There is tremendous pressure to take part in circuits of intimate exchange through courting connections with other young men and women. If one person has a partner, so too all their immediate colleagues are expected to do the same. At the same time, specific structural factors, that is to say, the implicit nature of the social space these workers inhabit, contribute in diverse ways to how these affective practices take on value.

Firstly, relationships occur under pressure in a very literal sense. As in the other border zones I described earlier, time is of the essence. Workers have one day off a month, which may or may not be in sync between different factories. The search for time together is an ever-challenging exercise. Workers will come together in the dorms or in the rented rooms, pretending one or the other is sick during the time when others are doing overtime. They will cross the river to short-time hotels in Myawaddy where they pay for the room by the hour. More often they will disappear into the nearby woods or fields. Staff and town residents describe either seeing couples themselves, or evidence of trysts, in spaces surrounding factories, as one resident drily noted: "Sex in the fields is very common in the dry season, one can see condoms and underwear left behind in the flattened fields where we grow peanuts and soy." Somchai describes further

> Some factories are very closed, they don't let the workers out except for one-two days a month. These ones tend to have less couples inside because everyone knows each other so well. Then on their day off they have to race to get together with their lover [Thai: *faen*] – organized through networks of friends and mobile phones – and there is a lot of pressure to have sex. Sometimes it only takes two or three days after knowing someone before they sleep together. In the more open factories, couples come together far more commonly within the worksite dorms or even factory sites. It is easier to meet others in and around the workplace.

As in the casinos, the management of time is a strongly determinative aspect of life in the factories. Life's very fragility means that spans of time become a commonplace measure used by workers to adjudicate exposure to life in Mae

Figure 4.4 Social connections take place in the streets

Sot and the readiness for intimacy. Explanations of constantly changing partners often begin with temporal descriptions. Hun, born in Mae Sot just after his parents arrived in 1990, offers his own version of the typical trajectory of youngsters from Myanmar:

Guys usually start to have sex around 14–15 years old, sometimes it takes a while, but by 20 all have had sex. On the other hand, only about 50 percent of 20-year-old women will have had sex. At first, it takes a long time for a girl to acquiesce to sleeping with her boyfriend, maybe one year, but if they split up then sleeping with the second and third boyfriend gets much quicker, only a month or even a few weeks. Splitting up is easy. Plenty of choices. In fact, women end relations quicker than guys. There are so many other guys around, so many choices. Guys with money do better than handsome ones. Everyone is thrust together; it's so very easy to flirt. In fact, it is getting easier and easier to flirt with girls, they are much more open, easier to sleep with them.

Lha, an older married woman, notes a similar picture:

After five or six months 70 per cent of women will have boyfriends but only 30 per cent of these relationships will last more than a few months. Likewise about 30 per cent of married couples here split up. No need to go to Myawaddy to be together, they can be together in the fields, or back in rooms when others are doing overtime.

In addition to time constraints, social and physical pressures take a strongly formative role in relationships. We mentioned abuse can occur at the hands of authorities when one is caught in public spaces or in factory raids. Violence, real or threatened, is an ever-present dimension to migrant life in Mae Sot, from overt violations to vicious prejudice and degradations. Within the factories, those in positions of power can pressure women to be their partners. Some women choose, or acquiesce to, a long-term relationship on the promise of more concrete workplace benefits. Others do it for protection. As Nut, a young seamstress, noted:

Some women curry favour with the Thai managers or their Burmese assistants for special attention, protection, security. But in the smaller factories these girls would be looked down on by other workers so it tends to happen with managers from other factories who provide assistance from a distance.

The need for a partner who might provide security is a pervasive sentiment in Mae Sot. Women working in factories learn very quickly that having a boyfriend is not only a source of affectionate pleasure, it is also a source of protection. Abuse does not only emerge from collisions with Thai predators, but can also ferment within the workforce itself. Dtim, a security guard at a textile factory employing close to 4,000 male and female staff workers, described how male workers take photos of women unclothed in the makeshift bathrooms and circulate them on their phones. Other forms of violence are more acute. A-bert added that: "When guys finish work and drink in or around factories then they often get rowdy and sometimes violent with women. Women need to say they have got someone who will protect them or to be able to say they have someone who watches out for them." Lha elaborated further:

Women need a boyfriend to protect them, more so when they are outside than within the factories. One time, we were walking down by the river and we could see a girl, 17, raped by a 20-year-old male friend; she didn't want to have sex but he forced her. No one dared to intervene, it was just us girls watching, what could we do?

In sum, pressure to have partners is insidious and derives from two directions; on the one hand, the need for security is a feeling shared widely and learned quickly by the vast majority of women who join the ranks of migrant workers. On the other hand, desire for a partner is escalated by peer pressure as a means to establish one's place in the social order of Mae Sot life by publicly displaying one's proficiency at intimacy. This is felt by both men and women as they are pressured to demonstrate prowess amid the pursuit of many partners, demonstrated by ability to attract (and discard) at will. Governing this climate of hyper-elevated emotional and physical bonding, Mae Sot relationships are rushed at many levels in both a physical (pressure to have sex) and temporal sense (lack of time and space). These connections are often also short-lived as lack of trust builds from the constant turnover of attention. A-bert described how he met a girl the day before:

I liked her so we exchanged numbers. She said she was single. Next day she asked me for some money – I pitched in with my friend and gave her 100 baht. The day after that I called her and a guy answered the phone, he said he was her boyfriend! I don't trust factory girls. They are too 'easy'.

With the intense concentration of bodies in factories and sleeping halls, de facto criteria are made paramount in the humming circuitry of social connections as young men and women pay close heed to one another. Discourses of masculinity and femininity are strongly conditioned in this environment and they partake of two key parameters: ability to make money and aesthetic appeal as men and women become party to a core set of understandings about what life and its affective pursuits in Mae Sot entail. Dtim, the textile factory security guard, elaborated on the volatility underlying intimacy in these spaces:

Women need to have a partner, doing this is the best way to get ahead. It helps them stay here. Some women will have two boyfriends in separate factories – perhaps one will have less money and one [Thai: *gik*] might have more. Women won't reject the first until she is sure the richer one will take her as his girlfriend. Some guys from Burma have a good education, they are not all poor, women like this sort very much. Some guys can make decent money at the textile factories, depends on how hard they work, how strong they are. If they don't make so much money they will be teased as being 'gay', not man enough and not rich enough, girls don't like this sort of male. Girls 14–15 don't know about guys yet, guys invite them, they don't know anything, they go with guys who can take advantage of them, seduce them, force them. One woman was accosted by a group of men and when one guy didn't want to join in, they all said he was 'gay'. This type of thing, rape, is not uncommon, there is very little women can do.

Women confirmed not only the ever-present substrate of violence fracturing intimacy's appeal, but also, more generally, the time-bound mechanisms of partner selection. Lha's friend Min, a 31-year-old seamstress, relays a similar trajectory of appeal:

> Up to roughly the age of 25, the girls choose based on looks – after that money becomes the most important, here everyone worries about financial security, girls get bored easily, looking for money, if the guys don't take care of them, they also go for good looks. Handsome guys can get girls wherever, whenever. Girls want guys to take care of them, buy gifts so it can be seen by others.

Marriages take place from some of these relationships, but given the precarious environment where life is characterized by perpetual uncertainty and movement, many couples split up as quickly as they come together. Factory workers cite a core set of reasons that underscore intimacy's implicit instability, as Aye Aye Moe notes:

> It happens when one of the couple changes worksites and it is harder for them to see each other and there is the appeal of so many new young people around, or otherwise disagreements, if girls get pregnant, guys just disappear. They look for money and 'beauty'; they also like people with secure jobs. Guys split up more easily because they move around so easily, so easy to find girls.

Lha brings it home to pressure of a different kind:

> One major reason for splitting up is refusal to have sex. If a guy wants sex and the woman refuses then he will threaten to leave. Guys expect sex and if it doesn't happen he will look elsewhere. It is emotional blackmail! But actually women can be easily persuaded to have sex for money and gifts and security. In fact, girls end the relationships more often because of guys' behaviour; guys misbehave so the girls end it.

The above descriptions evoke a seemingly progressive degree of freedom to be with whom one wishes, but partner-seeking and partner-redundancy cannot be divorced from the hyper-intensified sense of dehumanization that surrounds life in Mae Sot. It reminds me in a superficial way of *Emergency Sex* (Cain et al, 2006), a book that suggested NGO staff under serious emotional distress seek intimate contact as a coping mechanism. Obviously there are limits to this argument. But in Mae Sot it has a high degree of relevance. Some seek relations overtly for material or physical comfort but the key characteristic is that nearly all do it for security and one simple premise: relationships succour. It is not just freedom, but the need for some connection that is pleasant in face of all others being oppressive. Just as fear of the other circulates as an economy, so too desire circulates. A key dimension to self-making processes within the precariat is the constant sense of vulnerability that "intensifies a sense of alienation and instrumentality in what they have to do. Actions and attitudes, derived from precariousness, drift towards opportunism. There is no 'shadow of the future' hanging over their actions, to give them a sense that what they say, do or feel today will have a strong or binding effect on their longer term relationships" (Standing, 2011: 12). In turn, anger and anxiety accompany this alienation and insecurity (ibid: 19). As we have seen there are numerous demonstrations of these dimensions of life in Mae Sot. But, and this is the important point, negative emotions are not the only affective response born of these surrounds. Other forms of sentiment proliferate in precarious zones such as Mae Sot. As we have been describing above, finding pleasure in intimate unions is a ubiquitous and concrete response. Young migrant workers come together often, and in sometimes urgent ways. Life's hardships generate a counter-demand for closeness and demonstrative emotional and sexual openness and this should not be underplayed as a source of desire and joy. I started by suggesting it is incorrect to view the precariat as somehow having less meaningful relations. Let me add that there is nothing trivial or superficial about the often fleeting intimacy young Mae Sot couples use to buttress life, even as it is never divorced from the demeaning circumstances in which it emerges.

Significantly, the quest for security that generates this marketplace of partners also has profoundly embodied costs as sex becomes a passage to emotional attachment. Finding 'safety' in the guise of someone close and dear is an ever-present affective practice found throughout the factories, but, so too, vulnerability to health dilemmas emerges as an unwanted and unanticipated consequence. This derives from the commonplace practice of young men and women entering into serial sexual relations with alternating partners. Reasons for relations to be short-lived are many: relocation to different worksites; pressure to have a local partner who can provide material and/or emotional support; sheer range of choice as many thousands of workers are thrust together in close quarters. This rotation has repercussions. A further characteristic of life in the precariat is the inability to ultimately be in control of one's physical safety, not just in terms of coercion and violence either within the worksite or town, but also within one's own sexual connections.

Reproductive health and infectious threats

The factory environment generates a wide range of sexual unions, many of which take place without health precautions. As a result, there is an ongoing spread of infectious diseases and many young and single migrant women become pregnant. The reasons for inadequate protections are summarized by most informants as twofold: first, young women are too shy to seek contraception and boyfriends will think they sleep around if they do; second, the urgency with which unions take place sometimes means they are haphazard and unplanned and therefore men do

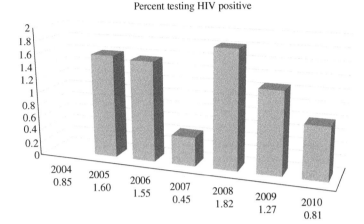

Percent testing HIV positive

Figure 4.5 Rate of blood donors testing positive to HIV in Mae Tao clinic
Source: adapted from Mae Tao Clinic Report on HIV/AIDS Patients and Services 2010

not prepare condoms, or choose not to, based on their personal preferences and lack of knowledge. As a result, STIs spread. HIV, for example, has been detected among the factory workers by surveys conducted by Mae Tao clinic. This clinic is a bustling complex at the edge of Mae Sot, and has for many long years been a beacon of hope and public health assistance for ill and suffering Myanmar people on both sides of the border. Mae Tao is aided by donor assistance and volunteers but is largely staffed by local Myanmar medics led by Dr Cynthia Maung who has deservedly received international acclaim and, perhaps more importantly, local trust and veneration. It is the centre of both ambulatory care and outreach to the huge numbers of displaced people who have limited access to health care and social support. Mae Tao clinic runs a blood donation programme in order to maintain its stocks of albumin. The donors are factory workers conducted through cooperation of 26 factories in the Mae Sot area (with a workforce of nearly 17,000). This programme provides a window into the presence of sexually transmitted diseases among this population.

In 2010, more than 2,300 workers volunteered to donate blood. Over 100 were excluded after behavioural risk assessment and health surveys, leaving 2,211 who donated blood (53.7 per cent were female). Of these 2,211 donors, 0.95 per cent (21 cases) tested positive to syphilis and 0.81 per cent (18 cases) to HIV. While lower than numbers of migrants testing HIV positive at Mae Sot hospital, these figures nonetheless offer a clear indication that HIV is present in factory environs. Numbers might have been higher if those with known sexual risk practices had not been excluded. Voluntary testing (VCCT) data from Mae Sot hospital shows significantly higher levels of HIV among migrants being tested than among Thai for the three years from 2007 to 2010. This is not a random sample and some have

Table 4.2 HIV detected during voluntary testing at Mae Sot hospital

Mae Sot hospital VCCT results	Thai Number tested/Number positive	Non-Thai Number tested/Number positive
Oct 2007–Sept 2008	3,515/126 (3.58%)	2,766/188 (6.79%)
Oct 2008–June 2009	2,674/114 (4.26%)	2,193/203 (9.25%)
Oct 2009–Sept 2010	2,579/82 (3.18%)	2,050/185 (9.02%)

Source: Mae Sot hospital

been referred for testing based on other symptoms, so we cannot compare the two as generalizable evidence of infection levels among Thai and migrant communities. But it does give an indication of a significant presence of HIV among migrants.

Health programmes run by NGOs are seeking to address the spread of HIV and condoms are made available in many factories, but such initiatives are often impeded by owners/managers who wish to avoid outside scrutiny. A further reproductive health dilemma is the persistent number of women who suffer serious complications from backyard abortions. In Thailand, the abortion rate among migrant women has been 2.4 times higher than that of Thai women (D'Souza, 2007: 27). In Mae Sot, health staff told us that at least four female migrants arrived at Mae Tao clinic each month haemorrhaging or suffering other severe symptoms related to abortions. Other sources confirm this picture. There has been an increasing incidence of women seeking help from Mae Sot hospital, where on average more than ten migrant women per month were treated for complications of induced abortion in 2004 rising to 15 per month by 2009 (Phadthaisong-Chaipanit, 2010). In 2007, 55 per cent of maternal mortality at Mae Tao clinic was caused by post-abortion complications (Kusakabe and Pearson, 2010: 27).

Numerous factors prompt the lack of precaution and subsequent decision to end pregnancy. Inevitably, in and around Mae Sot, these emerge from a hostile workplace where some combination of poverty, refusal of support or abandonment by the father, fear of loss of employment, lack of or incorrect use of contraception, and pressures from family and friends bring about the decision to terminate. Young men and women workers confirm this picture where abortion is a commonplace consequence of life in the precariat. A local health volunteer noted:

> About 80 per cent of women in sexual relations have abortions at some point, they go and see a local midwife either here or in Myawaddy, it costs 300–350 baht for each month of pregnancy. The most common reason is the failure of the father to agree to marriage.

Others suggested that it becomes necessary when the pregnant woman might already be married and away from her husband or for the many women who simply misunderstand how to take the pill every day. Gruesome details add to the depredations of life in this work zone. A-bert described how he had seen aborted foetuses lying in the sump behind the bathrooms by the factory walls. Lha noted simply, "no one takes care".

Methods used by migrant women to induce abortions might include herbal medicines, injections, massages and/or the insertion of objects. So too our inform- ants noted the widespread advertising of 'hot' medicines used to induce menstrua- tion across the river in Myawaddy, supplements that can also be purchased in local markets. While young women may try to induce a miscarriage themselves, others also turn to local midwives for help. Factory workers described the ease with which one can find a migrant resident supposedly skilled in such services. We visited a Shan midwife living on the outskirts of Mae Sot who described how she would only assist women to give birth but not terminate, but she was quick to add there are other local women who will do this. "Some women who visit these abor- tionists are only a few days pregnant; some are five-months pregnant. The method they use is to insert a small papaya tree twig into the vagina. The cost ranges from 2,000 to 3,000 baht." Like others before her, she echoed conventional perceptions that migration is the core to these outcomes:

> They would not sleep with a man easily because they have families and others in the community to take care of them. But when they came to Thailand, this changed. Now there are increasing cases of abortion. These are young women of about 17–18 years old. They work in the factories in this area. I hear about at least two to four cases of abortion each month.

Many go wrong.

Conclusion

I started the chapter with Berlant's reminder that intimacy carries with it an ever- present presentiment of vulnerability as we are surrounded by insistent reminders that our quest for emotional closeness carries no guarantee of longevity. It is a sensation that people anywhere in the world recognize. But in the Mae Sot precariat this insecurity is exacerbated exponentially due the environment of instability and subjugation. This is not to say migrants carry no hope for long-term relations. Couples marry and either seek work in a factory that will accommodate families or leave children with grandparents. More broadly, life in Mae Sot fosters an insistent presentiment that one has the opportunity to explore new ways of life even as its overarching constraints keep one acutely aware of the limits of this thinking. Kusakabe and Pearson (2010: 24) describe: "Although they faced constraints on their mobility, those who had managed to negotiate some degree of freedom within the town valued the relative autonomy they had as workers in Thailand, in contrast to the strict nature of family and community vigilance and control." Hence, the quest for intimacy in circumscribed circumstances takes on a number of permutations. Men and women seek companionship to buffer the predatory insecure nature of life in Mae Sot. The need to persistently buttress instability creates volatile attachments, fleeting pleasures and sometimes unforeseen anguish.

There is also a rich vein of intimate connections that take place beyond the normative male–female couples, but similarly predicated on the pursuit of pleasure outside of social and community oversight. So too health consequences are deeply implicated in the nature of these relationships. Sometimes male factory workers at Mae Sot will cross the border to Myawaddy to meet other men there. We talked with Miu Miu, a Burmese *kathoey* (transgender) and his friend, Mo Mae, who work at a beauty shop just across the river: "These days many men come here to work like us, there are numerous beauty parlours where men come to find sex. There is a lot of commerce. Many men come to Myawaddy to seek male partners." Data from Mae Tao clinic shows high levels of HIV among the few transgender that have been tested. Risk is foreshadowed more diffusely by the large number of migrant men testing HIV positive at the clinic who indicated they had engaged in male sex at some point in their lives. Thus, as in the other border zones we have discussed, material and intimate economies overlap in multiple dimensions. Here, more prominently than elsewhere, mobility and anxiety combine to generate new partnerships oriented to a sense of overt security. But at the same time, the quest for safety introduces other modes of risk and danger. It is to the ways that human capital and commercial intimacy are deployed within other examples of male–male relations and mobile unions that I turn now.

Notes

1 www.exim.go.th/doc/newsCenter/41901.pdf (accessed 9 May 2013).
2 www.ftiprovince.or.th/index.aspx (accessed 16 May 2013).

5 Poiesis of the intimate encounter: dormitory exchanges and bed-sit affairs

More radically put, my human capital is me, as a set of skills and capabilities that is modified by all that affects me and all that I effect.

(Feher, 2009: 26)

We are not selling sex, but selling life.

(Dai masseuse in Hat Yai)

The previous chapters describe how intimacy and its connections are intricately entwined with the development initiatives, policy roll-outs and infectious aspirations in frontier areas of the Greater Mekong. In some respects, the capitalization of affect as it fuels expanded socio-sexual networks, special zone acrobatics and embodied vulnerability of the precariat is a modern-day rendition of age-old processes. Graeber, in his treatise on the history of debt, notes that in most 'human economies' – which have long pre-dated market economies – "money is used first and foremost to arrange marriages" (2011: 131). In a broader context, a voluminous literature describes intimate interactions tied to other forms of exchange ranging from commercialized sex through to monetized courting or social conventions such as bride-wealth or dowry that still to this day require massive investment. In short, sexual intimacy and varied forms of exchange are dual, frequently locked-at-the-hip (pocket), aspects of the social order. Of course, what I wish to underscore is that while the intersection of the material and the intimate might not be new, it is never homogenous over time and space. Looked at historically, for example, we see that institutions and meanings associated with commercialized sex have consistently evolved in different cultures and epochs from ritualized privilege through to sometimes pathologized and often stigmatized secular pursuits. Furthermore, as we saw in Mae Sot and the rubber-clad hills of northern Laos, the valorization of intimacy very often encompasses far more than commercial sex.

Recently, as neoliberal forms of capital appreciation have become the touchstone for understanding social standing, Hakim (2011) argues that aesthetic, social and sensual skills can be deployed by women competing for wealth, asserting: "Erotic capital is the least understood personal asset, one that is completely visible yet at the same time overlooked. Those who possess erotic capital have

Figure 5.1 Kathoey and gay: identities in motion in downtown Laos

a big advantage." To uncover the erotic as a form of value is, in and of itself, a valuable move. The terms by which it is able to operate as strategic currency in contemporary Western life (or anywhere) is far less transparent. Less controversially, Illouz (1997) describes how young people's romance rituals gradually became interwoven with capital over the long years of Western industrialization and modernization as courting became ever-more associated with consumption of leisure technologies – going to the mall, going to movies and so forth. Similar changes can be detected in recent decades all over the GMS. Previous courting encounters from a couple of generations ago that might have been characterized by carefully staged interactions (the evenings on a straw mat outside the young woman's village house under the hovering watch of parents) and sharp repartee as "the remnants of a world of linguistic artistry, eloquent palaver and magical speech persist in the verbal courting battles" (Klausner, 1987: 252) have been replaced by new trappings. Across Asia (as elsewhere), the motorcycle, mobile phone and social network technologies have radically reshaped courting opportunities and affectionate exchanges in rural and urban environs. As a further example, Valentine's Day with its bestowal of flowers and expectations of intimacy demonstrates a heartily commercialized aura for Asian teenagers due to diffusion of global pop culture. More broadly, increasing numbers of cross-border marriages, migrant care-givers, domestic and sex workers demonstrate multiple ways in which reproductive labour is commodified within global networks (Constable, 2009). This chapter builds on our previous discussions of affective economies by probing further into the interpenetration of intimate relations and changing economic conditions, not solely in border zones. I do not focus on erotic capital per se, but rather wish to concentrate on particular mechanisms that foster the (self-) appreciation and the value of a human capital to set the stage for how we then think about approaches to risk that constellate as neoliberal forces infiltrate aspects of self (and the ways in which capital is deployed).

We firstly consider the commonplace incidence of male–male sexuality in Laos and document how cultural formations and expectations give shape to physical pleasure and intimate longings. Against a backdrop of national-level mobility prompted by recent economic transitions, the movement of money shrouds profound moments of emotional interplay within male–male relations. For these men, gendered subjectivity and pursuit of long-term intimacy is embedded within an economy of desire being refigured by internal migration and global flows of people, media and capital. This chapter then looks further into how forms of family and domestic relations are reconfigured by ways in which human capital, as the tool for self-advancement, becomes deployed in ways not anticipated by development planners. We consider this by focusing on one area of southwest China where Dai women have turned captive work in Thai massage parlours, previously controlled by traffickers, into vibrant networks of local recruitment. Many of these women are married; their husbands remain at home tending to children while their wives seek new partners as a means to financial accumulation. Demonstrating capitalism's prolific ability to find new structuring relations, Dai women utilize human (being married), social (kin and ethnic connections) and cultural (Chinese language) capital to find material support through relations with Chinese Malaysian men at the Thai–Malay border in ways quite different from conventional models of commercial sex in Southeast Asia. At the same time such manoeuvres, ostensibly encouraged by state economic reforms, do not go unnoticed. In an era of resurgent concern with cross-border infections, the Chinese state is increasingly monitoring, controlling and stigmatizing Dai women for the health threat their mobile and supposedly 'unruly' bodies represent.

We thus detect in the ways Lao male sexuality is valued within an extractive economy of exchange (semen and money) and the ways Dai women simultaneously subordinate and exalt sexual autonomy in the name of economic independence (finding new partners, while still supporting their husbands who also find new partners), enormously resourceful modes of fashioning a resilient sense of self. As in the previous chapter, where structural violence intersects in complex ways with entrepreneurial aspirations, here too we see that changing economic frameworks bring with them complex configurations of intimacy and what to expect from it. It brings us back to the question: if migrants and mobile individuals, or simply those whose lives have been radically transformed by development initiatives, are the valued vessels of values, then precisely what type of value is being established by unstable and often ambiguous intimacy within economic endeavours?

The poetics of the encounter

Desjarlais has brought our attention to the merits in thinking about lifeways, and the gamut of emotions everyday life typically entails, through the age-old Greek notion of 'poiesis'. What interests him, in particular, is its generative presence in our everyday attempts to make something of ourselves. He makes clear the inadequacy of seeing only practicality in the mundane, and pushes us to think of the artistry in commonplace endeavours.

> The term poiesis has come to designate any making or doing beyond purely practical efforts. Poiesis is involved in the crafting of poems and the art of shipbuilding. It implies a begetting, a fabrication and bringing forth, of some new form or reality; something that was not present is made present.
>
> (Desjarlais, n.d.: 16)

In this sense, poiesis foregrounds the creativity in giving shape to one's aspirations – creativity in the sense that everyday life is forever moved forward by forging new ways of being and understanding – the very stuff of dreams, hopes and desires. Hence, just like the lives of male lovers in Vientiane and Dai migrant masseuses in Hat Yai and Dan Nork, poiesis may be underemphasized, but it is close to omnipresent.

> Poiesis is found in the strivings of all peoples – and, perhaps, of all life forms more generally. Poiesis is there in the urge we have to make something of, and in, our lives, both individually and collectively … It's evident in the ways people fashion something out of the elements of their lives, even if those elements are bone bare, at times. We are always going beyond what is given to us, in one way or another. The capacity for generating is built into us. There is a creative tendency in life itself. Poiesis is found in moments of joy and suffering, and of life and death.
>
> (ibid: 19)

From this vantage point, the sexual and the intimate become creative under-pinnings of ways people fashion a sense of self and seek to make something out of their lives, in particular as economic stimulation broadens strategies to access a consumer market across Southeast Asia. As mentioned earlier, Spinoza noted long ago that the capacity to be affected is absolutely central to the capacity to act. Spinoza was arguing that for effective political action to take place emotional engagement based on what he termed "adequate ideas" is crucial. I will return to a discussion of what might constitute adequate knowledge, but here we can follow Spinoza's directive to emphasize the central role of emotionally engaged connections, not in purely political terms, but in the ways opportunities and opportunism together with expanding capital flows afford new forms of intimate bonding. In other words, I wish to uncover the 'poiesis of the intimate encounter' as development processes ferment desires and channel opportunities for individuals that profoundly embody attempts to become 'modern'. One might not think of intimate relations as endeavours that typically rely on the combination of craft and artistry, but as market forces insinuate themselves within processes of self-making it becomes clear that connections are indeed 'fashioned' through interlocking rubrics of desire and opportunity. So when Wetherell (2012: 118) reminds us that "Affective practice can disempower in the guise of empowering, but it can also be genuinely novel and generative", we need to be able to identify how emotional connections can provide opportunities for self-appreciation. In this light, sexuality is always an affective practice that draws on shared meanings and, at the same time, always subject to active and creative figuring of precisely what meanings gain value in different modernizing spaces.

Dating in Downtown Laos

Bodies do not come with ready-made sexualities. Bodies are not even attracted to other bodies – it is human subjects who are attracted to various objects including bodies, and the features of bodies that render them desirable to human subjects are contingent upon cultural codes, social conventions and the political institutions that structure and inform human subjectivity itself, thereby shaping our individual erotic ideals and defining the scope of what we find attractive.

(Halperin, 2002:106)

As anywhere in the world, in Laos men have intimate and sexual relations with other men. But the specifics differ. Money, pleasure and desire for emotional and physical connection are obvious concerns. Like anywhere, these entailments are not gained automatically. They emerge from local understandings about what sex between men means and what practices it requires. Social conditioning shoehorns homoerotic intimacy into certain forms of relationships as it governs the choices available to men in terms of partners and where they might find them. In turn, social narratives surrounding male sexuality become embodied in very specific ways. These days in Laos, so it is described, young straight men have sex with non-heterosexual (in local terms *kathoey* or transgender) men for money. 'Why else would they?' people explain. In fact, there are many reasons. Under the guise of 'doing it for money' men seek connections with other males, at the same time as mobility coupled with modernizing affective economies allow new shapes and channels of exchange. The following examples from an earlier study (Lyttleton, 2007) bring our attention directly to elements of self-fashioning that underpin sexuality and intimate exchange.

> Late in our research, we are sitting in a small salon – several beauticians are tending to customers. It is some way down a winding road – cut open as plumbing pipes are being laid – on the outskirts of Vientiane. Inside, Suk is attaching hair extensions to a customer in front of a mirror. A woman lies prone being attended to by a soft-faced man named Phe – his hair is short, her hair is being washed. We are talking with Maew while others carry on crafting beauty. Suk herself has flowing hair and skin that is only possible after months of hormone intake (in local practice taking huge numbers of contraception pills). Like her customer Suk calls herself *kathoey*. Phe is not sure which word is better, but he prefers 'gay' over *kathoey*. He has a Western boyfriend. It is popular knowledge amongst Lao men who are looking for Western lovers that they prefer men with short hair. It was a scene we encountered often. Beauty shops are the prime locale associated with both work and sociality for *kathoeys*. Although today wearing jeans and a tee-shirt, the evening before Suk had paraded a sequined gown while at a fashion show organized by a health programme that works specifically with *kathoeys*. At the party she said she was about to go to Thailand (again). If she can't 'sell well' in the red-light town of Pattaya this time she will go to Phuket, a different sort of tourist zone. She wants to meet more Westerners – there is more money with these men she tells us and maybe more chance of longer-term emotional and financial support. But she will have to try being 'gay'. Only old men come to see *kathoeys* in Phuket, she says. Short hair she can do – but more than that she says she does not know. Can she do 'gay' in sexual terms? She is unsure.
>
> Several weeks earlier, we had been in a northern province, the capital of which is nowadays recognized in global gay networks as a popular and pleasurable tourist destination. Some distance down a dusty road outside of the town we reach Ee's house tucked behind some rice-fields. Here people have never heard of gay and have no idea what it means for changing understandings of sexuality. In this respect, we might be anywhere in Laos. Across the road is a boarding school for students from remote rural areas. Young men (Lao: *phu bao*) in their late teens often hang out at Ee's house which is a welcome source of satellite television and socializing away from the concrete, unadorned and crowded dorm rooms. Ee usually has beer or whiskey to drink. Quite possibly several *kathoeys* will visit from the nearby city. Sex often takes place at some point in the evening between the various visitors. It

is casual, common, hardly private and usually involves a number of rotating partners. Ee is 28 and unabashedly *kathoey* although he dresses as a male and has short hair. When he was younger he slept with women after he was dropped by a boyfriend but now has sex exclusively with males. Some married men pay him. "It's easy to get guys here – the students have nothing else to do, they come and hang out and want sex; in the towns, the *phu bao* are much more into the game, they always want money."

These vignettes reveal a number of points. There is no uniform version of 'Lao' male–male sexuality that we can refer to (even choosing he or she pronouns is awkward). There are multiple cultural logics that shape how men who have sex with other men understand and experience their lives. Moreover, a sexualized identity entails intersections of localized belief systems and global sources of identification and capital flow. Sometimes people move freely between different subject positions, for example some men will have sex with other men one day and with women the next – the much commented 'fluidity' of Asian gender/ sexuality. Underlying this flexibility are complex self-making processes in which the sexual is central. Usually meanings associated with these connections are discussed within public health arenas based on the fact that how two people perceive their relationship is a key determinant of whether sexual health risks are also present. And in fact, these risks have been confirmed by epidemiological studies that have detected significant levels of HIV – 5.6 per cent prevalence in 2007 (Sheridan et al, 2009) and 4.2 per cent in 2010 (CHAS, 2011: 25) among men who have sex with men (MSM) in certain Lao cities. Notably, these studies show that considerable numbers (39 per cent) of men having sex with men also had sex with women during the previous three months. These are hardly trivial details, but, rather than discussing the spread of HIV per se, in what follows I wish to pursue a deeper discussion of vulnerability that lies within the complicated ways material exchange dovetails with intimate interactions. It is here that poiesis resides, and here that the rubrics of social change become key determinants of the volatile value of bodies and relations. This is, of course, not a new process even as it partakes of new configurations of physical and occupational mobility.

Prior to the revolution, colonial Vientiane was famous for its *kathoeys*. One elderly Lao *kathoey* described to us his astonishment when he first moved to Vientiane during the war years in the 1960s and saw literally "hundreds of long haired and beautiful *kathoeys* congregating around the fountain" waiting for Western partners in the centre of the small city. He told us of a Frenchman who picked him up and took him to a bar where he was consigned to refill this gentleman's opium pipe before returning to his hotel for slow and somnolent sexual play. After the revolution in 1975, the number of *kathoeys* plummeted as they either left, hid their predilection for femininity or were sent to rehabilitation camps. Since the early 1990s this trend is being reversed. While there is no way of knowing in comparative terms whether male–male relations are on the increase, there are perhaps a number of overlapping reasons why male–male sexuality is more visible in

Laos than in the past. First, mass media from Thailand and the West, including a wide range of gay pornography, is making male–male sexuality fashionable and exotic – in the words of teenagers 'it is cool [*tae*]' to hang out with *kathoeys* or gay men. Second, there is a growing recognition of a market for male sex fuelled by increased visits from Western and Asian gay tourists. Third, there is an increased public visibility of Lao men who in earlier years closer to the post-revolution period would have felt obliged to be more discreet in public demonstration of homoerotic desire. And finally a growing number of young men try male–male sex under the guise of economic need or experimentation.

Increasing visibility has a number of effects. Same-sex male relations are widespread and quietly accommodated in Laos (female–female relations are more stringently disavowed) but prejudice remains a subtle backdrop. Men who exhibit non-normative sexual desires, primarily *kathoeys*, are sometimes regarded as bad luck, and environmental misfortune, such as lack of adequate rain, is commonly attributed by an older generation to their growing numbers. At a more personal level, parents try and 'cure' their sons by making them act more 'masculine'. In face of such pressures, many *kathoeys* move to cities for greater freedom. Many take wives as a means of gaining social acceptance. For others, greater social visibility is itself liberating and a diversity of connections becomes more possible. Even with these changes, male intimacy remains overdetermined by specific affective practices that structure how large numbers of Lao men experience male–male sex at some point in their lives. In this context, I will concentrate on the relatively common occasions of sex between young 'straight' men (*phu bao*) and transgender males (*kathoeys*). Even as gay models from the West gain traction, this more conventional dyad remains the most prominent version of homoeroticism present in Laos as it continues to discursively channel desire within same-sex engagements. There is no doubt identifiable elements of 'gay' identity have become more obvious in developing countries through a globalization of identity politics (Altman, 2001) and, at a more prosaic level, international HIV programmes. In turn, this transnationalism of identity might be understood as either empowering or belittling to local versions of sexuality (Boellstorff, 2005: 27). Jackson (2009) shows us that transgender identities in Asia have certainly altered under the modernizing spread of market capitalism, but not through a uniform import of global 'queer'. In Laos, modernization plays a significant role in evolving sexual subjectivities through processes of mobility, wage labour, urbanization and their combined loosening of social constraints, trends that have been identified in the history of sexuality in many countries. But, as Jackson notes, there is nothing homogenous about queer modernities.

Configuring male–male sex

Men who enjoy sex with other men may be from any walk of life anywhere in Laos. Overlying this, there are geographic, age-based and economic factors that structure expression of male–male desire. As we have seen in other chapters, space shapes relations. Laos is still an overwhelmingly rural society and one consequence of recent modernization is that large numbers of young people migrate to further their education or to look for work. There are dormitories all over Laos for young men and women who move closer to urban or provincial centres, becoming the hub of the 'landscapes of desire' that Hubbard mentioned earlier. Dormitories are sites where semi-transient men have sex with each other and where transgender men find many partners. The majority of estimates in our earlier research suggested between 30 and 75 per cent of young men in dormitories all over Laos have engaged in sex with another male. One student told us that of ten of his friends, five would have had sex with other men and of these about two would do so regularly, about ten times per month. Other studies have indicated that nearly 20 per cent of men in Vientiane have experienced sexual interactions with other men (Toole, 2004). While numbers are important to some parties as a means to gain conceptual and programmatic grasp of 'transgressive' sexuality, my interest is elsewhere. These connections are first and foremost meaning-intensive practices that illuminate what is being exchanged and, in the process, how one might gain (or lose) material and symbolic value through modes of intimacy.

In addition to spaces with concentrated numbers of males, age plays a core role in how these affective practices take place. In most rural settings, male–male sex is regarded as both experimental and situational. For instance, an 18-year-old *kathoey* student described key elements that underpin male–*kathoey* relationships in his home village:

> Here, *kathoeys* tend to hang out as a gang. Young men in the village also congregate in groups as well. At times they meet up at festival events or parties, or just outside the village and then they pair-off for sex. One *kathoey* who owns a small restaurant will sometimes take sex instead of money for payment from young men who eat there. From what I can tell about 50 per cent of young men in villages in my province sleep with *kathoeys* – most of them just want try sex before they sleep with women. Overall more men lose their virginity with *kathoey* than they do with women.

This commonplace depiction highlights the role played by *kathoeys* rather than women in socializing young men into sexual activity. To sleep with women is considered a precursor to an ongoing relationship. This entails emotional and material support and commitment to a joint future. Sex with men is understood as just sex (albeit more varied and exotic) as emotional investment in male–male relations is precluded in popular narratives for many reasons. Ed is a young man who lives near an army camp just outside the city. He has relations with other men whom he regards as friends: "I go with men and it's just about sex, just about release. As soon as the sex is finished it is over, we don't think of anything else. If I have sex with a woman it is just the start of things. With men it doesn't mean anything, with women it always does."

In fact, I wish to show that sexual intimacy between men does indeed mean many things, even if these are defined in part by the brevity of relations. Bee, a

Figure 5.2 Dorms are temporary home to thousands of mobile young men all over Laos

male student in Vientiane, observed: "It takes two to three days of courting to be able to have sex with a woman, it takes 30 minutes with a *kathoey*." These distinctions take place as a result of social traditions: in lowland Lao culture it is still widely held that a young woman should not have sex before marriage. As in other parts of Asia this is rapidly changing, but throughout Laos there remains a social model that defines premarital sexuality as a transgression for women and polices it by social sanction on the young woman's reputation. A sexual interaction between a young man and a *kathoey* or other male is more acceptable on a number of fronts. Like many cultures, the Lao regard male sexuality as a hydraulic drive that is damaging to repress; sex with another male relieves sexual tension in ways that are conveniently regarded as devoid of any meaning. In so doing, young men's interactions with *kathoeys* protect normative female sexuality (marriageable daughters and sisters) at the same time as they validate male sexual experimentation. This feeds into forms of ongoing sexual desire that are formatively age-structured wherein for many *kathoeys* a desirable partner is a young novice who might be 'taught' the ways of sex. The appeal is both emotional and material as the *kathoey* is expected to 'take care' of his younger charge. These patterns transfer with little change into urban settings when young men and *kathoeys* meet up at dormitories, restaurants, nightclubs or just in the street.

Age structures notions of desirable partner and how power and status are employed. Youth is something young men capitalize on and they typically receive money from *kathoeys* based on their physical appeal and sexual rawness. Conversely, older, usually married, men will pay for sex with *kathoeys*. This reverse occurs as both a recognition of status and because older men are deemed less aesthetically desirable. More often, the *kathoey* (and to some extent gay man) pays or gives gifts to a young '100 per cent' male (Lao: *phu xai tem loi*) for sex, who in turn justifies his need for money based on lack of resources to pay university fees, living money, or funds to entertain his girlfriend. There is little stigma. Certainly, people feel that 'full' men are lazy and uncouth for receiving money in this fashion, but they are seldom considered sexually transgressive in any fashion. For others, having sex with both men and women is, in fact, a sign of masculine prowess. Thus, in sum, Lao *kathoeys* receive money from a small number of older (married) men for sex but pay for a greater number of fleeting relations with younger 'straight' men. Notably, this basic form of exchange differs from neighbouring GMS countries where *kathoeys* are more predominantly associated with receiving rather than forfeiting money in sexual interactions (Jackson, 2009; Morineau et al, 2004). Importantly, these divergent equations allow financial exchange to be integrated into the relationship as a means of fashioning and masking sexual and emotional appeal.

Typical dormitories at educational colleges throughout Laos

In line with the social immaturity of the young male, typical descriptions highlight the *kathoey* as the seducer – vivacious conversation and suggestive caress plus direct offer of financial assistance. Pong, living outside a provincial town, noted:

> The guys around here chase money less than they do in Vientiane city. But you still need cash or drugs to 'get' them. Here one pill [of *yaba*] will do. Young men want money from the moment they hit puberty these days. In the past they waited until they had a job before they would think about sex and relationships. Now it all starts much earlier. Sex and money go together; guys want cash, so they can buy things and have girlfriends. In the countryside some things are more relaxed. In Vientiane, the older you are the more you pay.

Financial exchange is discursively placed at the heart of relations. At the same time, the narratives that condition male–male sex build on larger tropes of modernization. They revolve around the way notions of human and social capital are deployed. First, these exchanges establish the burgeoning idea that underresourced young men recently relocated to the city can gain money through sexual interaction. The need for money provides an ostensible logic for this group to be having sex with other men that doesn't require or make prominent homoerotic desire. Because it happens fleetingly and casually it is not seen as commercial sex, but instead associated with material immaturity of youth who are newly mobile but not yet able to make an adequate living. Second, it entrenches the idea that the *kathoey* is purchasing something, which requires that the young men have something desirable (youth/masculinity) to be consumed. This, in turn, constitutes an object of value to be 'gained' by the *kathoey*. Local language always describes the relations as the young man 'losing himself' (*sia tua*) in the exchange rather than the fact he gains money. These men say they need to compensate for loss – of semen (*sia nam*), the fact he has been possessed/conquered (*sia piap*), loss of face (*sia na*) and possible regret (*sia jai*). A *kathoey* obtains something more important than the forfeited money – a fleeting sense of dominance in a world that typically denies the *kathoey* social respect (and social capital). Finally, as the monetary economy gains prominence in all sectors of Lao society (after years of socialist penury) it privileges the notion that sexual desire is one-way and that 'straight' men are doing it for material gain rather than sexual pleasure. While sexual satisfaction is clearly implicated, it is secondary to the masculinized traits of experimentation and entrepreneurialism (making money as best one can). The *kathoey*, on the other hand, is supposedly responding to innate sexual needs. For the *kathoey*, what are at stake are sexual contact, possession and subjective pleasure. Taken together these facets of capital accumulation intersect in resonant ways with notions of fluid expenditure/accumulation and its link to sexual identity. These widespread narratives have very specific embodied effects.

The affectionate and the financial

I have been describing that popular understandings of what constitutes desire in male–male relations in Laos defer to broader structural issues: money, age/ beauty and power exploitation. But although far less spoken, desire is also deeply embedded in ways of understanding and experiencing one's body and its potential for gendered emotional exchange. In turn, this has profound implications for the types of relations that sustain in popular imaginary and everyday life. In each instance, their relevance is central to understanding the cultural nature of sexuality, the deployment of human capital (in Feher's sense, mentioned at the beginning of the chapter, of the composite skills and capabilities that make up one's sense of self), and also vulnerability to HIV spread born of the instabilities of intimacy. Duang, a strapping 23-year-old, originally from a northern province, works in a large Vientiane beer restaurant with about 15 other waiters and cooks. His descriptions of sexual adventurism illustrate many of the above points. Duang sleeps in a room at the back of the restaurant. He says about five or six other men at the restaurant will, like him, sleep with *kathoeys* when the occasion arises.

> My first time of sex with a *kathoey* wasn't that pleasant – I accompanied him to a guesthouse when I was drunk. We hugged and kissed and had oral sex. I wanted to know what it was like with a *kathoey* but ended up feeling pressured to have sex, I was a bit anxious. I wanted to try because I had seen other

guys at the restaurant wearing jewellery and getting other gifts and money from *kathoeys*.

Lots of very beautiful *kathoeys* come to the restaurant – sometimes I am not even sure they are *kathoeys* and not women when I go out with them. Usually I get between 50,000 and 100,000 kip [$5-$10]. The most I have been given is 1,000 baht [$30]. Money is the main reason I will have sex with a *kathoey*. The second reason is for the sex. Some of my friends like the emotional support they get and I can see what they mean. But one problem is that you cannot get too close to them – they drop you after one or two times together. So I don't want to get to like them too much – I will just end up getting hurt. It is easy to feel comfortable with a *kathoey*. They talk to us like a guy will talk to a girl. They treat you very well.

I am usually drunk when I am with a *kathoey* – so they do it all. Sex is at least three times more active with a *kathoey*. Sweat is everywhere. You get three times as tired – they suck all the strength out of you. Your joints end up sore – as if all your juices have been sucked out. You end up getting thin, your arms and legs lose strength and your face looks really thin. Overall I don't think it is worth the money. They will hit you if they are angry; and they drop you easily. There is no security with a *kathoey*. They get bored so easily and are always changing partners. They change because they feel that they have already had you. They always say – "I have had him already I want someone new."

Overall I prefer women – there is more physical attraction even if *kathoeys* take better care of you. My parents could never accept me being with a *kathoey* as a partner – we could never be a real couple. We couldn't have children. But even so, I do feel strongly when I am with a *kathoey*. When you sleep with girls you have to give everything; it always costs you in some shape or form – when you sleep with a girl you have to pay for everything. It takes a long time to get a girl. If I get money from being with *kathoey* I will sometimes split it with my girlfriend, but I would never tell I have had sex. I tell her they give me money for hanging out with them.

Duang's narrative highlights many commonplace understandings in Laos. While occasional descriptions cite a confluence of male and female energies in the *kathoey's* body as prompting an elevated desire, most explanations are biological. Many believe *kathoeys* have 'excessive' sexual desire (usually described as lust, *tanha*) based on a need for male semen to reclaim a functioning masculinity as Nun, a 19-year-old student, summarizes: "*Kathoeys* get semen from guys. They need it because their bodies cannot produce it. They are always chasing men and they spend a lot of time trying to suck it all from them." This stereotype is further abetted in circulating tales of a *kathoey's* voracious sexual appetite, group sex and the perpetual quest for a new partner (described further in Lyttleton, 2007). What these narratives reveal is that, based on perceived scarcity, semen is a resource with exchange value within the intimate economies connecting young men and their transgender partners. Desires underpinning these relationships have deeply symbolic value, which, in turn, take on market value in the circulation of bodies and body fluids.

Populist explanations underpinning *kathoey* desire for sex are telling. One crucial factor is that *kathoeys* 'performing' properly are not supposed to get erections. This is not to say, sexual pleasure is not important, simply that it cannot (or should not) be demonstrated physically through mutual genital stimulation. To show physical arousal indicates a still functioning form of masculinity (and the ability to sire children) and this troubles the overarching femininity that is meant to characterize the *kathoey* as a 'second type of woman' (*praphet thi song*). Thus, it is widely believed within Lao society in general, and by many *kathoeys* themselves, that a 'proper' *kathoey* does not have erections – to do so means one has not taken on the performative existence of being 'not man' adequately (even as many *kathoeys* themselves know the reality to be different). Many transgender men thus try to suppress, hide or deny physical arousal. Importantly, the reverse perception also holds – men who sleep with other men in the active and insertive role are not feminized. Any man could have sex with another man and remain a 'man' so long as he adheres to certain pro-forma sexual scripts – the 'straight' male has the erection and the orgasm (Jackson, 1997). The *kathoey* is the one who services his partner's sexual arousal and satisfaction. If the *kathoey* has an erection there is no intrinsic difference between the two – and *phu bao* cannot cope with this recognition. To see an erection is too confronting, too shocking and in their words absolutely "disgusting". This disavowal of the presence of more than one erection can make things complicated between two men who see themselves as friends: for example Uan, a *phu bao*, tells us:

> The main reason I sleep with other men is for sexual release. I often share a bed with friends, particularly soldiers from the nearby army camp after we have been drinking together. We only hug and kiss. Usually I want him to touch me because I get horny, but I would never think of touching him back – this is disgusting. But if the other guy is a 'full' man he won't touch me either; if he is not 100 per cent male he will. Because I won't touch him, the other man will usually just masturbate himself – I never masturbate in front of another man.

It is not just straight men but significantly *kathoeys* who also strongly reproduce this image of unwanted arousal. They note that their partner will immediately reject them and furthermore spread the word that this is not what a *kathoey* should be. Sri, a highly effeminate *kathoey*, explained the definitive difference: "If a guy sees that a *kathoey* has an erection he would think he is not a real *kathoey* and could instead be with a woman. If the guy tries to touch my penis I will stop the sex immediately." Many *kathoeys*, therefore, put active effort into not getting or not showing erections for fear of being labelled a 'failed' *kathoey* who, in turn, will get no partners and no satisfaction. *Kathoeys* and some gay men thus described how they will never remove their own clothes so that their genitals are not disclosed during sex; others suggested it is easy to hide erections by lying face down during anal intercourse. Others told us they take hormones both for breast enlargement and skin clarity but also very clearly to decrease the intrusion of physical arousal. Unlike in Thailand, where body modification is a commercial windfall and aesthetic pinnacle for many *kathoeys*, very few in Laos opt for surgery. We should note that this form of embodied typecasting is being challenged by some forms of gay identity, in which physical arousal is able to be enjoyed mutually. This is precisely what Suk meant in our prelude when she said she was unsure if she could do 'gay' – maintain and share enjoyment of mutual excitement.

Value in numbers: pleasure in possession

The politics of sexual arousal have profound implications. One outcome leads directly to the pursuit of multiple partners. Instead of their own climax, some of those who disdained having erections told us that satisfaction lies instead in the orgasm of their partner. Sri explains further:

> My pleasure [Lao/Thai: *khwamsuk*] relies entirely on that of the guy, I get pleasure from his pleasure – I like to do oral better because I can be more active and guys like it more also. *Kathoeys* have more desire because they have no climax [Lao: *bo mi jut rabay*], they have to keep looking for more men to satisfy their desire.

Others elaborated that in lieu of their own orgasm, pleasure rests in ensuring they are able to access their partner's semen: "You only completely possess [*dai*] the man when you 'swallow' his semen." Thus, for many *kathoeys* the act of 'possession' entails receiving semen inside the body, a dynamic that poses obvious challenges to HIV prevention.

Conveniently, 'full' men interpret this as a physiological need for sperm on the part of the *kathoey*. In so doing the narrative of elevated lust and the need for a constant stream of partners is efficiently perpetuated. The social order has thus created a supremely effective – and cuttingly exploitative – model whereby the *kathoey* sublimates his/her own pleasure and in turn this creates a ready source of sexual access for 'full' men whenever and wherever they want. In a subtly elegant fashioning of power, the heterosexual structuring of society makes *kathoey*s ever-available by creating a role that subordinates their pleasure through that of their 'straight' partners. Some might argue that this typifies patriarchal patterns in hetero-normative relations the world over; but what is different here is the production of a deficient and overtly sexualized identity that (apart from the way female prostitutes are often typecast) cannot be labelled on women in general. Importantly the lack of specific climax means that for many *kathoeys*, pleasure is figured through 'having' many partners. Hence pleasure is not just sublimated; it is produced in such a way as to increase sexual availability and contact. These understandings are shared and internalized and, as such, just like Ahmed's networks of fear, circulate as an economy of desires.

On the one hand, *kathoeys* (and by extension gay men who in many people's eyes are one and the same) are credited widely with being potent and resilient individuals, possessed of heightened social and practical skills made most evident in their ability to keep paying young men for company. But, on the other hand, through a combination of perceived characteristics – either physiologically defi-cient (inadequate semen) or endowed (combined male–female energies), full of lust, emotionally prohibited from long-term partners, socially competitive, bound by stringent age constraints – a *kathoey's* life becomes above all a highly sexual-ized social identity. In practical terms, it means there is a constant change in part-ners based on the way the need for satisfaction is created. It also means *kathoeys* are denied any possibility of long-term relationships, because their social identity is totally shaped by the ethos of short-term sexual contact with many men. Of course, there are exceptions: some *kathoeys* profess love for only one man and refuse to engage in multiple sexual contacts. Others find ways to get comeup-pance on *phu bao*, drawing satisfaction from ditching them after one encounter, or flaunting their power to say yes or no to their attentions. Nor should we interpret these dynamics as meaning there is no pleasure: none of the men we spoke with indicated that lack of orgasm meant no sexual pleasure.

Instead, this narrative construction invigorates a market logic of commodity exchange that suffuses deeply within self-making processes that link sexuality and subjectivity. These economies are built on two structural elements: a large pool of single young mobile men in want of money and a smaller pool of transgen-ders whose identity is centred on sexual interactions with a large number of men. Importantly these relations are increasingly monetized and associated with urban modernity (characterized most visibly by mobile young men in mushrooming dormitories across Laos) in contrast to 'undeveloped' rural settings. Exchanges of money and semen become the means by which such relations are fashioned, capitalized and deemed functional in modernizing Lao society. There are however further dimensions to the poiesis of intimacy at play here.

Because ongoing intimacy is regarded to adhere in male–female relations, male–male sexuality is considered no more than a fleeting interaction within a vibrant and highly dynamic sexual marketplace. Shared affective practices create a sense of communal solidarity for *kathoeys* who attempt to possess as many men as possible as a public badge of pride. For their part, 'full' men explain their sex-ual interactions in terms of money, experimentation and pressing need for sexual release. But, as so often in the realm of sexual practice, these connections evoke a number of conflicting responses and affective counterpoints. Even as *kathoeys* are begrudgingly given respect for the fact they can always afford to pay, money exchange masks the ongoing exploitation of a manufactured social identity for the sexual desires of normative masculine men. Likewise, transience and mate-rial gain shrouds the emotional weight that intimacy carries for the young men. Many men relish sex with other men based on the appeal of having a partner who can share a sense of maleness, be enormously solicitous and offer supposedly far greater and more exciting sexual variety than women. These combined pleasures lead men to readily, as some put it, 'cheat' *kathoeys* out of their money.

Fear and desire

There is another hugely important element underlying attraction that defies the preservation of such safe explanations and that further emphasizes the fundamental instability of intimate configurations. Pleasure in gender reversal is also central to the *phu bao*'s desire for a male partner and significantly undermines the idea that male–*kathoey* relations are a homology of male–female relations. Young men emphasized a very direct reversal of attention as they themselves felt feminized by the active and solicitous attention from the *kathoey*. This takes place in several ways: financially, it is the *kathoey* who provides the material exchange; emotionally, it is the *kathoey* who does all the expressive leg-work, so to speak; and sexually, it is the *kathoey* who is active in terms of seduction, suggestive behaviour and sexual initiation. In this rendering, the feminine *kathoey* takes on male roles, just as the overt male relishes his feminization. Xai, a student in Vientiane, summarized neatly: "Just as man is to woman, so *kathoey* is to male – we *phu bao* become the women in this context, this is what is appealing." In this dynamic, the *kathoey* is gaining something from the man – his sperm, his pleasure (and, in some men's eyes, his shame) – in ways that assert control of the relationship that are not applicable to a woman (who always 'loses' herself to the man), just as the *phu bao* gains pleasure from the not having to uphold forms of social manliness through which intimate relations with a woman take time, effort and money.

Thus, despite the prominent claims to conventional masculinity being preserved by an insertive role in sexual practice, other transformations take place. Importantly, this extends beyond the 'straight' male–*kathoey* dyad I have been describing and includes a wider range of men being comfortable with each other sexually. A number of men described to us how easy it was to be with another man (friends or peers), how easy it was to understand each other and how easy it was not to have to achieve gendered expectations of pleasing a woman. In similar vein, one young woman mentioned that she felt second-best to *kathoeys* in competition for a male partner because "they have a tremendous advantage because as a male they know exactly what another man likes sexually. For women it is much harder to know how to please a man, we know it is important but we are not taught about these things."

Underscoring their complexity, there is an ebb and flow within these economies of desire that makes them such awkward dynamics to capture either conceptually or in programmes seeking to address health consequences. Juxtaposed against *phu bao* desires for affinity and support and their (entrepreneurial) inclinations to turn sex into cash, we see deeply embedded fears at being subsumed by overwhelming appetite of 'caring' *kathoeys* to the point that the body (and psyche) is at risk. In Laos, the belief that semen is a limited commodity is still widespread and as we have seen this informs perceptions of why *kathoeys* desire sex. At the same time, considerable numbers of men worry that losing semen weakens them and potentially precludes having children. Thus, for example, in addition to its enticement and exoticism, oral sex is considered to be intrinsic to a *kathoey*'s needs (and not something women, apart from occasional sex workers, do). But

Figure 5.3 Kathoey hair extensions in a Vientiane beauty shop

like Duang's comments earlier, descriptions from a range of young men suggest a number of debilitating effects associated with this need.

> A *kathoey* needs the sperm from men so their penises will get strong again and they can have children … A *kathoey* will want to have sex all night. They

will wake me up and keep trying to get me to have another erection – two or three times at least. A woman only wants it once; *kathoeys* want it much more … They suck all your juices and it makes your joints hurt … You can tell who has been having sex with a *kathoey*; their faces get thin and their skin gets yellow … With a woman your semen will emerge naturally, and there is still some left, but a *kathoey* has to suck it out and in the process takes it all … If you let a *kathoey* suck your juices you yourself will become homosexual.

These vampire-like metaphors of intrinsic essences being consumed shout widespread anxiety. Hence, as much as there is recognition of sexual freedom and experimentation and multiple levels of appeal, there are pressures to preserve boundaries that protect 'masculine' integrity. In the sexual encounter, the *kathoey* threatens the *phu bao*'s integrity through removal of the fundamental essence of maleness – semen, understood as a primal commodity the *kathoey* is lacking. Thus, coupled with desire we can also detect a profound fear and a deeply entrenched and resonant rationale for distancing. The *kathoey* remains relegated to brief and controlled sexual excursions; figured through the logics of tremendous appeal and tempered by an equal and opposite worry over loss of bodily integrity. Thus the distance between subject positions and the contingent nature of intimacy is preserved through classic tropes of desire and countervailing anxiety over untrammelled pleasure that circulate as central elements within affective economies that shape intimate practices. None of this, however, is locked in stone and, under the sway of modernization with its global flows of money and ideas, the very instability of intimacy becomes the means by which the underlying poiesis of the sexual encounter is transforming self-making processes.

A shift in terrain

Even as relationships are predicated on ambivalent money/semen exchange, significantly, and making obvious the extent to which sexuality is linked to broader flows of capital and people, the emergence of local versions of 'gay' provide alternative choices through variations of sexual pleasure and emotional longevity. The term 'gay' is not yet widespread in either linguistic or subjective terms in Laos (nor many parts of Asia), but is slowly becoming more common, in part as a result of increasing internationalism of experiences, narratives and practices via media and pornography, people mobility and market forces. There is (currently) no civil activism around sexuality and no gay or lesbian political movement in Laos. While Edmund White might have wittily remarked that the 1968 Stonewall riot was a 'swish' that was heard around the world, it is sobering to remember that in much of the GMS the more prominent sound at the time was exploding ordnance. Instead, gay is a more recently budding social category that allows men to be more open in non-normative sexuality, but in complicated ways that maintain links to normative masculinity with its social pressure to become part of a domestic social unit – the family. In Laos, its growing presence as a subjective category is stemming from the breakdown of the above pigeonholed narratives of sexual practice.

At a sensual level, 'gay' means to engage in alternating sexual roles and pleasures. The increased number of Western and other Asian gay men coupled with widespread pornography are providing mobile and alternative models of male–male sexuality. These are based primarily on the notion of two homosexual men enjoying sexual and emotional relations with each other. In Laos, 'gay' has very specific bodily connotations: it means physical arousal with another man while at the same time enjoying one's own physical arousal (*pliangarn het*), an experience at odds with the stereotyped *kathoey*–'full' man model. This recognition takes on a tremendously prosaic dimension. In Laos an ability to have an erection while desiring another man sexually is interpreted to mean the ability to get married and sire a family. Thus, in the social landscape I have been describing, many men, who do not feel themselves to be *kathoeys* because they become physically aroused with other men, also imagine they will take wives and raise a family as a means to long-term emotional connection. As gay becomes a subject choice, it is less bounded in emotional and physical terms than more traditional models of male–male sexuality and this is where human capital and its link to intimate economies become even more relevant. For, as cross-border and international movement means relations with men from other countries become more commonplace, and as media broaden local perceptions, so too notions of family and domestic love become more complex.

Under globalization, the fashioning of self offers new potential for intimate relations because one's human capital as a composite of all skill sets we carry (in this case, the ability to provide emotionally and materially for another) can be deployed in a larger set of engagements than previously. Speaking generally, in most Asian societies love between a man and woman is usually seen as complementary; whereas love between two men is considered less feasible in any long-term fashion. To have a wife and, even more so, to have children and raise a family, is perhaps the most powerful symbol of social reproduction. All other forms of domestic union are denied legitimacy and any form of social longevity. There is huge pressure for men to marry to achieve social maturity and become an acceptable member of society, to satisfy one's parents' wishes and to have children that might assist in domestic security when one is old. In Laos, love between men is not seen as a domestic alternative, but rather as intrinsically competitive rather than complementary and fraught with tensions over who might be the leader of the 'family'. In other words, it is seldom imagined possible that two men share life together as a couple in an ongoing emotional and practical sense. In addition, due to the elevated lust that is taken to generate homoerotic desire, monogamy is never deemed possible. Thus, short-term relationships have been regarded as the only viable means to enjoy male–male sex.

But, this is changing precisely as forms of modernity usher in a greater array of identity choices; and the opportunities for fashioning one's life become more diverse. Nowadays, men who desire other men in Laos are able to imagine longer-term relations with the object of their desires. The changes are reminiscent of Beck's argument, mentioned earlier, that as the traditional gives way to modernity so too processes of self-formation gain more autonomy, leading to his well-known formulation: we are in an era of self-designed biographies and do-it-yourself identities. Gay as a mode of social identification is gaining social visibility and increasing its constituency from both *phu bao* and *kathoey* for a number of reasons linked to changing subjective positions. As Suk indicated at the outset as s/he is about to go to Phuket, there is indeed a 'creative' air to this: a poiesis of the erotic as men fashion new subjective possibilities. While the social order has by no means relinquished its talon-like hold on the trappings of identity options available for Lao *kathoeys*, the landscape is broadening. *Kathoeys* who enjoy erections and reciprocal sex now have the option of thinking of themselves as gay rather than having to suppress this arousal. There is a perception that Western men prefer gay rather than *kathoey* partners because of reciprocal sexual roles, and a growing recognition that long-term gay relations are possible that are more materially secure and emotionally satisfying than short-term relations with 'full' men. Straight men who never thought they might be *kathoey* now wonder if they are gay because they enjoy emotional support and sex with other men. There is a growing sense that male–male relations are possible without overt femininity and that being gay also does not exclude the possibility of marriage. In short, options are far less closeted than in the recent past.

Our argument is that creative management of bodies and emotions becomes obvious in the increasingly diverse styles of male–male eroticism in Laos, as sexuality and desire and money circulate. This then offers another dimension to the arguments that human capital is the driving mechanism in the ways neoliberal sensibilities smuggle the market into emotional interactions. Indeed, the increased commodification in everyday life is providing no shortage of concerns over what it means for our personal engagements. Hochschild, for example, in her *Commercialisation of Intimate Life* flags "the emotional dangers of global consumer capitalism for our experiences of identity, gender, sexuality and family life" as she warns of a deteriorating fabric of private life through unbridled narcissism (quoted in Elliot and Lemert, 2009: 45). My interest here is not to declaim the loss of some idealized and preferred past, nor do the people of whom I write. Refusal to be cowed by social prejudice is plaintively echoed in the refrain of a well-known Thai song: "What you notice these days is a *kathoey*'s tears, But please don't think that *kathoeys* will perish. What you notice these days is *kathoey*'s tears. Do not think that *kathoeys* will cease to breathe." Understanding how individuals continue to breathe is to recognize the resilient energy in processes of self-fashioning as constrained as these may be. From the point of view of embodied implications, there is no doubt that clear apprehension of demographic trends, shifting identities and changing modalities of pleasure and material exchange are crucial for health programmes wishing to assist with optimal mechanisms to ensure modes of self-fashioning include self-protection, especially given these men in Laos are now seen as the key driver of an expanding HIV epidemic for many of the reasons we have been examining. But rather than discuss concrete facets of male sex and disease spread – this has been done elsewhere in detailed fashion – I wish here to take the discussion in a different direction, by linking the multiple types of exchange I have been describing in male relationships in Laos to a broader consideration of capital and sexuality and health. To do this we return to the Thai–Malay border I discussed earlier.

Commercial intimacy: migrant capital south of the border

There is a growing clamour in popular presses that sense of self in a globalized world is increasingly 'isolated, adrift, anxious and empty', collectively distancing attitudes to love and sex in "today's high-risk relationships market" (ibid: 45). In the final section of this chapter I wish to bring our attention back to relationships, markets and risk but in a way that focuses us on self-making processes evident in the entrepreneurialism and aspirations inspired by modern-day mobility. The above discussion emphasized that sexuality, and its role in a sense of self, is pliable and that this pliability is anything but idiosyncratic. Instead, it is best understood as a combination of deeply interiorized affects and strongly politicized discourses that are together embedded in modernizing social formations and their particular affective practices. In other words, everyday pursuit of wants and needs meld subjective desires with material choices – thus inescapably poetic in the Desjarlais or even ancient Greek sense. This is true for men finding intimacy in Laos, just as it is true elsewhere. The lives of Dai women who move back and forth to southern Thailand add further nuances to the seemingly mundane manner in which sexuality and aspirations coincide.

If one of contemporary capitalism's characteristics is the "diversity through which women and men of varied class niches and racial, ethnic, national, sexual and religious positions negotiate power and inequality" (Tsing, 2009: 152) then women from one particular border county in southwest China concretely exemplify this complexity and its complicated negotiations. Just as Suk and Phe in the dusty Vientiane street reflected on changing options and opportunities, so too Yan, a 34-year-old Dai woman in her home village close to the border with Myanmar, describes evolving dynamics of exploitation and exploration in her pursuit of capital.

> Yan's daughter was four months old when her Han Chinese husband left her; Yan was 18. Her mother persuaded her to go to Thailand in 1997 when she was 22, citing other Dai women making substantial amounts of money. An agent arranged for her to be taken to a massage shop in Central Thailand. She was unable to repay the compounding debt and was too scared to leave. After many months of sexual servitude, she called her mother who organized relatives working in Bangkok to assist. They asked owners of another massage shop to cover her debt and Yan relocated to Bangkok. Here she had a series of Chinese/Malaysian boyfriends and after two months she repaid her new employers with money made as temporary girlfriend to this core group of clients.
>
> Yan returned occasionally to make merit at the temple, renovate her parents' home and began to buy land in her village. In 2002, in Bangkok, she became mistress to a Singapore man and travelled to many Asian countries

Figure 5.4 Dai Water Festival brings many migrant women home

as his companion. She had a son in order to consolidate the relationship but the reverse happened. He ensconced her in an apartment in Singapore and took another mistress. She returned home. He occasionally sent substantial amounts of money so she could begin a business venture in her village. Nowadays he no longer visits.

Yan is well-known locally as an enterprising woman. Her highly visible investments have prompted many others to go to Thailand and she cautiously assists some in this endeavour. Nowadays, across the county, remittances from migrant women allow their husbands more latitude in their own endeavours and many end up relying extensively on their wives as a source of support. Yan is not kind in her summary of local men: "They are lazy, they like the money." Yan for her part recently returned to Thailand: "I only have a few years left to make money – I am getting too old to have much market value." Thus, just as male lovers in Laos feel that strictures of age strongly determine intimate opportunities and channels of capital, how migrant Dai women fashion life also entails thinking through what knowledges and what bodily practices allow affect to be exchanged for wealth.

Sigley tell us that "the emerging global order demands that China embraces global capital and develop strategies for producing docile labourers on the one hand and entrepreneurial citizens on the other" (2006: 500). Dai women, just like

Yan, embody these contemporary tensions. Their transnational mobility poses instructive differences in the self-making required to adjust to these demands. Both similar and different to other ethnic zones in borderland GMS, this one county bordering Myanmar is the site of the contagious formulation of a very specific 'entrepreneurial self'. Here a distinctive mode of transnational intimate commerce takes shape as neoliberal expansion with its emphasis on human capital builds locally on changing cultural and economic formations. But at the same time, in an important counterpoint to market freedom, stereotyped assumptions concerning 'ethnic' sexuality and its link to disease spread have generated localized and abrasive forms of surveillance and control of this movement. These Dai women come from a small rural county and, as mentioned, move in large numbers to seek work in massage parlours near the Thai–Malaysia border. Many are married, leaving husbands and families at home. The growing exodus emerges directly from desire to access the concrete fruits of modernization becoming evident throughout China. Some return with money from men they befriend to build large houses, others provide ongoing support to husbands, parents and children, still others never quite realize their dreams of material wealth. They do not consider themselves to be prostitutes, even as sexual relations are commonly part of their work, and carefully distinguish themselves from Lao, Burmese, Han Chinese and Thai sex workers in these tourist zones. Instead they profess to offer a different sort of market appeal based on their ability to be a mature companion in broader social settings. They, so they say, engage in commercial intimacy rather than commercial sex and suggest their emotional and cultural appeal is based on the fact they are not (as) young and that they have already married. Significantly, these distinctions highlight how self-proclaimed capabilities can be deployed as a highly flexible resource. Even this remote area in Chinese borderlands shows certain characteristics of a globalized neoliberal ethos and its potential to transform "citizens into self-governing subjects whose human capital becomes a passport toward realizing individual freedom in diverse transnational realms" (Ong, 2006: 231).

Going extraterritorial and extramarital

Enduring cultural and linguistic affinity with Tai populations south of the border gives migrant work particular appeal to Dai women from this county. For example, Pak has worked in a Hat Yai massage shop for more than four years, which she describes as "like not leaving home – one meets so many Dai". Whereas Hat Yai is famous as a site of cross-border relations and has over the past decade or so been the site of massage parlour employment for many Dai women, an increasing number nowadays work at the small border crossing of Dan Nork (about an hour outside of Hat Yai), where the atmosphere is more freewheeling and the possibilities and risks more volatile.

> Pak returns to her home county each year during rice-planting season for one or two months. In Hat Yai, she earns an average of 15,000 baht a month

(US$500) and her husband is happy that she support him and their child. In the massage shop, there are about 70 women, roughly 50 of them come from her county, and a few from other Chinese counties – only three or four have not yet married. She notes that there are even more women from her county at Dan Nork. They either send money home to their husband or have separated and aim to find a Malaysian partner/husband. Even some who are married look for a long-term Malaysian boyfriend or 'husband'. If they manage this they will stop working and return home and host occasional visits from the new partner or alternatively spend time with him in Hat Yai and Malaysia.

The presence of so many women from this one county in these worksites builds on networks established over the past 20 years when it was difficult to move within China and, although dangerous, travel through Myanmar was a practical and lucrative choice. Now, many local Dai women choose this route rather than arduous work in local fields or service industries in urban China. As Chinese travel restrictions eased in 2002 making cross-border travel legal, female migrant labour increased notably. We conducted a survey in 2010 in 27 Dai villages with a total population of 10,436, representing 40.8 per cent of ethnic Dai in this county. Overall, one-third (912) of a total of 2,738 women between the ages of 15 and 49 had worked in Thailand. In some villages, this includes more than half of reproductive-aged women. While social and mobility patterns continue to evolve, Dai women in this county typically marry at an early age soon after school and consider migrating after that. Dai men for their part seldom move either internally or across borders. Notably, Dai women from other counties do not migrate in anywhere near the prevalence found in this county. The reasons for this are based on the ways networks have evolved and specific values, geared to place and work, have become entrenched within local economies.

In part, choosing Thailand rather than internal migration within China is a product of social prejudice where, alongside other rural migrants, ethnic minorities are deemed to have low education and social quality (Chinese: *suzhi*) facing discrimination and disdain when seeking work in urban enclaves (Loong-Yu and Shan, 2007). One woman, who had left an unhappy marriage, explained that Thailand is preferable because "no one can track you down". In similar vein, local Dai carefully avoid mention of sexual commerce. This is considered a sensitive topic as many migrant women are married, their husbands left at home to tend fields, livestock and children. Men repeatedly told us they never ask their wives what they do while away. But while this ostensible silence might preclude public discussion, assumed multiple partners is an accepted facet of life in this county. Growing numbers of women who migrate confirm that there is little overt stigma within Dai communities for these practices in large part due to visible economic success, but there is no doubt people notice. The same cannot be said for inter-ethnic prejudice as many Han Chinese label Dai women as 'promiscuous' and inevitably 'diseased' due to their independence. As mentioned, despite outside perceptions, most women who work in massage parlours do not consider themselves as sex workers. Instead, in seeking to establish long-term relations with Malaysian or

Singaporean clients, Dai women regard themselves as demonstrating a particular example of self-enterprise based on competitive human capital. That is, they feel they can offer something for exchange that others cannot.

While Ong regards Chinese neoliberalism as inducing a self-enterprising subjectivity primarily to 'elite subjects' and not available to uneducated rural masses, at the same time she notes, "the promiscuous entanglements of global and local logics crystallise different conditions of possibility" for different groups (Ong, 2007: 5). When we consider the narratives of Pak and Yan and their many compatriots we see that even in remote parts of the GMS, a propensity to dream, plan and mobilize around a future different from the everyday, at levels simultaneously more immediate, far-reaching and pervasive than in previous times, is an irreducible aspect of the proliferation of neoliberal sensibilities. It would be overstepping the mark to describe scenarios where women use their bodies as a means to capital accumulation as innocuous neoliberal 'freedoms', but it remains undeniable that under Chinese and regional market reforms Dai women are finding greater room for creative fashioning of self, and furthermore that the entrepreneurialism in evidence is, just as in the backstreet dorms of Laos, heavily sexualized.

Underlying my arguments in preceding chapters is the suggestion that privatizing and internalizing a combined sense of freedom and risk is central to trajectories of modernization. In China, even as individuals are encouraged to take on new livelihoods – a corollary of the Great Western Development regime that energized much of Southwest China (Nyíri, 2006) – the essence of 'open up' (Chinese: *kaifang*) poses an inherent ambiguity as it takes on embodied physical and emotional characteristics. The conduct of individuals and their proliferating desires becomes the focus of state surveillance based on an ongoing concern with maintaining and policing bounds. In the frontier areas I have been describing, this anxiety is fixed around notions of cross-border contagion. As a case in point, based on stereotyped notions of gender and ethnicity, local authorities assume that Dai women are not able to self-monitor their status as suitable citizens adequately. And yet in the paradoxical ways capital finds new forms, it is alternative readings of ethnicity and gender that are most readily used by the Dai women in the border massage shops to derive a new life and livelihood.

Massaging the intimate encounter

In much of the GMS, where networks of social and cultural identity interpenetrate across borders, social and linguistic affinity is close within most Tai-speaking groups. Historically Dai (Tai Lue) peoples have been able to assimilate alongside mainstream Lao and Thai populations virtually at will throughout the Upper Mekong borderlands. In contrast, Dai identity in China is heavily characterized by exotic and eroticized otherness. In tourist sites in Yunnan (and beyond), one encounters pictures in restaurants and postcards of Dai women posing semi-naked in 'traditional' attire. An eroticized Dai femininity has become an increasingly marketable commodity and a further economy of alterity. This has led to a curious subterfuge in Xishuanbanna where migrant Han sex workers dress as Dai to

Figure 5.5 Posters of Dai women can be seen in many Chinese restaurants

capitalize on Han men's erotic fantasies (Hyde, 2007). In the border county I am describing the tourist market is still small, prompting female mobility rather than local investment; but in so doing Dai women also harness a sexualized imaginary. Responding to changing articulations of enterprise and value, what began as people trafficking is becoming voluntaristic ambition as Dai women from this county utilize intimacy as part of off-shore work relations. Just as male tourists seek out ersatz Dai women, migrant Dai travel to the Thai–Malay border to become magnets for men seeking tall, pale-skinned, Chinese speaking 'sensual' companions. In this instance, they become ethnic *flâneurs* rather than ethnic 'frauds'. They utilize cultural capital mobilized as part of an expanded affective economy to establish relations with foreign men.

Sometimes the money they have earned allows them a degree of economic diversification (running small hotels, building hostels). Bao went to Hat Yai five years ago and tells a complex story of emotional entanglement.

> Almost all women have left to Thailand in our community, only those over 40 stay at home ... I worked in a massage shop but because I didn't sell sex I didn't earn much money and after two months I decided to return home. I met my current 'husband' just before I left. He is a 56-year-old Malaysian man with a factory and a family in Singapore. He also had another woman in Malaysia. He supported this mistress and her two kids but she betrayed him, having affair with a young man. In order to abandon him completely, this woman paid for bewitching him. When I met him, he was exhausted and sick. He came to our shop saying he was tired. He asked me to massage his head and he slept for four hours. He gave me a 5,000 yuan tip. He said that he was going to die and would never come back to Thailand so asked me to keep the money and also requested my phone number in China. After returning home, he called me in China almost daily, sometimes at midnight. He could not sleep well because he was bewitched. Both his health and business were depressed. He told me repeatedly he was going to die, so I asked him to send me his clothes and some money, and I found someone to release the spell. He gradually got better. He thought I saved his life. He wanted to help me, opening a karaoke shop in Dan Nork for me. I did not accept his gift at first, but one of my friends persuaded me. He never asked me for sex but, later on, I thought he treated me so well and I should give him something. So I slept with him. Later, he helped me to build bungalows for rent. I know he won't support me forever but at least I can get money for living from renting these rooms.

Other women who have yet to find long-term partners feel their aspirations are best served by sustained periods in Thailand punctuated by short-term returns. Village temples overflow with ornate prayer flags embroidered by women during idle hours in off-shore sites and proffered alongside monetary donations when they return to make merit during New Year festivals. There are, of course, multiple affective dimensions to these forms of life, including satisfactions and regrets as Quan describes:

I got married when I was 17. We worked hard for few yuan a day. I saw many women go to Thailand. My husband wouldn't let me go, so I left secretly with my friend and when I called home he said: "I did not agree with you but you still left. In this case, you must come back with money." I chose Thailand because I am illiterate. I don't know where I can find a job in China, but I heard I can do massage in Hat Yai with no need to write. Massage doesn't make much money, but some clients gradually become frequent visitors and ask you out. After six months, I met two men who are willing to take care of me. They send me allowance every month, and visit me in Thailand occasionally. Sometimes, if I am home, they might call me to go back Thailand for their visit. Actually, I prefer to live away from China. Life here is totally different from Thailand. After I left, my relationship with my husband became cold. We assume each other has new lovers. At first, I regretted leaving but now my family is getting better and better because of me. Villagers call me 'landlady' (Chinese: *laobanniang*) because of my new house and we also bought a car.

Underpinning these narratives is the manner through which liberalizing economic structures permit development of an 'enterprising subject' in the midst of complex ethnic and gendered tensions. Encouraged entrepreneurialism and the prevalent desire for development together generate contagious appeal for forays south of the border. Throughout the county, Dai women share navigation points built by a growing network of family or village associates with experience in Thailand who provide a checklist of information on finding work, organizing transport, transferring money, handling clients or escaping oppressive work environments. Likewise, as numbers of migrants increase in every village, the prominent concrete and glass houses clumsily overshadowing older more gracefully arched wood abodes have become an acknowledged spur to competitive accumulation. Collectively, migrant women now become exemplary development agents, in the sense they migrate and remit substantial resources allowing the material development of the community. But if we turn to them as remitters of values we discern a more complex package. In some respects, the values of independence and enterprise are indeed nurtured. But subservience, family disruption and proximity to disease are awkward bedfellows. In such cases, affective labour (the commercialization of intimacy) and the capitalization of self is central to their evolving engagement in a money economy.

I mentioned earlier that a defining feature of spreading neoliberalism is the "rise of human capital as a dominant subjective form" (Feher, 2009: 24) and the now seamless merging of the intimate realm with that of the market. The Dai women heading for Thailand demonstrate par excellence these conflated dimensions as they become 'entrepreneurs of themselves'. Utilizing a wide set of skills well beyond menial massage they appreciate, in the sense of increase, their value as both breadwinners and autonomous subjects. They set themselves apart from other women catering to Chinese/Malaysian tourists in Hat Yai or Dan Nork through a set of nested capabilities noting that they are not prostitutes like the younger Han

Chinese, Thai or Lao women but instead deliver (sexual) companionship premised on marital maturity and intimate solicitude. They do not compete via modalities of youthful sexuality, but rather what gives Dai women a market edge is their ability to create long-term emotional relationships with men who are looking for substitute or second wives, using language and social skills as well as aesthetic appeal. The evidence of their success in these endeavours is the large numbers of Dai women from this county that do in fact gain significant material support from 'second' husbands.

In the West, a new acronym has been coined for this type of sentimental cum commercial appeal. Clients of sex workers often seek more than physical gratification and desire emotional intimacy and companionship, "a brief but meaningful human connection", to such an extent that escort services now market the provision of 'the girlfriend experience (GFE)' (Weitzer, 2009: 227). While economic diversification can create a niche out of a stunning array of service provisions, there is no doubt Dai women are market leaders in the GFE in the border areas of the GMS. In so doing, they employ age, ethnicity and gender as dimensions of human capital to be appreciated and self-appreciated. Importantly, managing self-value is at heart always speculative. Accordingly, Dai women use their 'selves' to strategically gamble at bettering their everyday lives, through money, through freedom, through comparative improvement of their minority status. Most of all, in demonstrating the ability to showcase wealth, they are able to achieve a foothold on the ladder of social mobility in China as they claim the "legitimacy of the aspiration to appreciate or to value oneself" (Feher, 2009: 40). Many now have the enviable ability to assert themselves as successful, laying claim to demonstrable progress towards the 'good life' as the normative value in contemporary times. Juan describes this competitive and prosaic self-enterprise further:

> Everyone has their own reason to go to Thailand. We do not go to sell our bodies but work hard in proper massage shops. We are not flirtatious women. Other [Han Chinese] women moved here before us. They are shameless and do anything for money. Even though men dislike them, they stick like limpets. Some of us get wealthy not because of sex but because 'kind men' [Chinese: *haoxinren*] help us. We meet them in the massage shop and become friends if it feels right …When I lived with Mr Li, he did not ask for sex. He said if he wants sex, he would call a sex worker. Instead, he said, being with me was destiny.

Likewise Lin notes:

> In Hat Yai, there are many brothels [Chinese: *jidian*]. In the past, some Dai women were trafficked and worked in these places until they repaid their debt, but now no local women do this – only women from Myanmar, Thailand, Laos and Han Chinese. In Hat Yai most Dai women are married – they know how to take care of men. The men do not like young girls who are 18 or 19. They also don't like flirts. The clients take us out not just for sex but also

dinner with friends. We always dress properly. If your dress was too sexy their friends would think you are a '*ji*' [sex worker]. The clients say we look like their girlfriend or wife.

Importantly, these explanations show that aspirations flourish in transformation of adversity. With its booming economy, Thailand was regarded as a highly fantasized site of employment in the latter part of the twentieth century. But due to the need to pay an agent to assist with dreams to travel south of the border, a number of women from this county ended up trafficked to Thai brothels in the 1980s and early 1990s; in Feingold's words "migration gone wrong". The stories of those returning were, in fact, not a deterrent, but rather the money they eventually made and displayed prompted more to go. Over time, sustained mobility has resulted in stronger support networks and more flexible work choices. Since the late 1990s, trafficking cases from this county – increasingly policed and prosecuted – have mostly been replaced by deliberate movement into sex work (Peters, 2002; Beesey, 2001). What were once harrowing tales of deprivation and subjugation south of the border have been refigured as compelling narratives of personal gain. Indeed, some women feel they benefit at many levels. Men from Malaysia and Singapore seek out Dai women as second wives for the reasons indicated above, even as the Dai women seek them out as second husbands based on ongoing support. Yan told us: "I never felt like a woman until I went to work in Thailand and met wealthy men: now I know what it is like to be offered levels of emotional and material exchange I had never felt before." But it is important to note that even as strategies are individualized and privatized, the lines between (self-) exploitation and opportunism are blurred as operating parameters of regulated production become internalized and actors replicate structures of dominance. In fact, this is where the capacity to aspire runs into the insidious reality that exploitation is hard to defuse even when it is configured in more creative fashion. So too, as this local pattern becomes ever more embedded in local expectations as a fertile income stream, trajectories continue to evolve. More and more unmarried women are going to Hat Yai and mainly Dan Nork. Sometimes mothers take daughters – some as young as 14 – in the hope off-shore work will furnish a secure future.

   Thus, one can argue that even as human capital – incorporating a variable compilation of skillsets and capabilities – becomes the tool to advancement, for Dai women gender subordination (marketing male satisfaction) remains a key structuring element in how aspirations are achieved through idealized fantasies of male support. The irrevocable duality of development processes can be seen as the 'experimentations with freedom' and implicit poiesis within self-making processes south of the border together produce ambiguous outcomes as human experience is now subject to 'appreciation' that includes both gendered subservience and female independence. We also see conflicting outcomes in the fractures that emerge in families back home. The fact that a majority of migrants are married, and that this is used as market advantage with men looking for long-term companions, significantly distinguishes these networks from most other sex-related migration in Southeast Asia wherein women tend to be single or

Figure 5.6 Offshore money: village renovations in southwest Yunnan

separated. However, experiments with marital independence and increased intimacy with transnational partners do not sit seamlessly within domestic relations. Female migration is simultaneously an extension of female entrepreneurialism, long regarded as a hallmark of Dai women (LeBar, 1964), and a departure from traditional family arrangements wherein the wife is now absent for long periods. While some women are divorced prior to leaving, others emphasize domestic strife as both a precursor to departure and an ongoing element to relations back home. Left-behind husbands begin affairs of their own, often with sex workers, and often using money from their wives in Thailand. These circuits raise complicated questions about HIV risk and vectors of transmission (Deng and Lyttleton, 2013). Indeed, enforced testing has shown that Dai migrant women have significant levels of HIV – roughly 2 per cent – but it is unclear whether infection occurs when away from home or during their intermittent returns. Either way, we cannot portray these sojourns in Thailand as devoid of physical and emotional hardship. Quite the reverse. Likewise, it is immediately apparent that, following typical gender prejudices, Dai women bear the brunt of designated disease control and not-so-subtle ethnic stigma. Little epidemiological attention has focused on male behaviour as a risk factor. But increased surveillance from state authorities has at times heavy-handedly denied Dai women over the age of 18 access to travel papers for a period of several years (which had the adverse effect of motivating many women to leave before they reach this age) and pointedly targeted them as 'returnees' in need of enforced epidemiological surveillance (ibid).

Conclusion

Rofel (2007: 3) has shown how neoliberal techniques of the self in China build on liberation of the desiring subject who is increasingly free to pursue "sexual, material and affective self-interest". As Dai women cross borders with the hope of meeting the 'right' man in the hyper-sexualized markets of the southern Thai borderlands, rather than freedom per se it is more accurately an expanding 'capacity to aspire' that fuels willingness to utilize intimate human capital as the bargaining chip in a world of loosening bounds. But, even as aspirations incite this movement, so too regulations concerned with proliferating contagion seek new modes of intervention. At a local level, Dai women's movement to Thailand refashions various social structures from agricultural modes of production and wage labour through to kinship modalities and hierarchies of family support. Women transform prior modes of 'victim-based' sex trafficking into entrepreneurial agency. But in their capacity to provoke both fear and desire of what lies across boundaries, Dai migrants also reflect how "tensions between local and global rules, structures and processes governing ethnicity and sexuality have heightened as the speed of globalisation has increased" (Nagel, 2006: 546). Across the GMS, mobile female bodies are considered 'unruly' in numerous ways, while at the same time, they are encouraged to partake in numerous practices of value speculation. China's White Paper on National Minorities Policy states that ethnic minorities are encouraged to adopt "new, scientific, civilized and healthy customs in daily life" (quoted in Nyíri, 2006). But the actual manifestation of their choices continues to provoke anxiety. Within the affective economies prompted by consumer desires, and the role of intimacy in achieving these, just as in our earlier descriptions of fear of migrants at other border zones, anxiety proliferates that Dai women are causal vectors of disease. If one is a 'returnee', even a common cold is enough to generate accusations of HIV infection.

Meantime in Laos, entrepreneurialism evolves as men pursue their own material aspirations and experiences through intimate relations. There is no doubt the heightened mobility and sexual plasticity is part of a global shift in changing subjective connections to the world around us. A broader market horizon also has emotional and social implications at a profoundly embodied level. In Laos, having many partners is seen as an internal benchmark within the social world of *kathoeys* and gay men. In circumstances where social status is denied on most fronts, criteria for self-worth are recalibrated within forms of male–male sociality.

Similar to the Dai women, one might flag a reconfiguration of oppressive forces into celebrated modes of accumulation. Here *kathoeys* notice, comment and keep tabs on how many partners they and their peers have. This becomes a means by which achievement is measured: it becomes the accumulated value that is seen as more significant than the money expended. It reinforces a particular form of social status, sexualized and to some extent stigmatized, but flexible and self-affirming nonetheless. Moreover, like nearly all our examples, there remain contradictory dimensions to the self-employment of human capital in an expanding market. This confronts us with the embodied ambiguity of development trajectories in unavoidable detail. And, as in the case of the Dai women, outside forces muster regulatory impulses to curtail the threats of intimate entrepreneurialism. Scrutiny on the potential of male–male sex to be a disease threat is gathering speed in Laos and, given the increased public profile and the fact that many of these men also have female partners, is generating growing anxiety.

For the individuals themselves, adventurism and aspiration muddy the inclination to be cautious. In both the above settings, as one becomes an entrepreneur of the self, sexual safety is manipulated. There is enough diversity and lack of certainty about intimate relationships that gives individuals a huge range of possibilities to avoid thinking about HIV protection and to not consistently use condoms. It takes place in the interconnected ways in which capital accumulation and exchange is not simply monetary, but social and emotional. It is abetted by the fact that intimacy is always itself vulnerable. In Hat Yai and Dan Nork, Dai women seldom use condoms with regular boyfriends, as one woman told us:

> After cohabitating with my 'current husband', we gave up using condoms. I don't know how many women he slept with in the past, but I believe now he only has me and his wife. I also believe he is a good person since he helped me a lot. I should trust him. Condoms are weird.

Meanwhile, back home she will seldom use condoms with her husband who in turn frequents sex workers in her absence. Her example is repeated by hundreds, perhaps thousands, of other Dai women who make the trip south of the border in the interests of new relationships. In Laos, similarly aspiring to many partners affirms a different sort of entrepreneurial identity, not as a means of Western civil advocacy based on minority group difference, but as having something valuable to offer to 'straight' partners: solicitude, money and sexual experimentation. In both cases, possession is the key trope of intimate engagement; possession in both a physical and emotional sense and that this is a contemporary value to be appreciated within the affective economies of pleasure and exchange. But at the same time, what is exchanged, including bodily essences, in these contingent interactions is crucial to the ways sexual health becomes compromised. Understanding these currents is central to apprehending the optimal mechanisms to reconfigure modes of self-fashioning into self-protection.

The potent mix of capitalism and (sexual and/or ethnic) minorities both labelled as 'promiscuous' highlights an ongoing paradox of contemporary life

Figure 5.7 Merit flags made in Thai massage shops float in local temples in Dai villages

in the GMS. Locals are encouraged to take on new livelihoods, and many deploy forms of human capital that are emotional and sexual, which, put another way, simply shows us that intimate economies foreshadow much of what current developments in the GMS aim to achieve. But at the same time, such pursuits are

regularly portrayed as problematic to the state body precisely because they conjure images of perilous disease invasion. This, in turn, crystallizes the inherent
dilemma in so much of health preventive work: how to both ration and rationalize desire in environments where aspirations are the emphatic lifeblood of global
consumer culture and (self-) negotiating risk is a defining parameter of entrepreneurial freedom.

6 First do no harm

Threat is as ubiquitous as the wind, and its source as imperceptible. It just shows up. It breaks out. It irrupts without warning, coming from any direction, following any path through the complex and increasingly interconnected world.

(Massumi, 2011: 23)

Plague metaphors dominate our times. More than 20 years after initial panics of pandemic spread riveted Thailand and the world, the title of a recent expose in a Thai newspaper remains luridly on song, 'HIV scourge spreads from red lights to white collars'. It refers to a Centers for Disease Control report warning "that the spread of the virus in Bangkok has become an 'explosive epidemic' and that an increasing number of sufferers are not sex workers, but ordinary people whose lifestyles expose them to risk" (*Bangkok Post*, 7 July 2013). In the cited report, the lifestyles belong to men who have multiple male partners, many of whom have, quite possibly, moved to Bangkok from other regions of the country. Lifestyles have been the focus of our preceding chapters, collectively demonstrating that underlying vulnerabilities for infectious health threats such as HIV are not located only in urban settings. Lifestyles, in our instances, are also shaped by space, by mobility and most of all by new economic formations with an expanded range of social relations, many of which, like the men in Bangkok, inculcate forms of intimacy. Taken together, they highlight that mobility, health and sexuality intersect in crucial but complex ways as development and modernization structure vulnerability.

It is not simply a question of representation that concerns me here, although there is much about marginalization, minorities, disease and stigma that relies on discursive entrapment. It is also about the skein of connections in our hyper-capitalized world and how social constellations and risk are part of a broader approach to global health. New approaches suggest we should imagine disease spread from a 'syndemics' perspective, which argues that disease is always rela-tional and "sustained by social inequality and the unjust exercise of power, which channels and sustains damaging disease clusters in disadvantaged populations" (Herring and Swedlund, 2010: 5). An emphasis on connections also flags the ways in which people actually think and feel in states of ill-health and mobilize to ward off such threats. Here we return to Spinoza once again and his evocation of the need to address emotional connection as the core to the capacity to act. He was specific that this was most fulsome when born of shared affect in which 'joy' served as the impetus and affirmation of effective action. This takes us to the importance of affective economies that structure the ways emotions circulate and direct behaviour in the new economic and social landscapes of the GMS. The potency of emotional appeal as a means to influence behaviour is a fact long known to marketing wizards who seek to optimize sales through visceral appeals to pleasure; so too to health promotion advocates who suggest that positive public service messages deliver more impact in the long term than short-term negative and fear-based emotional assaults. But if, in turn, we focus attention on the ways affect interacts with disease(s) vulnerability from a syndemics point of view that emphasizes connections within the surrounding bio-social environment, it also moves us into the more difficult terrain of risk profiling and assessment.

My arguments, thus far, link health, mobility and sexuality through a number of propositions that all, sooner or later, direct us to issues of risk and, thereby, given our discussion of programmed assistance, rubrics of responsibility. First, material and immaterial economies belong together in analysis of social transformations. This is because affects move. As we have seen, circulating sentiments run the gamut of inclusionary desires and aspirations through to exclusionary expressions of prejudice and hatred. In this respect, shared hopes and yearning for a better life prompted by development and modernization programmes jostle uncomfortably alongside collective fear and distrust of mobile populations, minority peoples or new social engagements. Second, we can identify emotional substrates emerging alongside infrastructure and demographic changes taking place across the GMS. Importantly, it is the complex interplay of these emotions that, on the one hand, fuels the constant willingness to engage in experimentations with new opportunities, and, on the other hand, promotes opportunistic exploitation and sometimes vicious reactionary responses, all of which are fostered by manoeuvres to promote 'connectedness, competition and community'. Third, as self-making processes are ever more stimulated by global trends and neoliberal sensibilities, the often indeterminate ways that affective practices permeate the everyday are central to new social formations required by expanding capital. As such, they create forms of sociality and embodied experience that rely on the intimate. Fourth, if affect lies at the core of modernity's push for more attachments and connections to things and people, then at the same time, intimacy's very instability defies ready-made prescriptions of order and control, largely because of its association with the ephemeral and the unseen. Hence, even as affective labour is elevated within many entrepreneurial endeavours, emergent emotional dissonance raises an uneasy presentiment of risk and uncertainty. There is always an evocative and discursive power implicit in these connections: "By extension, *inter*personal relations – above all, sexuality, from the peccadillos of presidents to the global spectre of AIDS – come to stand, metonymically, for the inchoate forces that threaten the world as we know it" (Comaroff and Comaroff, 2001: 15). There is also a distinctly embodied impact for us to consider as illness and disease spread between people and groups at least in part because of the conduits and fractures created by affective connections and collisions.

Finally, therefore, we see that attempts to confine the potency of intimacy and stabilize its charge become targeted on specific bodies. Controls occur at a number of levels ranging from policy and institutional practice through to social discrimination and individual stigma. The logic of applied surveillance often centres on the assumption that entrepreneurialism among certain groups cannot be trusted; freedom for experimentation becomes the worrying licence to transgress, in particular among those who are considered as not adequately socialized to the demands of appropriate citizenry or nationalist belonging. Attention is drawn to these individuals through a prominent rubric of health wherein being mobile and/ or from a minority group are key triggers to the assumption that this combination equals disease. I mentioned that the Chinese state attempts to constrain the bodies of Dai women who head south precisely because they are considered unable to control their sexuality. These are the women who are tested for HIV, not the numerous other mobile peoples in the county nor their husbands. I described how social stereotypes pigeonhole *kathoeys* in Laos into tightly bound and delimited roles of prescriptive sexuality that maintain a public and therefore (supposedly) manageable identity. Transgenders are targeted in HIV policies as a sub-category of high-risk MSM, but the complicated tropes of possession and exchange of semen allow a more insidious worry to percolate – that their harder-to-identify 'straight' partners are in fact the conduit of spread to a broader population. In frontier zones, mobile and ethnic women are the focus of public health campaigns based on assumptions that they are unable to appreciate the threat their sexuality represents even as public health authorities are prejudicial in their ministrations. Suggesting ethnic women should no longer wear 'exotic' traditional attire (as has occasionally happened) as a means to reduce sexual risk is, put kindly, misguided at best. Special zones orient themselves to exploiting itinerant workers in factories, casinos and red-light districts, but, at the same time, those that benefit most from their presence offer little in the way of social or health safeguards. 'Unruly' or ill individuals more typically suffer alone or get sent back home. Hence, alongside state public health manoeuvres, when development agencies bring mitigation activities into the equation as a means to dampen concerns over unwanted and out-of-control outcomes, the question becomes 'what precisely is their target?' and furthermore, what constitutes 'adequate ideas' that might pre-empt negative consequences in the first place for these diverse and disparate groups?

Confronting negative externalities

Preceding chapters have outlined how marginalization is central to tropes of affect and value even as effervescent hopes draw ever more people into circuits of mobility in the GMS. But, what I wish to also make clear is that the supposed amorphous threats that borderless bodies represent never go away. Even as exclusion or control is sought as a means of control, the very ethos of connectionism in the new economic structures is made concrete by the legal channels and physical thoroughfares that channel migrant flows. And yet, the potential for transgression exists at every turn. This is the very dilemma that affective economies generate. They do not rest within specific bodies; they circulate – so the rubrics of control are forever confronted by the recognition that regulations cannot ultimately control the mobile body, its capacity to host hopes and dreams and its evolving intimate practices, even as they try to do just this. Hence, development policymakers and programmers actively seek to make safeguards part and parcel of planning for change. For example, the ADB's mid-term review of the Strategic Framework of the GMS programme notes that:

> Further measures are required to minimize and mitigate the adverse impact of subregional economic integration. Indeed, costs and benefits are involved in subregional cooperation and integration, but the experience so far has demonstrated that the benefits of working together far outweigh the negative externalities. Nevertheless, pre-emptive measures are necessary to address the potential negative 'side effects' of subregional integration.
>
> (ADB, 2007: 12–13)

These 'side-effects' include a checklist of commonplace culprits that surface in areas of rapid social and economic change in many parts of the world: spread of HIV and AIDS and other communicable diseases; drug trafficking; illegal labour migration and the related issues of human trafficking and child labour, environmental degradation, increase in land prices and landlessness (ibid). And so on. While the report concludes that the list of negative externalities require more comprehensive mitigation, other embedded concerns are also raised. Poverty is considered a local and entrenched problem. Thus, the ADB review stresses that more emphasis on programmes that assist the poor, in particular ethnic minorities in remote areas, to take advantage of the new infrastructure developments is also necessary. "It will be important to continue to find ways of integrating the poor into the mainstream of economic development and prevent them from being 'crowded out' in this process" (ibid). Here we reach the crux of our discussion. Obviously, it is important not to create new barriers or hierarchies that make poverty even more intractable. Few would disagree with this proposition. But here's the rub. What this distracts us from is an adequate consideration of the terms by which poor people are in fact *included* within new social and economic formations rather than being simply 'crowded out'. This is a fundamental and confronting shift in focus, for it requires that we face head-on the role that affective practices play alongside the structural channels that either afford or delimit opportunities. If we acknowledge that specific forms of emotional connection circulate within different social formations then we must also attend to the types of belonging they create, the specific styles of intimacy they engender and, most crucially for development planners, the conditional terms by which relationships are negotiated and experienced. It is this latter context where the rules of the game, the parameters of the 'good life' and the means to get it, are informed and controlled by global development processes. Berlant (2007: 278) summarizes the arch outcomes of 'political and affective economies of normativity' for the poor and bereft beautifully, "so many bad jobs contingently available to so many contingent workers and never enough money, never enough love, and barely any rest, with ruthless fantasy abounding". Choosing not to turn away from this image requires we think more closely about the role of mitigation and its ability to reframe the picture.

ADB has sought to address identified negative externalities in the region. For example, over the past decade it has implemented multi-million dollar programmes aiming to lessen the risks of people trafficking and HIV spread, in particular facing ethnic minorities and migrant populations. It has spearheaded the extension of a Memorandum of Understanding between GMS governments confirming a commitment to continue regional cooperation in the planning and implementation of HIV activities addressing migrant workforces and cross-border mobility. Through grants and loans to GMS countries, the ADB has sustained attention on marginal groups living in border areas where, as has been discussed, vulnerabilities emerge in diverse circumstances as new relations between mobile and non-mobile populations create opportunities for disease spread. I mention these to make the point that, in many respects, a focus on diverse and disparate groups such as these swims headfirst against a current trend in HIV programming. Throughout the region a dramatic shift back to risk-group targeting has seemingly swept aside the manoeuvres of preceding decades to take a broader approach to vulnerability than those defined solely by identity-based behaviours. This marks the (re)ascendancy of drug-oriented and medical rather than behavioural modes of intervention. In very simple terms, distinctions can be made between different levels of response to the presence of HIV and AIDS: biomedical modalities prioritize clinical interventions and drug treatments, public health methodologies tend to focus on proximate risk behaviours such as an individual's use/non-use of condoms or clean needles. For their part, development approaches, that have in the past characterized a large portion of HIV work globally, would consider social and structural triggers that prompt or preclude safe behaviours. Others have classified delivery mechanisms as points along a health system continuum, such that:

> High-road solutions typically address the disease and people as patients, focus on cure, treatment and pharmaceutical programmes, are noteworthy biomedical and technological, typically seen as 'hard' and top-down. Low-road solutions typically promote health and wellness among communities, focus on care, prevention and educational programmes, are often noteworthy rights-based and holistic, typically seen as 'soft' and bottom-up.
>
> (Vanwesenbeeck, 2011: 289)

HIV and AIDS work has shifted noticeably in recent years to the higher and harder end of this scale following an argument that donor money is best spent on high-impact initiatives such as anti-retroviral drug roll-out for both treatment and prevention targeting specific groups, while framing more general population disease control as something best managed through strengthening national and local level health systems. Inroads making affordable anti-retroviral drug treatment available to growing numbers of people with HIV around the world is a tangible and positive outcome and, while not without legal and politicized problems, a critical marker of success. It is within the arena of prevention that the ground remains murky.

The justification for shifts in targeting away from population-based prevention initiatives is simple, and in many instances, persuasive. Global and regional funding for HIV and AIDS has decreased noticeably in recent years, as have numbers of new infections in many parts of the world. Intent to refocus on key affected populations (KAPs) with measurably high levels of risk is easy to understand at a pragmatic level. A combination of donor fatigue and global financial ruptions have ensured that efficiency in use of financial resources is paramount and to be verified through numbers of people saved or treated. A summary of regional trends in Asia and the Pacific notes the need for customized responses in a context where "prevention resources are inadequately targeted towards key populations"; Southeast Asia, as a case in point, had only 20 per cent of funds allocated to high-impact prevention among key-affected populations, whereas "high-cost interventions with relatively low-impact in terms of number of HIV cases averted receive at least one third of HIV funding in Asia in general" (UNAIDS, 2011: 17). This line of thought builds on the influential Asian AIDS Commission report which noted bluntly that interventions focused on so-called 'MARPS' (an alternative acronym meaning most-at-risk populations) should form the core of HIV prevention programmes (Commission on AIDS in Asia, 2008: 103). Most countries in the region have followed this recommendation for a sharpened focus of project spending on the three main KAPs: men who have sex with men (MSM), people who inject drugs (PWID) and female sex workers (FSWs). This is a global trend. Indeed, there is no doubt a long-term and comprehensive focus is needed for these groups given their dynamic and changing nature – there is a constant movement of women across borders or from remote areas into commercial sex in towns and cities throughout the GMS; male–male sex practices are increasingly incorporating young men from rural areas who move into city environs for education or employment; people who inject drugs is an expanding group of prior opium users and a younger generation of urban substance users throughout the GMS. One might readily concede this is a defensible position from a budgeted programme point of view, but it also highlights a bigger and as yet unresolved question of how and what risks are focused on in seeking to lessen infectious health threats.

Refocusing risk

In this respect, it is largely overlooked that the AIDS Commission report also notes that challenges should not be oversimplified, given that neither behaviours nor intervention contexts occur in a vacuum. It follows that there is a danger in overemphasizing so-called 'most-at-risk' populations if we think of them as programmatically and behaviourally discrete 'communities' and ignoring broader social as opposed to identity-based drivers. For example, the Lao national AIDS

Plan (2011–15) notes the logic behind the shift to comprehensive KAPs-based programming:

> For some current target audiences for HIV prevention (e.g. ethnic groups, students, migrants), insufficient evidence of their vulnerability is available. Ethnic groups, young people and migrants are large populations, consisting of many subgroups, and targeting them all with comprehensive prevention services is not cost-effective.
>
> (NCCA, 2010: 9)

This position is common in other countries in the GMS where ethnicity and migration are mostly sidestepped as a prioritized focus of attention for HIV programmes, in particular those that might reach undocumented migrants (although mobile men with money are occasionally mentioned). In the absence of broader targeting, national prevention programmes are assumed to reach ethnic groups and migrants nonetheless: if minority or migrant women sell sex they will be reached by FSW programmes, if minority or migrant men use drugs they will be reached by PWID programmes. But a generic approach underplays the ways in which ethnicity, mobility and migration independently structure access to health services as well as myriad underlying risks – the very issues we have been covering in preceding chapters. This applies not only to HIV but broader reproductive health or other infectious disease. There also remains a convenient inconsistency. Insufficient evidence does not mean vulnerability does not exist; it simply means there is not yet enough information to decide and one can debate whether it should be the basis for assuming programmes are not needed.

A further issue haunts provision of health services in the economically and ethnically diverse GMS. Notwithstanding a few current interventions, difficulties in isolating and measuring risk for infectious disease spread associated with ethnicity and/or caused by migration is a major obstacle in generating sustained funding and long-term targeting. For example, HIV surveillance data is almost never disaggregated in terms of ethnicity, usually on the rationale that to do otherwise is tantamount to reproducing discriminatory stereotypes. Likewise, with the exception of some trucking routes in Africa, there is limited longitudinal epidemiological data linking migrants to higher risk of HIV infection than non-migrants. And yet, despite this, there is a growing body of qualitative data that suggests there are important connections. A summary review of academic literature on HIV and migration confirms that vulnerability is indeed generated in ways that conform to a fairly standard checklist of determinants including:

> prolonged and/or frequent absence, financial status, and difficult working and housing conditions ... cultural norms, family separation, and low social support ... substance use, other STIs, mental health problems, no HIV testing ... needle use, limited condom use, multiple partnering, clients of sex workers, and lack of HIV knowledge.
>
> (Weine and Kashuba, 2012: 1614)

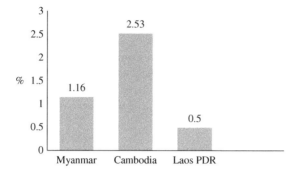

Figure 6.1 Percent of male and female migrant workers testing HIV positive in select Thai worksites in 2010 (adapted from Mendoza, 2013: 12)

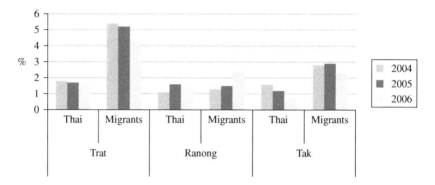

Figure 6.2 HIV prevalence among Thai and migrant pregnant women in select Thai border provinces (adapted from IOM, 2010: 29)

The important point is not our familiarity with these factors, but the fact they are ongoing at a global level. Deane et al (2010: 1458) also note that comparatively few studies demonstrate the relationship between HIV spread and migration in a systematic way, suggesting an equally familiar directive: "Future research on mobility and HIV transmission must incorporate an understanding of migration and mobility as dynamic processes and link different patterns and forms of mobility with location-specific sexual networks and HIV epidemiology."

As in the above figures, a smattering of studies in Thailand have managed to link HIV epidemiology to migrant health status in specific border sites. Outside of these we have only a general sense that migration affects the spread of HIV in the GMS. Take Laos for example. In 2011, migrants rank as the second highest 'occupational' category of identified HIV positive people in Laos (CHAS, 2011) and more than 50 per cent of known HIV cases have a reported history of migration to a neighbouring country, with a larger percent of female migrants with HIV (58 per cent) compared to male migrants in the 15–24-year-old age bracket (UNGASS, 2010: 19). The UNGASS report further notes that Lao female migrants show the second highest levels of seroprevalence (0.8 per cent) after MSM and surpassing that of FSW (0.4 per cent). Despite such indications, the difficulties in tracking migrant bodies over time and space mean that mobile populations usually fall through the cracks of sustained sentinel data collection. Or when data is collected, causal links are sometimes unclear. Dai communities in southwest China are a case in point. Here similar numbers of Dai men and women are infected with HIV. As I described, it is almost universally assumed that migrant women are the key vector. But the epidemiology is not so clear-cut. It is unknown whether husbands and wives have become infected from each other or from other partners. Migration is part of this picture, but simple movement is not in and of itself the problem. What is clearer is that when the need to migrate in turn fractures families, fissures occur and HIV (and other health problems) can enter. Coming back to an earlier point, I stressed that it is not so much that the poor are excluded but the means by which they are included that is important. Here, in the types of relations born of rapid social change, HIV is hardly a negative externality in people's lived experiences. Rather, a wide combination of political, social and cultural factors contributes to higher vulnerability to sexual/reproductive dilemmas and disease spread more generally. This, then, is where a broad-based low-road approach to risk seeks to seed notions of community resilience and safe migration. This is, in turn, the arena that the concept of mitigation draws our attention to. This move, however, highlights that the integration of empirical risk targets within a landscape of proliferating existential threats is a problematic project in concept, access to funding and implementation. The difficulties should not distract us from its importance.

Pre-empting peril

At its most basic, mitigation is, or should be, about preventing or reducing risks that occur, in this case, from development processes, including but not restricted to health threats. Its need derives from the outcomes of impact assessment, which is typically defined as "processes of analyzing, monitoring and managing the intended and unintended social consequences both positive and negative of planned interventions and any social change processes invoked by those interventions" (Vanclay, 2003: 2). In the attempt to disentangle consequences, a necessary first step is to distinguish social impacts that "are experienced or felt in corporeal or perceptual terms" from a broader set of social change processes that are themselves the basis of all development activities that seek to alter people's lives – demographic, economic, geographical, institutional and legal, emancipatory, socio-cultural and so forth (Vanclay, 2002: 200). This is where the difficulties begin. Any instrument that seeks to comprehensively evaluate the ways subjective and material aspects of life intersect within this wide array of social change processes will be fraught with methodological and conceptual challenges. Frequently such challenges lead to streamlined packages delivering only readily measurable impacts, such as demographic movements, overt health indicators or shifting employment statistics.

This strategic reduction in the target of impact adjudications brings us to a broader problem facing risk assessment. Historically, so it is argued, there has been a gradual shift from seeing danger as external and resigning ourselves to its damage, to a desire to master risk through our own devices. We have recalibrated our conceptual warning systems from outside danger to sensitivity to uncertainty and threat that we, as humans, have created. This in turn creates a set of reflexive concerns associated with modernity that circle the ubiquity of danger that Massumi pointed us to earlier – we know enough to worry about our future but not enough to be confident we can fix it. As Schmid (2006: 3) explains, modern risk discourse "is based on the perception that risk is not only related to danger but also brings with it opportunities and gains. Thus, to risk something is a conscious choice and not a fate." While our intimations of potential danger are, at best, perched on shaky ground as they are simultaneously internalized and stretch out well beyond our spatial and temporal grasp, what is recognized in increasingly excruciating detail is that ongoing transformations in material and social realities carry serious implications for our futures.

Understanding and seeking to intervene in individuals' and institutions' risk and uncertainty has become a potent growth industry. More and more resources are devoted to the business of assuaging anxiety. Risk management is therefore part and parcel of globalizing formations where, "with its vested interest in catastrophism, neoliberalism is … intent on profiting from the 'unregulated' distribution of life chances, however extreme" (Anagnost, 2011: 233). So too development programmes seek to achieve similar relief for donors, who are aware of development's chequered history, and for stakeholders who are nowadays approached (at least by the OECD donors) with something akin to a development-speak Hippocratic Oath – 'first do no harm'. Hence, the goals of environmental impact assessments (EIAs), for example, are typically defined as in part "securing a prediction of the future" (Wilkins 2003: 402). But there is a highly troublesome element at play here. If EIA is viewed as a "tool to make informed decisions on specific development proposals, then it is virtually unworkable" Wilkins asserts, because "knowledge of the environment will never be sufficient to accurately predict the exact impacts of the project" (ibid: 402–3). Social impact assessments share the same intrinsic problems as social life and subjectivity, and especially affective practices, are immune to empirical assessment. "Neoliberalism wrestles with the complexity of an uncertain, neo-conservatizing environment in which risk is not only endemic but is inexpungible and ultimately unknowable" (Massumi, 2011: 36). What element of immaterial labour or intimate connections could or should one measure? Thus mitigation, as an institutional practice based on pre-emption, can never be more than a narrow and overly simplified attempt at redress, quite possibly, in some instances, missing the very targets it is aiming to address.

Seeking to solve some of these methodological difficulties in targeting negative externalities, Cernea, a long-time sociologist at the World Bank, made valiant attempts to turn mitigation into a project with enough integrity to satisfy the demands of 'self-defeating' potential damage. He devised an influential model for dealing with adverse social and livelihood outcomes that make life worse for individuals or groups affected by infrastructure development (Cernea, 1996). His strategy rests on a simple premise: if one can categorize and quantify unwanted consequences, then one can mitigate their impact through a series of corrective measures. But, as in EIAs, the problem lies in accurate prediction and measurement. According to its critics, models that rely on a compensatory logic – assess and then reduce or fix the damage – can only deal with quantifiable forms of 'loss' and cannot take into account larger issues of social marginalization or other forms of exploitation and social suffering that so frequently occur as part of programmed change. Hence, Dwivedi (2002: 718) reminds us of the fundamental flaw at the heart of this approach: "While some losses can be computed, others cannot; assets and livelihood losses can be valued, but identities and networks cannot. Only those losses that can be computed can be prevented." Marginalization and its various deleterious trickle-on effects is not one of these.

Making threat personal

What remain unmeasured are the subjective aspects of potential or real damage. Theorists commonly depict contemporary societies as characterized by 'risky freedoms' and management of uncertainty as a lifelong project wherein the individual has to cope with an increasing variety of risks ranging from technological and environmental through to health issues or social problems (Zinn, 2010). This point has long been used to characterize everyday modernity that shifts a sense of supposed control away from the social onto the individual. This is an ethos spreading throughout the GMS alongside economic changes, wherein "individualisation does not aim to insure individuals against risks, but to constitute an economic space in which individuals individually take upon themselves and confront risks" (Lazzarato, 2009: 118). Within this unstable situation, the role of subjectivity is a perpetually confounding factor in the ability to understand and assist in channelling risk-averse motivations and practices. A commonplace assumption is that people have biased perceptions and make flawed decisions concerning their own risks. Yet at the same time, we are expected to take responsibility in risk management precisely because we are led to believe that whatever happens to us is a consequence of the decisions we ourselves have made.

The role of dominant values implicit in modernization programmes, such as increased individualization, combined with subjective decision-making by its recipients, make the process of choosing appropriate navigational points to define and avoid risk a fraught project from the outset for donors seeking to pre-empt damage. This is particularly the case in terms of the intimate practices I have been describing in previous chapters. Risk research is clear about this point as it recognizes its lack of appreciation of "the reflexive/reflective practices arising from within the sphere of affect" (Henwood et al, 2010). To gain better insights into the role of subjectivity in personalized choices, forms of risk analysis have attempted to revalidate the status of lay knowledge and highlight factors such as values and power as well as trust, intuition and emotions and the role they play in decision-making (Zinn, 2010). But this doesn't mean it is achieved. Nor that those working in projects geared to communicating such insights to recipient populations have ultimate conviction that they might be in fact reaching people in ways that will reduce these more amorphous dimensions to contemporary risk. Rather it falls into the ever-present imbroglio basket that Latour described for us at the outset.

Thus, there are profound challenges facing mitigation at interrelated levels: which risks and how to minimize them at a macro level, and how people respond to these manoeuvres and warnings at the micro level. The ADB's regional HIV pro-gramme is a case in point that profiles the difficulties facing pre-emptive engage-ments, particularly in contexts of unseen and uncertain future risks. The intent to reduce the threats that could incur with road-building and its potential to prompt increased HIV spread face the insistent conundrum of how to measure success in preventing negative outcomes that haven't yet taken place, precisely because one has no benchmark for evaluating what has been avoided (in the absence of very tightly controlled comparison studies, the likes of which aren't available in the GMS). Part of the rationale for the interventions is to prevent groups of people from becoming 'risk groups' in the first place, not simply to focus on existing MARPs. In other words, the pre-emption involved here is to mitigate in the sense of preclude a potential outcome rather than reduce an already present danger. We might phrase the dilemma another way, what would be the risk of inaction in this situation in terms of subsequent disease burden and other forms of social suf-fering? Difficult to provide an answer to a donor requiring evidence of numbers of bodies saved. I earlier described that there is in fact evidence showing that itinerant labour and migrants can and do face risk for health threats based on the elevated levels of HIV infection in certain workplace sites. But how much risk they faced prior to leaving their home communities and how this becomes crys-tallized in the future and how much it might be reduced, if at all, by public health programmes are murky issues not readily quantified.

Unfortunately, the difficulties don't stop here. As mentioned, it is a basic tenet in risk research that we all make subjective assessments that inevitably misinter-pret the nature and severity of imagined threats, and then respond in ways that are not matched to the possible danger or undesirable outcomes. Part of the dilemma stems from the sheer scale of inclinations, admonitions and most importantly affect-driven value systems infiltrating people's everyday lives that collectively tailor what is desirable and what is to be avoided. In Chapter 1, I described Orn and the choices she made in aiming to run a small beer-shop/restaurant near a coalmine. What, indeed, are we to make of Orn's strategy? In many respects, Orn had been a perfect target of the anti-trafficking and HIV awareness projects conducted in her village during construction aimed at addressing 'negative exter-nalities'. But, in the terms addressed by these mitigation activities, she fails mis-erably. The messages seem to have missed their mark as she proceeded to recruit her two young nieces, both under the age of 18, with the potential, at least, to have them subsequently engage in multiple sexual relations. Instead, a far more potent discourse has inspired her. The appeal of livelihood improvement and modernity premised on material growth vastly overshadowed any cautionary lectures Orn might have received. It is not surprising, therefore, that she utilizes what human and social capital resources she has at her disposal – her knowledge of service provision in Thailand, and her family connections, to develop a mode of primitive capital accumulation. Moreover, it brings our attention to what Spinoza suggested centuries ago concerning the politics of 'inadequate ideas'. The capacity to act requires an underlying emotional affirmation. Top-down dissemination of knowledge (the HIV and anti-trafficking lectures) has limited effect; the more engaged response comes from a shared uptake of the dreams development is selling. Programmed mitigation aims for the smaller target of specific practices, but misses the larger point. The affective dimension of information flows in the GMS has not inspired adequate reflection on the nature of embodied risk to Orn herself or her nieces, but its reverse: throw caution to the wind and wishfully grasp opportunities in the quest for market appreciation. The ideal (self-) entrepreneur.

New economic corridors and border frontier zones have created numerous changes of this ilk as commodity capitalism infiltrates local communities alongside the shift from subsistence to wage labour and the growing mobility of a precariat workforce. In sync with these changes, people are actively embracing opportunities for engagement in a growing market economy prompting a huge array of new encounters. And in her version of what it means to become a self-styled entrepreneur, Orn is providing an answer to Wetherell's earlier question. Here she is seeking to show that affective practices – service with a smile and her nieces' proximate companionship – can indeed be exchanged for material value, in this case money from waiting truckers. Many of the new opportunities we see across the GMS reproduce this pattern of problematic outcomes based on provision of manual and/or immaterial labour: the bar owner visiting a Khmu village to look for more hands to work in her restaurant, the mothers who bring their daughters to bars in Dan Nork, the endless chains of cheap labour arriving at border factories, the men who give women sex drugs as a means to enhance their own intoxication in frontier casinos. It is easy to discern that in these vignettes a capitalist logic of commodity exchange might reign supreme, but as Tsing reminds us this is not a closed system. In fact, forms of intimate exchange demonstrate the persistent point that "capitalist commodity value is everywhere created through tapping and transforming non-capitalist social relations" (Tsing, 2013: 21). The GMS is a wide-open playing field for these dynamics and intersections.

The important point is that not all players are positioned to engage evenly in the competition underlying each of these relationships, and this in turn has specific implications for wellbeing, including health. People are willing to engage wholeheartedly in the larger promises that the GMS dreams represent, to embrace the spread of market values while at the same time reproducing entrenched forms of hierarchy. Villagers are seemingly happy to turn rice or forest land over to outsiders to plant rubber, pledging the next generations of their kin to lopsided agreements. Bar workers accompany Chinese men into casinos where they face the threat of drug-crazed violence. Female students haunt nearby drink-shops as part-time escorts to make money from passers-by, passers-by take advantage of ethnic subordination to ensure they have ready access to a steady flow of young impressionable female bodies, whom they pressure into unsafe sex. Men rotate partners in border factories premised on the supposed security they can offer: the women for their part give up control over their health. Young women bring relatives and friends into the world of male predators along the new thoroughfares. Mothers bring daughters to massage shops as a doorway to livelihood security and broader choice of partner. Brothers introduce sisters to cross-border rubber traders in the hopes social reciprocity will give them market advantage. Young men gain money from other men in exchange for semen: one after the other. All are considered market niches – each of the above perfectly logical entrepreneurial responses conforming to trends of economic accumulation. Is there a downside to this when it comes to wellbeing, embodied health threats and/or dignity? The unfortunate answer is yes!

Value and remittance

Hence, we can elevate to a more general level the conundrum of mitigation's ability to only address what can be categorized and measured ahead of time, as well as the unfortunate outcome of unilaterally missing the health threats and exploitation present in most of the preceding examples. I indicated at the outset that there is a tension between a neoliberal subjectivity that promotes a sense of individualized risk-taking and an institutional ability to simultaneously ensure that safeguards forestall negative outcomes. Each subsequent chapter brought our attention to the ways these diverse enterprises implicate embodied hopes and dreams as well as intimate attachments to people and places. This ethos by definition moves human behaviour well beyond the rubrics of programmed risk pre-emption as much as state bodies would prefer it didn't. Cernea (1996) cites marginalization and social disarticulation as key variables in the downward spiral that carries disenfranchised peoples into poverty and its physical and emotional distress. But, while mitigation interventions might aim to instil safe resource management, safe migration and safer sex in its toolbox of pre-emptive measures, there is nothing – and I have no intention of sounding trite – that would imply that expanding capitalism itself needs some careful management in order to render it 'safe' for those caught up in the swell of livelihood changes sweeping the region. Precisely what safety might even look like in these circumstances is not part of the conceptual repertoire that fuels the radical transformations taking place. This type of thinking is simply not within the scope of current damage control planning.

What I am suggesting here is that mitigation, as both concept and practice, should, of necessity, be about more than material and/or economic compensation and more than superficial attempts to patch over obvious dilemmas, even as one must recognize this is exceedingly difficult to achieve. It requires we consider a far broader range of impacts and intrusions and brings us back to the point made earlier about migrants as bearers of values. It is not just migrants that bring back new ways of thinking and feeling, and new values that in turn seed changes back home. This is exactly what development programmes do. They instil new values, although this is a tangled and partial project. Social and economic transformations in the name of an expanding free market are works-in-progress not finally or finely formed. "Free market exchange is a value rather than a fully realised practice" wherein "expansion of the market can lead to a growing dominance of economic values and to the gradual obviation of alternative values with serious political implications" – a situation leading Otto and Willerslev (2013: 15) to conclude: "All questions of value are also questions of morality and ethics." In this light, as the upsurge in rights-based discussions has reminded us, all questions of controlling development's impact are (or should be) also questions concerning human dignity and its connection to wellbeing.

The very reason that development, as an institutional practice, came into being was premised (ideally speaking) on doing something to address morally alarming inequities at a global level. How it does this is another matter. Some have argued that ensuring fundamental capabilities of even the most disempowered populations is the non-negotiable road to guaranteeing the most basic element of a good life, envisaged in this instance as a life that has at its heart a non-negotiable sense of dignity. Linking capabilities allowing a "fuller human life" – often thought of as entitlements to education, bodily integrity, physical, cultural and spiritual sustenance and so forth (Nussbaum, 2004: 13) – and the more amorphous capacity to aspire charts a difficult path that sometimes undermines confidence that the litmus test of human dignity is being preserved (or in fact allowed). Despite the rise of new advocacy movements and international social justice tribunals, dignity is not usually a value that forms the basis of development planning and measurement. More often, the value of mobile values and their moral weight as development tool is simply taken for granted. And yet there is no end of paradoxes in this assumption. Levitt and Lamba-Nieves (2011) offer a summary of the bewildering contradictions within global flows of social remittances from transnational migrants. It seems that just like so much of development's equivocal promises and deliverables, there is no uniformity to outcomes. Comparing a range of data from a range of sending countries they show that migrants as 'bearers of values' do many things: sometimes migration increases birth rates, sometimes it lowers them; migration influences maternal behaviour but not always in positive ways; migration can improve or hamper educational outcomes; social remittances can challenge inequality by changing values and norms but so too they can reproduce or strengthen gender hierarchies; the movement of new ideas can both encourage and inhibit development through consumer consciousness; migration can both stimulate and weaken local reservoirs of human capital. In other words, if any of the above sectors are part of capabilities to be improved by the remittance of values, that might, in turn, ensure dignity is fostered, the record is all over the shop (so to speak).

As always the devil is in the detail (or lack of). While the GMS programme relies on faith in markets and neoliberal competition to improve livelihood conditions across the region, at the same time, planners recognize that this entails sustainability of wellbeing in a broad sense of the word, 'so the poor don't get crowded out'. But, if there is to be any meaningful and sustainable control of negative externalities occurring in the process of infrastructure development, be they HIV-related or otherwise, then one has to consider the parameters defining one's approach to negative outcomes in the first place. Rao and Walton have argued that understanding social and cultural dimensions to change must "confront difficult questions in terms of *what* is valued in terms of well-being, *who* does the valuing, and *why* economic and social factors interact with culture to unequally allocate access to a good life" (2004: 2, emphasis in original). Donors usually accept that social consequences are undesirable if they lessen rather than improve one's ability to access resources. The process by which they occur, and how this is linked to the broader question of what is being preferentially valued, or where dignity fits into the picture, is harder to either examine or curtail. Further confounding well-meaning attempts at mitigation, individuals' subjective risk assessments concerning mobility and human capital as a ticket of entry into commodity-based forms of supply chain capitalism are obstinately inscrutable, making the politics of seeding 'adequate ideas' even more complicated.

Regardless of conceptual challenges posed by the risk horizons I have canvassed, some certainties remain. One can still, following Fekete, assert that values are omnipresent within the social order.

> No aspect of human life is unrelated to values, valuations and validations. Value orientations and value relations saturate our experiences and life practices from the smallest established microstructures of feeling, thought and behaviour to the targets established by macrostructures of organisations and institutions. The history of cultures and social formations is unintelligible except in a relation to value orientations, value ideals, goods values, value responses and value judgements and their objectivations, interplay and transformations.
>
> (Fekete, 1988: i)

While we might take fleeting comfort in the notion that collectively the very presence of values or, for that matter, the 'value of values' for our social makeup might demonstrate an "irreducible orientation towards the better, and revulsion from the worse" (Connor, 1992: 2), this appears an unstable position at best. For, there is also no doubt that the reality of conflicting or radically different values, and the practices that follow, can bring misery and hardship as much as life improvement. Marxism might have sought to dismantle hierarchies of economic value, and feminism the same for systems of gendered value, but development studies and development planners for their part devote little time to questioning forms of valorization within capital and its flows. Berger (2007: 41) offers a poignant reminder of dimensions so often missed: "Consumerist ideology which has become the most pervasive and invasive on the planet, sets out to persuade us that pain is an accident, something that we can insure against. This is the logical basis for the ideology's pitilessness."

The material in preceding chapters therefore requires we consider how one might, in fact, approach values within targeted development processes. And more precisely, what their role is in promoting the 'pitiless' management of life and its risks. From this standpoint, issues of governmentality and bio-politics enter the picture, as does the idea that being 'safe' means not just protection from infectious disease. Who has the power and obligation to take care of whom? Based on what set of criteria? What role is given to values and affect in planning and targeting mitigation interventions? Such questions butt up immediately against other machinations. Even as risk and responsibility for 'care of the self' is ever more privatized, larger ideological formations structure the management of risk within global supply chains and perilous work conditions where "risk is, in a sense, offshored to a space of underdevelopment that is being actively produced by the restructuring of the capitalist economy at its margins" (Anagnost, 2011: 224). So too, development programmes conjure symbolic capital, and at times a rationale for existence, based on their own advertised attempts at mitigation in the marginal zones. Rather than simple assessment of infrastructure impacts, the onus should also be on revealing what is discursively created through the rubric of mitigation and its choice of targets.

It is a well-rehearsed argument that value hierarchy is omnipresent in the functioning of development targeting and action. Taylor (2010: 562) suggests that in the opinion of the World Bank (as an example), 'irrational' societies and the "norms, values and practices they reproduce are perceived to retard the scale and scope of market activities, to block avenues for investment and entrepreneurship, and to breed socially exclusionary societies that violate liberal principles of formal equality". But, on closer scrutiny, in the very act of seeking to overcome 'cultural' impediments to market competition, the dynamics of global capital create their own version of non-rational, that is to say affective, exchanges through capitalist formations that rely on coercion and violence. This move, according to Taylor, requires the necessary participation of a 'precarious marginal mass' that must fall back on informal economies to stay afloat as their "activities are isolated from the circuits of capital and their processes of value expansion" (ibid: 572). In fact, as I have shown throughout, precariat and marginal populations are hardly isolated from affective economies and ways in which human capital takes on value; rather these economies provide the very motivations that make them constant players throughout the GMS. This is not to say their contributions are fairly valued as such, but that the ruthless fantasies of something better fuel their ongoing participation.

Conclusion

In either material or immaterial economies, in the factories in Mae Sot, the rubber fields of Laos, the brothel towns in south Thailand, or wherever one chooses to look, value hierarchies ensure that endeavour and risk are not simply a matter of individual assessment and control. Ideas and practices associated with free-market and wage labour expansion are never neutral, nor are those associated with health and sexuality, including the value of 'self-care'. Ascertaining ideological bias in how values are elevated or internalized is far harder to pin down, even as we rest our assumptions of global modernization on the premise of their restless remittance. Debates rage over whether it is possible to adequately represent and compare how values impact life, in particular, given the hyper-relativity of value in late capitalism, or more concretely whether exchange value is about to subordinate everything before it as economic expansion consistently remakes its boundaries. Nothing it seems is sacrosanct; bodies and their constituent parts are now 'fair game' as "biovalue is being produced out of the body's own vitality and thereby becomes a new frontier in capital accumulation" (Anagnost, 2011: 232). This impulsive terrain of mobile bodies, ideologies and (intimate) practices stimulates the incessant instability that mitigation seeks to sanitize. As funding for development becomes ever more competitive and OECD guidelines no longer globally dominant, it is a further uncertainty as to whether mitigation itself can be sustained as a programmatic gaze and practical endeavour in face of its constantly shifting target.

In sum, creativity and instability at the intersections of the intimate and material show the absolute inextricability of political economies and affective economies, and the fact that there's no simple directionality of one structuring the other. The scenarios I canvassed in previous chapters show that contradictions described by Levitt and Nieves are the norm rather than the exception. Khmu women head home to curry favour with parents and persuade peers that selling sex and its material gains make any presentiment of personal anguish worth bearing. They then bear the brunt of ethnic and social hierarchies diminishing dignity and producing ill-health. Dai migrants return with money and a sense of personal appreciation, but families are fractured and sometimes made ill by this ethos of off-shore accumulation. Adolescent Akha women want Chinese partners, their male kin assist in the process, but they learn in the course of their relations that some versions of modernity carry less durable appeal than they had been led to believe. Others are trafficked. Lao men appreciate the attention and coinage of effeminate men but are considered by their friends as succumbing to lazy and dissolute ways. More than a few become infected with HIV. Migrants in Mae Sot gain a sense of emotional and sexual permissiveness that is deemed anathema to family life back in Myanmar, and in turn suffer the perils of unwanted pregnancies and other health dilemmas. From any vantage point, travelling values and mobile aspirations trouble the assumption that social remittances are the touchstone of sustainable development.

This awkward conclusion brings us back to our earlier question. What is an objective measure of social value? Furthermore, what does it mean to do mitigation in face of the immutable fact that social values are ambivalent vehicles of change and, as such, subjective risk is inherent not only in social life (as it always has been) but also in the ways one inserts prescriptions for change. At heart, all economies carry risk, this is the nature of exchange as Connor, following Bourdieu, notes emphatically: "Every transaction (symbolic or otherwise) can go wrong, not only as a matter of accident but as a structural principle" (Connor, 1992: 91). We know that this is not an easy puzzle to untangle or inoculate against. So when it is argued that entrepreneurialism brings the magic of the markets to all, or that any negative externalities can be identified and controlled, or that migrants carry back social values as proudly as a new coat, none of the above is as straightforward as it might seem. What is new is the attempt to institutionalize risk management within development programmes even as it is uncomfortably recognized to be a fraught project. I do not wish to suggest that recognizing logical inconsistencies means development planning should give up mitigation and steam ahead untroubled by negative consequences. Rather, it needs to stake its claim on recognizing that the bedrock of human life is fragile and its intimacies are forever unstable, leading to the impossibility of only ever delivering the good life.

As such, we need a far closer evaluation of what values one is ascribing to in the economic expansion and imbrications of human capital I have been describing. In other words, the seemingly sanctified programmatic approach – that modernization's imbroglios are best left undisturbed because market logics suggest that each one of those at the coal-front must bear the brunt of their own decisions – must in and of itself be unsettled by the social and ethical implications of changes happening all across the GMS. Or a simple question: where is the dignity when Orn tells us with smiling pride that she has figured out how to improve her life, as her nieces sit mute next to her? A simple answer would note: interventions must comprehend affects or there will be no effect! Dignity requires safety. Safety requires nurturing. Nurturing requires adequate ideas, in Spinoza's sense, formulated with appropriate affect. Health is obviously more than just a spread of a virus in earmarked most-at-risk populations (especially given the fact that 'most' is a relative concept and that we could all be labelled as at-risk in one or another context). Health is a far broader condition of life that needs equally accommodating modes of adjudication to decide how to help or minimize the reverse of help. The way to intervene in the more diffuse corridors of illness? Through affective networks that can at least sense if not grasp the invaluable, incalculable and intangible ways we struggle together as humans.

References

ADB. 2007. *Mid Term Review of the Greater Mekong Subregion Strategic Framework 2002–2012*. Manila: Asian Development Bank.

——2009. *Migration in the Greater Mekong Subregion: A Background Paper for the Fourth Greater Mekong Subregion Development Dialogue*. Manila: Asian Development Bank.

——2012. *Overview Greater Mekong Subregion Economic Cooperation Program*. Manila: Asian Development Bank.

——2013. *Facilitating Safe Labor Migration in the Greater Mekong Subregion: Issues, Challenges, and Forward-Looking Interventions*. Manila: Asian Development Bank.

AEC. 2013. *Data on Per Capita Income, the Proportion of Age, the Population of the AEC*. ASEAN Economic Community http://www.thai-aec.com/37.

Ahmed, S. 2004. "Affective Economies". *Social Text* 22: 117–39.

Altman, D. 2001. *Global Sex*. St. Leonards: Allen & Unwin.

Anagnost, A. S. 2011. "Strange Circulations: The Blood Economy in Rural China". In P. T. Clough and C. Willse (eds) *Beyond Biopolitics: Essays on the Governance of Life and Death*. Durham: Duke University Press.

Appadurai, A. 1997. "Fieldwork in the Era of Globalization". *Anthropology and Humanism* 22: 115–18.

——2004. "The Capacity to Aspire: Culture and the Terms of Recognition". In V. Rao and M. Walton (eds) *Culture and Public Action*. Stanford: Stanford University Press.

Arnold, D. 2012. "Spatial Practices and Border SEZs in Mekong Southeast Asia". *Geography Compass* 6: 740–51.

Arnold, D. and Pickles, J. 2011. "Global Work, Surplus Labor, and the Precarious Economies of the Border". *Antipode* 43: 1598–624.

Askew, M. 2006. "Sex and the Sacred: Sojourners and Visitors in the Making of the Southern Thai Borderland". In A. Horstmann and R. L. Wadley (eds) *Centering the Margin*. New York: Berghahn Books.

Augé, M. 1995. *Non-Places: Introduction to an Anthropology of Supermodernity*. London and New York: Verso.

Baker, S., Holumyong, C. and Thianlai, K. 2010. *Research Gaps Concerning the Health of Migrants from Cambodia, Lao PDR and Myanmar in Thailand*. Nakhon Pathom, Thailand: Mahidol University and World Health Organization.

Beck, U. 1992. *Risk Society: Towards a New Modernity*. London: Sage Publications.

Beesey, A. 2001. "Return and Reintegration: Female Migrants from Yunnan to Thailand". In C. Wille and B. Passl (eds) *Female Labor Migration in Southeast Asia*. Bangkok: Asian Research Center for Migration.

Benko, G. 1997. "Introduction". In G. Benko and U. Strohmayer (eds) *Space and Social Theory: Interpreting Modernity and Postmodernity*. Oxford and Cambridge: Wiley-Blackwell.

Berger, J. 2007. *Hold Everything Dear: Dispatches on Survival and Resistance*. New York: Pantheon Books.

Berlant, L. 1998. "Intimacy: A Special Issue". *Critical Inquiry* 24: 281–8.

——2007. "Nearly Utopian, Nearly Normal: Post-Fordist Affect in La Promesse and Rosetta". *Public Culture* 19: 273–301.

Berlant, L. and Warner, M. 1998. "Sex in Public". *Critical Inquiry* 24: 547–66.

Boellstorff, T. 2005. *The Gay Archipelago: Sex and Nation in Indonesia*. Princeton: Princeton University Press.

Bourgois, P. 2002. "The Violence of Moral Binaries". *Ethnography* 3: 221–31.

Boym, S. 1998. "On Diasporic Intimacy: Ilya Kabakov's Installations and Immigrant Homes". *Critical Inquiry* 24: 498–524.

Brees, I. 2008. "Refugee Business: Strategies of Work on the Thai–Burma Border". *Journal of Refugee Studies* 21: 380–97.

Buck-Morss, S. 1995. "Envisioning Capital: Political Economy on Display". *Critical Inquiry* 21: 434–67.

Cain, K., Thomson, A. and Postlewait, H. 2006. *Emergency Sex (and Other Desperate Measures): True Stories from a War Zone*. London: Ebury Press.

Cernea, M. 1996. *Impoverishment Risks and Livelihood Reconstruction: A Model for Resettling Displaced Populations*. Washington: World Bank.

CHAS. 2009. *Lao PDR 2009 Surveillance Surveys: Behavioral survey among service women and Integrated biological and behavioral surveillance survey among men who have sex with men in Luang Prabang*. Vientiane: Centre for HIV/AIDS/STI.

——2011. *AIDS Situation in Lao PDR*. Vientiane: Centre for HIV/AIDS/STI.

Cohen, P. T. 1999. "Khruba Bunchum Yansuamror: The New Charismatic Ton Bun of Yuan Buddhism". Presentation at 7th International Thai Studies Conference, Amsterdam, 4–8 July.

——2013. "Symbolic Dimensions of the Anti-Opium Campaign in Laos". *The Australian Journal of Anthropology* 24: 177–92.

Colebrook, C. 2002. *Understanding Deleuze*. New South Wales: Allen & Unwin.

Comaroff, J. and Comaroff, J. L. 2001. "Millennial Capitalism: First Thought on a Second Coming". In J. Comaroff and J. L. Comaroff (eds) *Millennial Capitalism and the Culture of Neoliberalism*. Durham: Duke University Press.

Comaroff, J. L. and Comaroff, J. 2009. *Ethnicity, Inc*. Chicago: University of Chicago Press.

Commission on AIDS in Asia. 2008. *Redefining AIDS in Asia: Crafting an Effective Response*. New Delhi: Oxford University Press.

Connor, S. 1992. *Theory and Cultural Value*. Oxford: Blackwell.

Constable, N. 2009. "The Commodification of Intimacy: Marriage, Sex, and Reproductive Labor". *Annual Review of Anthropology* 38: 49–64.

CPPCR. 2009. *Feeling Small in Another Person's Country: The Situation of Migrant Children in Mae Sot, Thailand*. Burma: Committee for Protection and Promotion of Child Rights.

Deane, K. D., Parkhurst, J. O. and Johnston, D. 2010. "Linking Migration, Mobility and HIV". *Tropical Medicine and International Health* 15: 1458–63.

De Angelis, M. 2004. "Separating the Doing and the Deed: Capital and the Continuous Character of Enclosures". *Historical Materialism* 12: 57–87.

Deleuze, G. and Guattari, F. 1983. *Anti-Oedipus: Capitalism and Schizophrenia*. Minneapolis: University of Minnesota Press.

——1987. *A Thousand Plateaus: Capitalism and Schizophrenia*. Minneapolis: University of Minnesota Press.

Deng, R. and Lyttleton, C. 2013. "Linked Spaces of Vulnerability: HIV Risk amongst Migrant Dai Women and their Left-behind Husbands in Southwest China". *Culture, Health & Sexuality* 15: 415–28.

Desjarlais, R. n.d. *Subject to Death: Life and Loss in a Buddhist World*. Unpublished manuscript.

Dialma, E. and Le Roux, P. 2007. "The Chinese Diaspora and Prostitution at the Thai-Malay Frontier", in A. Leveau (ed.) *Investigating the Grey Areas of the Chinese Communities in Southeast Asia*. Bangkok: IRASEC.

DOE. 2011. *Statistics of Registered Migrant Workers throughout the Kingdom, 2011*. Bangkok: Workpermit Section, Department of Employment, Ministry of Labour (in Thai).

Donnan, H. and Wilson, T. 1999. *Borders: Frontiers of Identity, Nation and State*. New York: Berg.

D'Souza, C. 2007. *Review of Health Issues and Activities along the Thai-Myanmar Border, Report to the Border Health Program of the WHO*. Bangkok: World Health Organization.

Duncan, C. R. 2004. "Legislating Modernity among the Marginalized". In C. R. Duncan (ed.) *Civilizing the Margins: Southeast Asian Government Policies for the Development of Minorities*. Ithaca: Cornell University Press.

Dunlop, N. 2011. *Invisible People: Stories of Migrant Labourers in Thailand*. Bangkok: Raks Thai Foundation.

Dwivedi, R. 2002. "Models and Methods in Development-Induced Displacement". *Development and Change* 33: 709–32.

Elliot, A. and Lemert, C. 2009. "The Global New Individualist Debate: Three Theories of Individualism and Beyond". In A. Elliot and P. D. Gay (eds) *Identity in Question*. London: Sage Publications.

Evrard, O. 2011. "Oral Histories of Livelihoods Under Socialism and Post-Socialism Among Khmu of Northern Laos". In J. Michaud and T. Forsythe (eds) *Moving Mountains: Ethnicity and Livelihoods in Highland China, Vietnam and Laos*. Vancouver: University of British Columbia Press.

Faist, T. 2009. "Transnationalization and Development: Toward an Alternative Agenda". *Social Analysis* 53: 38–59.

FAO. 1993. *Challenges in Upland Conservation*. Bangkok: Regional Office for Asia and the Pacific.

Farmer, P. 2004. "An Anthropology of Structural Violence". *Current Anthropology* 45: 305–25.

Farole, T. 2011. "Special Economic Zones: What Have We Learned?" *Economic Premise* 64: 1–5.

Feher, M. 2009. "Self-Appreciation; or, the Aspirations of Human Capital". *Public Culture* 21: 21–41.

Feingold, D. A. 2010. "Trafficking in Numbers". In P. Andreas and K. M. Greenhill (eds) *Sex, Drugs, and Body Counts*. Ithaca: Cornell University Press.

——2013. "The Burmese Traffic-jam Explored: Changing Dynamics and Ambiguous Reforms". *Cultural Dynamics* 25: 207–27.

Fekete, J. 1988. "Introductory Notes for a Postmodern Value Agenda". In J. Fekete (ed.) *Life after Postmodernism: Essays on Value and Culture*. London: Macmillan.

Formoso, B. 2010. "Zomian or Zombies: What Future Exists for the Peoples of the Southeast Asian Massif?" *Journal of Global History* 5: 313–32.

Foucault, M. 1986. "Of Other Spaces". *Diacritics* 16: 22–7.

——2008. *The Birth of Biopolitics: Lectures at the College de France, 1978–1979*. Basingstoke: Palgrave Macmillan.

Galbraith, J. K. 1979. *The Nature of Mass Poverty*. Cambridge, MA: Harvard University Press.

Ganjanapan, A. 2000. *Local Control of Land and Forest: Cultural Dimensions of Resource Management in Northern Thailand*. Chiang Mai: Regional Center for Social Science and Sustainable Development.

Garcia, J. and Parker, R. 2006. "From Global Discourse of Local Action: the Makings of a Sexual Rights Movement?" *Horizontes Antropologicos* 12: 13–41.

Giddens, A. 1994. "Living in a Post Traditional Society". In U. Beck, A. Giddens and S. Lash (eds) *Reflexive Modernization: Politics, Tradition and Aesthetics in the Modern Social Order*. Cambridge: Polity Press.

Giddens, A. and Pierson, C. 1998. *Conversations with Anthony Giddens: Making Sense of Modernity*. Stanford: Stanford University Press.

Gillogly, K. 2004. "Developing the Hilltribes of Northern Thailand". In C. Duncan (ed.) *Civilizing the Margins: Southeast Asian Government Policies for the Development of Minorities*. Ithaca: Cornell University Press.

Glassman, J. 2010. *Bounding the Mekong: The Asian Development Bank, China, and Thailand*. Honolulu: University of Hawaii Press.

Glick Schiller, N. 2009. "A Global Perspective on Migration and Development". *Social Analysis* 53: 14–37.

Glick Schiller, N. and Faist, T. 2009. "Introduction: Migration, Development, and Social Transformation". *Social Analysis* 53: 1–13.

Graeber, D. 2011. *Debt: The First 5000 Years*. New York: Melville House Publishing.

Gregory, D. 1997. "Lacan and Geography: The Production of Space Revisited". In G. Benko and U. Strohmeyer (eds) *Space and Social Theory, Interpreting Modernity and Postmodernity*. Oxford: Blackwell.

Grieger, M. T. 2012. *Challenging Conventional Wisdom: Sex Work, Exploitation, and Labor among Young Akha Men in Thailand*. Master of Arts thesis, George Washington University.

Grimes, B. (ed.). 2000. *Ethnologue: Languages of the World* (14th edn). Dallas, TX: SIL International.

GTZ. 2003. *Study Report of Drug-Free Villages in Sing District, Luang Namtha Province*. Luang Namtha, Lao PDR: Lao-German Program, Integrated Rural Development in Mountainous Regions of Northern Lao PDR.

Hakim, C. 2011. "Attractive Wins and Ugly Loses in Today's Rat Race". *Evening Standard*, 22 August, www.standard.co.uk/news/attractive-wins-and-ugly-loses-in-todays-rat-race-6435454.html (accessed 8 August 2013).

Hall, D. 2012. "Rethinking Primitive Accumulation: Theoretical Tensions and Rural Southeast Asian Complexities". *Antipode* 44: 1188–208.

Hall, D., Hirsch, P. and Li, T. M. 2011. *Powers of Exclusion: Land Dilemmas in Southeast Asia*. Singapore: National University of Singapore Press.

Halperin, D. 2002. *How to do the History of Homosexuality*. Chicago: University of Chicago Press.

Hardt, M. 1999. "Affective Labor". *Boundary 2* 26: 89–100.

Hardt, M. and Negri, A. 2009. *Common Wealth*. Cambridge, MA: Harvard University Press.

Harvey, D. 2005. *A Brief History of Neo-liberalism*. Oxford: Oxford University Press.

Henwood, K., Pidgeon, N., Parkhill, K. and Simmons, P. 2010. "Researching Risk: Narrative, Biography, Subjectivity". *Forum: Qualitative Social Research* 11, Art. 20, http://nbn-resolving.de/urn:nbn:de:0114-fqs1001201 (accessed 27 November 2013).

Herring, A. and Swedlund, A. C. 2010. *Plagues and Epidemics: Infected Spaces Past and Present*. Oxford and New York: Berg.

Hilgers, L. 2012. "Laos Vegas: A Chinese Entrepreneur Crosses the Border to Build His Gambling Empire". *Good*, www.good.is/posts/laos-vegas (accessed 27 November 2013).

Hirsch, P. 2009. "Revisiting Frontiers as Transitional Spaces in Thailand". *The Geographical Journal* 175: 124–32.

Hubbard, P. 2001. "Sex Zones: Intimacy, Citizenship and Public Space". *Sexualities* 4: 51–71.

——2011. "Gender, Power and Sex in the World City". *L'Espace Politique* 13: 1–13.

Huguet, J., Chamratrithirong, A. and Natali, C. 2012. *Thailand at a Crossroads: Challenges and Opportunities in Leveraging Migration for Development*. Geneva: International Organization for Migration.

Hyde, S. T. 2007. *Eating Spring Rice: The Cultural Politics of AIDS in Southwest China*. Berkeley: University of California Press.

Illouz, E. 1997. *Consuming the Romantic Utopia: Love and the Cultural Contradictions of Capitalism*. Berkeley: University of California Press.

Irigaray, L. 1985. *This Sex Which is Not One*. Ithaca: Cornell University Press.

IOM. 2010. *Migration and HIV/AIDS in Thailand: Triangulation of Biological, Behavioural and Programmatic Response Data in Selected Provinces*. Bangkok: International Organization for Migration.

Jackson, P. A. 1997. "*Kathoey* >< Gay >< Man: The Historical Emergence of Gay Male Identity in Thailand". In L. Manderson and M. Jolly (eds) *Sites of Desire, Economies of Pleasure*. Chicago: University of Chicago Press.

——2009. "Capitalism and Global Queering: National Markets, Parallels among Sexual Cultures, and Multiple Queer Modernities". *GLQ: A Journal of Lesbian and Gay Studies* 15: 357–95.

Jameson, F. 2002. *A Singular Modernity: Essays on the Ontology of the Present*. London: Verso Press.

Klausner, W. J. 1987. *Reflections on Thai Culture* (3rd edn). Bangkok: The Siam Society.

Kleinman, A. and Fitz-Henry, E. 2007. "The Experiential Basis of Subjectivity: How Individuals Change in the Context of Social Transformation". In L. Biehl, B. Good and A. Kleinman (eds) *Subjectivity: Ethnographic Investigations*. Berkeley: University of California Press.

Kusakabe, K. and Pearson, R. 2010. "Transborder Migration, Social Reproduction and Economic Development: A Case Study of Burmese Women Workers in Thailand". *International Migration* 48: 13–43.

Latour, B. 2008. "It's Development, Stupid! Or How to Modernize Modernization?" www.espacestemps.net/en/articles/itrsquos-development-stupid-or-how-to-modernize-modernization-en (accessed 22 June 2013).

Lazzarato, M. 2009. "Neoliberalism in Action: Inequality, Insecurity and the Reconstitution of the Social". *Theory, Culture and Society* 26: 109–33.

LeBar, F. 1964. *Ethnic Groups of Mainland Southeast Asia*. New Haven: Human Resource Area Files.

Lefebvre, H. 1976. *The Survival of Capitalism*. London: Allison & Busby.

Levitt, P. and Lamba-Nieves, D. 2011. "Social Remittances Reconsidered". *Journal of Ethnic and Migration Studies* 37: 1–22.

Lewis, D. R., Lekfuangfu, N., Vojackova-Sollorano, I., Soda, F. and Natali, C. 2010. *Forecasting Migration Flows: The Relationships among Economic Development, Demographic Change and Migration in the Greater Mekong Subregion*. Bangkok: ADB/IOM.

Li, Y. 2013. *From Poppy Planters to Rubber Growers: An Ethnographic Account of Cross-Border Supply Chain Capitalism in Northwest Laos*. Doctor of Philosophy thesis, Macquarie University.

Loong-Yu, A. and Shan, N. 2007. "Chinese Women Migrants and Social Apartheid". *Development* 50: 76–82.

Lyttleton, C. 2005. "Market-bound: Relocation and Disjunction in Northwest Lao PDR". In S. Jatrana, M. Toyota and B. S. A. Yeoh (eds) *Migration and Health in Asia*. Oxon: Routledge/Curzon.

——2007. *Mekong Erotics: Men Loving/Pleasuring/Using Men in Lao PDR*. Bangkok: UNESCO.

——2009. *Build it and They Will Come*. Manila: Asian Development Bank.

——2013. "Linking the Social to the Economic: Broadened Ambitions and Multiple Mitigations in New Mekong Corridors". In O. L. Shrestha and A. Chongvilaivan (eds) *Greater Mekong Subregion: From Geographical to Socio-economic Integration*. Singapore: Institute of Southeast Asian Studies.

Lyttleton, C. and Nyíri, P. 2011. "Dams, Casinos and Concessions: Chinese Megaprojects in Laos and Cambodia". In S. Brunn (ed.) *Engineering Earth: The Impacts of Megaengineering Projects*. Dordrecht: Springer Press.

Lyttleton, C. and Sayanouso, D. 2011. "Cultural Reproduction and 'Minority' Sexuality: Intimate Changes among Ethnic Akha in the Upper Mekong". *Asian Studies Review* 35: 169–88.

Lyttleton, C., Cohen, P., Rattanavong, H., Thongkhamhane, B. and Sisaengrat, S. 2004. *Watermelons, Bars and Trucks: Dangerous Intersections in Northwest Lao PDR*. Vientiane: Institute for Research on Culture.

Massumi, B. 2011. "National Enterprise Emergency: Steps Toward an Ecology of Powers". In P. T. Clough and C. Willse (eds) *Beyond Biopolitics: Essays on the Governance of Life and Death*. Durham: Duke University Press.

Mendoza, A. 2013. *HIV among Migrant Workers: Policy and Program Issues*. Manila: Asian Development Bank.

MMN. 2013. *Migration in the Greater Mekong Subregion Resource Book (Fourth edition): In-depth Study: Border Economic Zones and Migration*. Chiang Mai: Mekong Migration Network and Asian Migrant Centre.

Mohanty, C. T. 2003. *Feminism without Borders: Decolonizing Theory, Practicing Solidarity*. Durham: Duke University Press.

Molland, S. 2010. "The Perfect Business: Human Trafficking and Lao/Thai Cross-Border Migration". *Development and Change* 41: 831–55.

Moore, H. L. 2011. *Still Life: Hopes, Desires and Satisfactions*. Cambridge: Polity Press.

Morineau, G., Ngak, S. and Sophat, P. 2004. *When You Fall in Love You Have to Pay for it: Men who have Sex with Men in Phnom Penh Cambodia*. Phnom Penh: FHI, Cambodia.

Nagel, J. 2000. "Ethnicity and Sexuality". *Annual Review of Sociology* 26: 107–33.

——2006. "Ethnicity, Sexuality and Globalization". *Theory, Culture and Society* 23: 545–7.

NCA. 2008. *Final Evaluation of NCA HIV/AIDS Akhawood Project in Luang Namtha.* Vientiane: Norwegian Church Aid.

NCCA. 2010. *National Strategy and Action Plan on HIV/AIDS/STI 2011–2015.* Vientiane: National Committee for the Control of AIDS.

NGO-Forum. n.d. "ABD's Involvement in the Greater Mekong Subregion". www.forum-adb.org/BACKUP/pdf/guidebooks/GMS%20main%20text.pdf (accessed 27 November 2013).

Nussbaum, M. 2004. "Beyond the Social Contract: Capabilities and Global Justice". *Oxford Development Studies* 32: 3–18.

Nyíri, P. 2006. "The Yellow Man's Burden: Chinese Migrants on a Civilizing Mission". *The China Journal* 56: 83–106.

——2012. "Enclaves of Improvement: Sovereignty and Developmentalism in the Special Zones of the China-Lao Borderlands". *Comparative Studies in Society and History* 54: 533–62.

Ong, A. 2006. "Experiments with Freedom: Milieus of the Human". *American Literary History* 18: 229–44.

——2007. "Neoliberalism as a Mobile Technology". *Transactions of the Institute of British Geographers* 32: 3–8.

——2008. "Scales of Exception: Experiments with Knowledge and Sheer Life Southeast Asia". *Singapore Journal of Tropical Geography* 29: 117–29.

Otto, T. and Willerslev, R. 2013. "Introduction: 'Value as Theory' Comparison, Cultural Critique, and Guerilla Ethnographic Theory". *Journal of Ethnographic Theory* 3: 1–20.

Peters, H. A. 2002. "Heaven is High and the Emperor is Far Away: Beijing Certainties Encounter Yunnan Ambiguities". Paper presented at conference, The Human Rights Challenge of Globalization in Asia-Pacific-US: The Trafficking in Persons, Especially Women and Children. Honolulu, Hawaii.

Phadthaisong-Chaipanit, L. 2010. "Second Generation Children of Migrants from Burma: Situation and Public Health Problems". Final Presentation Meeting: Status and Problems of the Second Generation Children of Migrants from Burma, Chiang Mai University.

Phrasisombath, K., Thomsen, S., Sychareun, V. and Faxelid, E. 2012. "Care Seeking Behaviour and Barriers to Accessing Services for Sexually Transmitted Infections among Female Sex Workers in Laos: A Cross-sectional Study". *BMC Health Service Research* 12.

Rao, V. and Walton, M. 2004. "Culture and Public Action: Rationality, Equality of Agency, and Development". In V. Rao and M. Walton (eds) *Culture and Public Action.* Stanford: Stanford University Press.

Reichl, A. J. 2005. "Fear and Lusting in Las Vegas and New York: Sex, Political Economy, and Public Space". In S. S. Fainstein and L. J. Servon (eds) *Gender and Planning: A Reader.* New Brunswick: Rutgers University Press.

Rigg, J. 2005. *Living With Transition in Laos: Market Integration in Southeast Asia.* New York and Oxon: Routledge.

Rodier, G., Greenspan, A., Hughes, J. and Heyman, D. 2007. "Global Public Health Security". *Emerging Infectious Diseases* 13: 1447–52.

Rofel, L. 2007. *Desiring China: Experiments in Neoliberalism, Sexuality, and Public Culture.* Durham: Duke University Press.

Rubin, G. 1975. "The Traffic in Women: Notes on the Political Economy of Sex". In R. Reiter (ed.) *Toward an Anthropology of Women.* New York: Monthly Review Press.

Ruddick, S. 2010. "The Politics of Affect: Spinoza in the work of Negri and Deleuze". *Theory, Culture & Society* 27: 21–45.

Sacramento, O. 2011. "Liminal Spaces: Reflections on the Proxemia of Cross-Border Demand for Prostitution". *Space and Culture* 14: 367–83.

Sadao AIDS Committee. 2011. "Summary Report on the Project of Strengthening Prevention of AIDS and STI, Sadao District, Songkhla Province, 2008–2011". Working Committee on AIDS and STI Prevention, Sadao District.

Saldanha, A. 2008. "Structuralism and the Heterotopic". *Environment and Planning* 40: 2080–96.

Santasombat, Y. 2008. *Flexible Peasants: Reconceptualizing the Third World's Rural Types.* Chiang Mai: Regional Center for Social Science and Sustainable Development.

Savage, M., Devine, F., Cunningham, N., Taylor, M., Li, Y. and Hjellbrekke, J. 2013. "A New Model of Social Class? Findings from the BBC's Great British Class Survey Experiment". *Sociology* 47: 219–50.

Schmid, G. 2006. "Social Risk Management through Transitional Labour Markets". *Socio-Economic Review* 4: 1–33.

Scott, J. C. 2009. *The Art of Not Being Governed: An Anarchist History of Upland Southeast Asia.* New Haven: Yale University Press.

Seidel, K., Phanvilay, K., Vorachit, B., Mua, L., Boupphachan, S. and Oberndorf, R. B. 2007. "Study on Communal Land Registration in Lao PDR: Land Policy Study No. 6 under LLTP II". Vientiane: Lao-German Land Policy Development Project.

Shao, J. 2006. "Fluid Labor and Blood Money: The Economy of HIV/AIDS in Rural Central China". *Cultural Anthropology* 21: 535–69.

Sheridan, S., Phimphachanh, C., Chanlivong, N., Manivong, S., Khamsyvolsvong, S., Lattanavong, P., Sisouk, T., Toledo, C., Scherzer, M., Toole, M. and Van Griensven, F. 2009. "HIV Prevalence and Risk Behaviour among Men who have Sex with Men in Vientiane Capital, Lao People's Democratic Republic, 2007". *AIDS* 23: 409–14.

Shrage, L. 1994. *Moral Dilemmas of Feminism: Prostitution, Adultery, and Abortion.* New York: Routledge.

Sigley, G. 2006. "Chinese Governmentalities: Government, Governance and the Socialist Market Economy". *Economy and Society* 35: 487–508.

Simana, S. 1998. *Kmhmu Livelihood: Farming the Forest.* Vientiane: Institute for Cultural Research.

Slesak, G., Inthalad, S., Kim, J. H., Manhpadit, S., Somsavad, S., Sisouphanh, B., Bouttavong, S., Phengavanh, A. and Barennes, H. 2012. "High HIV Vulnerability of Ethnic Minorities after a Trans-Asian Highway Construction in Remote Northern Laos". *International Journal of STD & AIDS* 23: 570–5.

Standing, G. 2011. *The Precariat: The New Dangerous Class.* London: Bloomsbury Academic.

Stiglitz, J. 2011. "Of the 1%, by the 1%, for the 1%." *Vanity Fair*, May.

Tapp, N. 2010. "Yunnan: Ethnicity and Economies – Markets and Mobility". *The Asia Pacific Journal of Anthropology* 11: 97–110.

Tayanin, D. 2005. *Being Kammu: My Village, My Life.* Bangkok: Matichon Press.

Taylor, M. 2010. "Conscripts of Competitiveness: Culture, Institutions and Capital in Contemporary Development". *Third World Quarterly* 31: 561–79.

TBBC. 2009. *2009 Programme Report.* Bangkok: Thailand Burma Border Consortium.

Thongmanivong, S., Yayoi, F., Phanvilay, K. and Vongvisouk, T. 2009. "Agrarian Land Use Transformation in Northern Laos: from Swidden to Rubber". *Southeast Asian Studies* 47: 330–47.

Toole, M. 2004. *Study of Young Men's Sexual Behaviour, Vientiane, Lao People's Democratic Republic*. Vientiane: Burnet Institute for Medical Research and Public Health and Lao PDR: Ministry of Health, National AIDS Centre.

Tsing, A. 2005. *Friction: An Ethnography of Global Connection*. Princeton: Princeton University Press.

——2009. "Supply Chains and the Human Condition". *Rethinking Marxism* 21: 148–76.

——2013. "Sorting Out Commodities: How Capitalist Value is Made through Gifts". *Journal of Ethnographic Theory* 3: 21–43.

Turton, A. 2000. "Introduction to Civility and Savagery". In A. Turton (ed.) *Civility and Savagery: Social Identity in Tai States*. Richmond: Curzon Press.

UNAIDS. 2011. *Universal Access in Asia and the Pacific: Regional Stocktaking Report*. Geneva: Joint United Nations Programme on HIV and AIDS.

UNDP. 2009. *Human Development Report 2009: Overcoming Barriers: Human Mobility and Development*. New York: United Nations Development Programme.

UNGASS. 2010. *Country Progress Report, Lao PDR*. Vientiane: National Committee for the Control of AIDS.

Vanclay, F. 2002. "Conceptualising Social Impacts". *Environmental Impact Assessment Review* 22: 183–211.

——2003. *Social Impact Assessment: International Principles*. IAIA Special Publication Series.

Vanwesenbeeck, I. 2011. "High Roads and Low Roads in HIV/AIDS Programming: Plea for a Diversification of Itinerary". *Critical Public Health* 21: 289–96.

Walker, A. 2009. "Conclusion: Are the Mekong Frontiers Sites of Exception?" In M. Gainsborough (ed.) *On the Borders of State Power: Frontiers in the Greater Mekong Sub-region*. Oxon and New York: Routledge.

Walker, D. M., Clark, C. and Folk, J. 2010. "The Relationship between Gambling Behavior and Binge Drinking, Hard Drug Use, and Paying for Sex". *UNLV Gaming Research & Review Journal* 14: 15–26.

Weine, S. M. and Kashuba, A. B. 2012. "Labor Migration and HIV Risk: A Systematic Review of the Literature". *AIDS Behavior* 16: 1605–21.

Weitzer, R. 2009. "Sociology of Sex Work". *Annual Review of Sociology* 35: 213–34.

West, J. and Austrin, T. 2002. "From Work as Sex to Sex as Work: Networks, 'Others' and Occupations in the Analysis of Work". *Gender, Work and Organization* 9: 482–503.

Wetherell, M. 2012. *Affect and Emotion: A New Social Science Understanding*. London: Sage Publications.

WHO. 2010. *Health of Migrants: The Way Forward – Report of a Global Consultation*. Madrid: World Health Organization.

Wilkins, H. 2003. "The Need for Subjectivity in EIA: Discourse as a Tool for Sustainable Development". *Environmental Impact Assessment Review* 23: 401–14.

Wolffers, I., Fernandez, I., Verghis, S. and Vink, M. 2002. "Sexual Behaviour and Vulnerability of Migrant Workers for HIV Infection". *Culture, Health & Sexuality* 4: 459–73.

Wynn, L. n.d. *Mimesis, Kinship, Gift, and Other Things That Bind Us in Love and Desire*. Unpublished manuscript.

Yan, Y. 2010. "The Chinese Path to Individualization". *British Journal of Sociology* 61: 489–512.

Yang, M. M.-H. 1994. *Gifts, Favors, and Banquets: The Art of Social Relationships in China*. Ithaca: Cornell University Press.

Yimprasert, J. and Hveem, P. 2005. "The Race to the Bottom: Exploitation of Workers in the Global Garment Industry". Occasional Paper Series, Norwegian Church Aid.

Zhang, J. 2012. "A Trafficking 'Not-spot' in a China-Vietnam Border Town". In M. Ford, L. Lyons and W. V. Schendel (eds) *Labour Migration and Human Trafficking in Southeast Asia: Critical Perspectives*. Oxon and New York: Routledge.

Zinn, J. O. 2010. "Biography, Risk and Uncertainty – is there Common Ground for Biographical Research and Risk Research?" *Forum: Qualitative Social Research* 11, Art. 15, www.qualitative-research.net/index.php/fqs/article/view/1512/3029 (accessed 27 November 2013).

Index